Pa... under
Pe... ...s
and Ideas!

Page 2 under
People,conditions
and Ideas chap 2

Women and (In)Justice

The Criminal and Civil Effects of the Common Law on Women's Lives

Sheryl J. Grana

University of Minnesota, Duluth

Allyn and Bacon

Boston ■ London ■ Toronto ■ Sydney ■ Tokyo ■ Singapore

Series Editor: Jennifer Jacobson
Editorial Assistant: Tom Jefferies
Production Editor: Michelle Limoges
Production Manager: Susan Brown
Compositor: Peggy Cabot, Cabot Computer Services
Composition and Prepress Buyer: Linda Cox
Manufacturing Buyer: JoAnne Sweeney
Cover Designer: Joel Gendron
Marketing Manager: Jude Hall

Library of Congress Cataloging-in-Publication Data

Grana, Sheryl J.
    Women and (in)justice : the criminal and civil effects of the common law on
women's lives / Sheryl J. Grana.
        p.   cm.
    Includes bibliographical references and index.
    ISBN 0-205-32163-1
        1. Women—Legal status, laws, etc.—United States.   2. Women—United
States—Social conditions.   3. Sex discrimination against women—United
States.   4. Women prisoners—United States.   5. Women lawyers—United
States.   6. Women—Crimes against—United States.   I. Title.

KF478 .G69 200s
342.73'0878—dc21   2001022664

Printed in the United States of America

10 9 8 7 6 5 4 3 2 1   06 05 04 03 02 01

For Brant, Kim, and Tyler—
my brightest stars

46- ON EQuality.
130- The cost of being female
+ discrimination

CONTENTS

46

LIST OF BOXES AND TABLES

PREFACE

I have spent many years looking for a book that combines a discussion of U.S. civil-justice and criminal-justice issues regarding women. It seems that such books are either "rights" oriented (that is, primarily civil) or criminal-justice oriented. This book attempts to combine the two. In some instances, the effort progressed well; in other circumstances, it proved less smooth because combining the two separate discussions illustrated their separateness. For example, a smooth segue from a discussion of the development of the common law to a discussion of "who is a criminal" turned out to be more challenging than anticipated.

Women and (In)Justice explores a number of different issues: the development of the common law; women's role in such development; legal rules about marriage, divorce, children, education, and "work"; theories about criminality and women criminals; women's prisons; violence against women; sexuality; and women lawyers, correctional officers (who many individuals refer to as "prison guards"), and police. The diverse topics are drawn together through the concept of *quadraplexation*, and with the ongoing discussion of "people, conditions, and ideas."

Each chapter includes a brief excerpt on "justice" from scholars in the field. Such excerpts are meant to stimulate readers to think about the variety of definitions of justice that exist. No wonder we have such ongoing debates about the issue; there are a lot of ways to think about it! Most chapters also include citations to U.S. Supreme Court (U.S.S.C.) decisions. I have chosen U.S.S.C. decisions because they apply to all U.S. citizens. In some places, I discuss state case decisions to make a point, but such discussions are less frequent. I do not spend a lot of time discussing cases, or the cases I cite; I believe it is in the reader's best interest to study the cases and their relevancy. I have also written this text in a colloquial style, preferring to have a discussion with the reader rather than make a formal presentation. Over the years, I have found that most of us are much more drawn to books that speak *to* us, rather than *at* us.

Many thanks to my colleagues at the University of Minnesota, Duluth. At times I would just shut my door and ignore everyone—and everything—to get this project finished. I appreciate these colleagues' patience and understanding. My family and friends deserve many kudos as well. Their support and encouragement always kept me going. The folks at Allyn and Bacon have been wonderful. Thanks especially to Jude Hall, for encouraging me to do this; Karen Hanson, for supporting the idea; and Jennifer Jacobson, for helping and understanding me. Many thanks to Kim Hearn for her patient editing of drafts, comments on content, humor in the tough moments, and candor. And to Helen Moore, for the courage and guidance you have taught me and given me over the years.

I hope you enjoy the text and learn something valuable from it.

SJG

1 Ideas about Women . . .

An examination of the lives of women in the United States must start somewhere. Given the length of recorded history, we could begin with ancient societies or with the Middle Ages or with European society as it was industrializing. Why is "where to start" important? Because the society within which women live provides important context. Societies, at different times in their histories, expect different things from women and men; ideas about gender change constantly because gender is socially constructed and societally based. This means societies actually determine and define what it means to be a woman and a man based on societal beliefs and attitudes at any given time. Context, then, recognizes that people, social conditions, and ideas all influence women's lives. In this chapter, we inspect the influence of these three variables on women's lives both before and after industrialization. We also examine the concepts of *quadraplexation* and *walking the line* to learn about their role in justice and women's lives.

People, Conditions, and Ideas

A crucial element in understanding humanity is the notion of the cultural context of human beings' lives. Grasping the cultural and societal milieu is the task of classic sociology but, in reality, it is also the crux of understanding who we are, how we got here, why we do what we do, and where we might be going. Some authors call these three elements the *social realities* (Grana & Ollenburger, 1999)—regardless of their "title," they are of utmost importance.

By "people," I mean that individuals influence one another's lives. "Conditions" are the social realities that influence people's lives, such as unemployment, war, economic depression, and so forth—those macro-sociological realities we all live with in our lives. The notion of "ideas" means that ideas in circulation at any given time in history influence people's lives and the social conditions within which they live. Granted, we can discuss these three things separately, but they are all intertwined as well. Ideas belong to people who live within certain social conditions; the

1

conditions influence the people and their ideas alike. This is thus an inter-dependent, circular relationship. Likewise, when we examine the lives of women, ideas, people, and social conditions influence the who, what, when, where, and why of our study. Of course, people, social conditions, and ideas also influence our ideas of "justice" and its meaning. Throughout time, justice has been defined and redefined.

Lady of Justice

The existence of the "Lady of Justice" provides an ironic twist in any discussion of women and justice. Interestingly, justice is represented by a woman, although her origin is not completely clear. Some believe she originally came from Greek mythology. She carries with her the "scales of justice" to remind us of the balance between justice and injustice. Traditionally, she also wears a blindfold to demonstrate that justice is blind, fair, and equitable.

Why a discussion of Lady Justice? Well, understanding "justice"—one of the words in the title of this book—is easier said than done. Throughout the text, I scatter brief discussions about what various authors think of justice. Indeed, researchers have recognized that women and men think about justice very differently (Pertman, 1994). They see evidence differently and espouse different "codes" of justice. Recognizing just this basic gender difference is eye opening—just imagine what different philosophers, criminologists, sociologists, and others think!!

Importance of Patriarchy

One thing we need to recognize is the importance of patriarchy in all of this. There are innumerable definitions of patriarchy—too many to list here. Sylvia Walby (1990, p. 20) suggests that patriarchy is a "system of social structures and practices in which men dominate, oppress and exploit women." Margaret Andersen (2000, p. 15) argues patriarchy is "a hierarchical system of social relations among men that creates and maintains the domination of women." The definition of patriarchy I commonly use is that patriarchy is a social structural arrangement whereby males, just by virtue of being males, have more privilege than women do in society. Moreover, this privilege often leads to greater power, access to opportunity, and better rewards for men. This privilege is therefore paramount. The above definition does not mean that all women are good and all men are bad. There are good and bad men and women. However, the definition helps us understand that within a patriarchy, some privileges are accorded to some folks and not to others.

The *accumulation of advantage and disadvantage* (see Valian, 1998) in a society adds up; very small differences in how we treat people can make a large difference in the big scope of things. "It is unfair to neglect even minor instances of group-based bias, because they add up to major inequalities" (Valian, p. 3). Thus, understanding the import of privilege in patriarchy— and its opposite, lack of privilege—is necessary to understanding women's lives in terms of everyday issues of justice, law, and so forth.

All of these definitions have a problem: They lean toward *essentialism*, or the idea that we can lump all members of one group under one label. In reality, of course, some men—white, upper-middle-class, heterosexual, Christian men, specifically—have more privilege than other men. Men with these characteristics tend to have a much more secure place in the social structure than men who don't fit those descriptions. But even in the face of these differences, the existence of patriarchy does benefit men universally by sheer virtue of their maleness. Differences among women are too numerous to list. We can examine differences in social class, race or ethnicity, sexual preference, age, marital status, and so forth. Though some people throw their hands up in the air as we lengthen the list, the fact that the list of characteristics is long must be brought to the fore. Indeed, the very length of the list tells us that all women are unique. (This is true of men, too.)

There is not a consensus on the emergence of patriarchy. Some say it has always been part of the human condition; others argue it emerged five thousand or so years ago for some reason. The answer to how it works also varies—from societal-level answers to institutional-level answers to psychological answers. The psychology of patriarchy is an area of concern and interest. What psychological effects, if any, does patriarchy have on people? Some researchers argue that the psychological effects are great. Others suggest that they are minimal and depend on how much individuals allow patriarchy to affect them.

I would argue that because of the characteristics of patriarchy, its effects are felt at many different levels—psychological, social, familial, institutional, and so forth. What are the characteristics of patriarchy? I define them as the following: violence, power, control, linearity, polarization, stereotyping, ideology, phallocentrism, and misogyny. (This last is integral to patriarchy.) These variables fluctuate depending on the patriarchal system that one is examining. For example, Greer Litton Fox (1977) argues that control is a major issue in patriarchal systems and that three different systems are used throughout the world to control women:

1. **Confinement:** constricting women to the boundaries of their homes, as in systems of purdah
2. **Protection:** allowing women access to the world beyond the home when accompanied by a chaperone

3. **Normative restriction** (which characterizes the United States and much of the Western world): instilling values and norms in women from the time of their birth about what "nice girls" do and do not do. This system pressures women to live up to such standards. Women who comply are guaranteed safe passage; those who don't, well. . . .

Women as "Bad"

The issue of control in patriarchy leads us to another integral idea in this sort of system—that women are bad and therefore must be feared, "dealt with," subdued, and dominated. Women's studies scholars often talk about the Mary/Eve dichotomy, an ideology that represents patriarchy's split analysis of women. Women are either the virgin mother (the "Mary" who gives life to, nurtures, watches over, and inspires us) or they're Eve (the Pandora of the world who brought on all "man"kind the evils that now face us). As with patriarchal thought, we have a dichotomous definition of all womenkind—she is either evil or pure.

Such an idea found tragic expression during the witch craze that struck the American colonies in the 1600s. Witches were the evil persons of society, the devil's workers. (Yes, there were some male witches, too, but most witches were women.) These bad women supposedly let Satan overcome them, and they then allowed themselves to do his task. While no evidence exists that any of the women accused, tried, and hanged (or any of the three) were in fact worshiping the devil, such was women's lot in life in this time and place.

Scholars of the craze note that accusations of witchcraft embodied the patriarchy which dominated colonial society. Puritan theology, a masculinist version of the world, saw a fine line between appropriate and inappropriate behavior. Many women accused of witchcraft were identified—often by men in their own families—as engaging in some kind of wrongdoing. Carol Karlsen (1987) argues that many women accused of witchcraft were marginalized. They were moderately poor, or old, or lacked male figures (husbands, fathers, brothers, uncles) in their lives. On the other hand, some accused witches were women of wealth and economic power, despised or envied in their communities. Men in this society felt compelled to control independent women.

Regardless of the alleged witch's economic status, age, or degree of independence, the key assumption here was the idea that women have the capacity for evil. Such a belief is an inherent part of patriarchy. Think about the many other ways women are defined as bad. . . .

Patriarchy and Quadraplexation

Juliet Mitchell's discussion of patriarchy led me to develop the concept of *quadraplexation*. In 1971, Mitchell wrote *Woman's Estate*, in which she argued that we can best understand women and their lives by examining the intertwining patriarchal and capitalist effects of four conditions in their lives:

1. socialization,
2. production,
3. reproduction, and
4. sexuality.

Mitchell saw these four variables as keys to understanding the condition of women in society. Like other theorists of the 1960s and 1970s, she believed that "traditional" notions of womanhood limited women's potential and trapped them in situations they did not choose. Her ideas, along with the social conditions influencing her writing, follow.

Socialization.   The *socialization of children* comes from the patriarchal and capitalist ideas we learn about being mothers. Mitchell argues, "Women's biological 'destiny' as mother has become a cultural vocation . . . and through this she achieves her main vocation" (p. 115). Socialization into the mother role often defines women's lives for them. Indeed, it becomes a primary focus for many women. Mothers are then evaluated as "good" or "bad" by a patriarchal and capitalist standard, often internalizing these judgments.

Production.   The word *production* refers to all issues dealing with women's labor—both paid and unpaid. Men dominate the economic and productive spheres of society because they control these spheres. Thus production is a key factor for understanding male dominance of women's economic resources. Certainly the notions of separate spheres and true womanhood, discussed later in the chapter, place women right in the middle of this notion of production. Mitchell feels that "far from woman's physical weakness removing her from productive work, her social weakness has evidently made her a major slave of it" (p. 104). Indeed, domesticity is all about women's production, or labor, in the home.

Reproduction.   This term refers to all issues pertaining to women's roles in reproduction, and the identifiable costs they must pay. These costs include not only carrying, bearing, and nursing children but also calling the babysitter, staying home from work when the kids are ill, losing wages, promotions, career momentum, and so forth. "The social cult of maternity is matched by the real socio-economic powerlessness of the mother" (p. 109).

Sexuality.   This term refers to the patriarchal and capitalist definitions of women's sexuality—what women can and cannot do in order to be viewed as "good," when women "ask for it" (invite rape), how much it costs

---

BOX **1.1**   Miller on Justice . . .

According to David Miller, we can discuss the notion of justice only if three conditions are met.

Outside these conditions, something may not be right, or may be uncomfortable or unfortunate, but it may not be called "just" or "unjust." The three conditions are:

1. There are at least two living, breathing people involved in a situation.
2. One person is carrying a burden, while the other is not.
3. The burden was humanly created.

Miller, *Social Justice*

---

women to make themselves sexually attractive to men, and so on. A patriarchal system restricts and defines women's sexuality; it sees women not as autonomous sexual beings but as beings sexually related only to men. Mitchell writes, "Women throughout history have been appropriated as sex objects . . . [the] sexual relationship can easily be assimilated into the statute of possession" (p. 110). If women disobey sexuality rules established by the patriarchy, they are punished. Keep in mind that patriarchy says not only that women should restrict their lives to the home but also that they should be beautiful and sexy, and should work to keep "their man" happy at the hearth side. It is the interplay of these four intertwining and interdependent variables that I call *quadraplexation.*

Throughout this book, I examine the effect of quadraplexation on women's lives. For example, what role does quadraplexation play in women's employment, education, and family life; the lives of women prisoners; and so forth? Does quadraplexation affect a lawyer who is a woman? The answer is yes. Because of patriarchy, all women are oppressed, even if they are not necessarily similarly oppressed.

Patriarchy and Oppression

What is oppression? Webster's dictionary defines it as "the bearing of a burden." Interestingly, that ties in with what David Miller says about justice (see Box 1.1). Often I look to the discussion of Florynce Kennedy (1972) for insights on this question; Kennedy defines four different kinds of oppression. First of all, there is *personal/psychological oppression,* or the kind of oppression that comes about when a person believes he or she is nothing because society says he or she is nothing. *Private oppression* is oppression in a private situation; for example, when a woman's boss tries to get her in bed. *Public oppression* is concerned with large-scale situations in which society makes blanket decisions that harm individuals' lives; for instance, when the government spends a person's money on war even though she needs it more for child care. Finally, *cultural oppression* is when an aspect of the culture trivializes, distorts, or omits from its history and collective memory the input, energy, and ideas of entire groups of people. For example, some history books attribute everything to white men.

These diverse notions of oppression reveal that oppression is not one thing—it occurs on many levels and takes numerous forms. And, it goes hand-in-hand with patriarchy; indeed, oppression is a major force fueling patriarchy. Patriarchy has influenced people's ideas about women and men for who knows how many years. But the ideas in patriarchy have varied, depending on social conditions and other factors.

I believe that many people, women included, are uncomfortable talking about notions of oppression. I sense this in classes when I teach, and in conversations I have with friends and colleagues. I believe this uneasiness with the topic stems from denial. Many women say they do not feel oppressed. They argue that women as a group are no longer discriminated against, or they recognize that some women may have a bad deal, but they themselves have not. As Valian (1998) points out, many researchers have coined the term *denial of personal disadvantage* (p. 164) to describe this phenomenon. With denial of personal disadvantage, a member of a particular group accepts the idea that the group as a whole is treated unfairly, but she believes that she herself has not suffered from unfair treatment. It is an interesting phenomenon, but as Valian continues, "what is not possible is that no individual has experienced discrimination even though the group as a whole has" (p. 164).

Patriarchy and Sex and Gender

Besides patriarchy, oppression, and quadraplexation, we should also talk about the role of patriarchy in the development of gender. Social scientists commonly make a distinction between sex and gender. Sex is often defined as what is biologically determined—the chromosomes that individuals possess. With sex chromosomes, women possess an XX configuration, men an XY configuration. (For variations on this configuration, see Andersen, 2000.) Gender, on the other hand, is the part of our identity that we learn from society. Gender is much more sociological and psychological in nature—it is about how we identify ourselves as women and men. Generally, sex and gender go hand in hand; that is, most individuals with XX chromosomes consider themselves women, and most with XY chromosomes consider themselves men. The following discussion of nature, biology, and gender schemas adds to this discussion.

"Nature" and Biology

The terms *nature* and *biology* are so important that they get a section of their own. Before we proceed with our discussion of social gender, we need to expand on our discussion of biology. We also need to add to that discussion the parallel topic of "nature." Often, we hear people say things like, "It's a woman's nature to want to stay home with the kids," or "it's just not natural if she does that." These comments rest on the assumption that there is a biologically determined, "natural" way to do things. Called *biological determinism*, this notion has been espoused by Charles Darwin and Herbert Spencer, and by judges, legislators, and presidents. This is an important idea to understand, because it has limited women's and men's behavior. If nature says a girl should be a mommy when she grows up, what do we do with her if she wants to be an astronaut instead? People have used the nature and biology argument to bolster the "true womanhood" and separate-spheres ideas we discuss later in the chapter.

Sociobiology, among other disciplines, supports such accusations. Sociobiology is the study of the biological basis of social behavior. Sociobiologists argue that biology indeed influences human behavior, through natural urges, instincts, hormones, and the drive to strengthen the human gene pool. Many sociobiologists use the language (albeit veiled at times) of natural selection and "survival of the fittest." The work of sociobiologists such as Edward O. Wilson (starting in 1975) and David Barash (1982) and others particularly explore the sexual behavior of women and men. These researchers suggest that men must spread their sperm around to continue the species, while women must carefully choose one mate to protect their children, and thus the species. Sounds like a double standard to me.

This discussion of biology and nature is part of the same debate as the nature versus nurture controversy. How much does nature (genes, biology) influence our behavior? How much does nurture (what we have been taught or exposed to)? Scientists and researchers, depending on their disciplinary bias, answer these questions differently. The answers vary by decade of scientific investigation (that "people, conditions, ideas" thing again!). In some decades, answers emphasize biology; in other decades, they stress the role of social learning. Such a pendulum effect suggests that we do not *know* the answer. The sociological perspective reflects the learning, or nurture, swing of the pendulum (of course, there are exceptions). On the other hand, many people like the biology, or nature, swing of the pendulum. Here's why: When we leave explanations for women's positions in society up to nature and biology, we do not have to take responsibility for women's secondary status. It makes our lives easy; this state of affairs is biology and nature's fault, not society's (our) fault.

Such ideas support the social ideologies that define men's and women's expected roles. They also legitimize decisions made by courtroom judges and by voting legislators. As we work through this book, we will come to realize just how powerfully such discussions have shaped women's lives.

Gender Schemas

Can women help the way they think about themselves? How and why do women think of themselves as they do? Where do their "guilt trips" come from—these ideas that they should clean the toilets, that they should call the babysitter if they want a night out? Researchers vary in their answers to that question. Nevertheless, the most widely disseminated *sociological* answer is that we *learn* this behavior and these attitudes through some kind of socialization process. This answer runs directly counter to the biological answer. True, there are several mainstream explanations of the gender-socialization process—identification theory, learning theory, cognitive-development theory, and symbolic interactionism, for example. I like the discussion of *gender schemas* as a way to answer this question.

According to Valian (1998), gender schemas are ideas we have about certain groups; often we call such ideas stereotypes. However, Valian prefers the word *schema* over *stereotype*, because she sees it as "more inclusive" (p. 2). We usually don't articulate gender schemas but nonetheless, they exert a major impact on our lives. Indeed, for women, gender schemas are extremely costly. They result in skimpier paychecks as well as negative self-images. Because a schema is a mental construct, it affects our perceptions, interpretations, and expectations of all human activity (p. 103). Schemas are powerful because they make it easy for us to construct and test hypotheses about daily life. In terms of gender, they help us decide what it means to be male and female. They give rise to our expectations about women and men, they interpret behavior for us, they supply explanations when data are missing, they point us to new information (p. 106).

Because a gender schema is a way for us to organize the world, it is also a way for us to limit ourselves. The *confirmation bias* only worsens these limits. This bias prompts us to pay attention to information that confirms a hypothesis we have about something and to discount information that doesn't fit in with the hypotheses. For example, when two names are listed on a checking account, and one name is preceded with "Dr.," the bias is to instantly assume that is a male. If that isn't the case, we may struggle for a moment with the new information. On a daily basis, we use this phenomenon to make sense of our world. Once we formulate a hypothesis, we find it very difficult to change or get rid of it (p. 106). For women, this reality can be disastrous both socially and individually.

Where do gender schemas come from? Sociologically, there are several answers. They may derive from our observations of people (p. 112);

what we see is what we learn. (Sociologists usually call this social learning, or observation theory.) Or perhaps we learn gender schemas through the sexual division of labor. We see the typical labor roles played by women and men and conclude that Mom is the cook and Dad mows the lawn. Or, perhaps we learn these schemas as a way to justify the existing division of labor. We really do not know. However, we *do* know that three processes work together to entrench the schemas in our minds.

The first process has to do with responding to physical differences (p. 118). Valian points out that if people look consistently different, then we conclude that they *are* different. Because women and men generally look different, well, there you go. Another way we implant gender schemas is taking an extreme example of something and considering it the norm (p. 119). This is how much stereotyped information gets engraved in our minds. We see a member of a group do something—even if it is extreme behavior—and we assume that person's behavior represents that of the whole group. We apply that same kind of reasoning to men and women. For example, we see very thin and beautiful women as *the* ideal woman and apply it to all women. Finally, our tendency to see the genders as dichotomous and mutually exclusive also implants schemas into our heads. Women are women and men are men. Period. If they do something that doesn't fit in with their gender, then we ignore that information or shift it elsewhere. It is much easier to dichotomize the world than to see "shades of gray."

Notice that all three of these devices are parts of the descriptions of patriarchy we talked about earlier. These three processes continually work together to reinforce and reconfirm our ideas about gender.

Though not impossible, it is difficult to evaluate the world *without* using gender schemas as one basis of the evaluation. Why? Well, for one thing, most people are pretty committed to their gender schemas. Thus they tend to see the world only through those eyes. Second, because of the often unconscious nature of gender schemas, we often don't even realize that these are "lenses" through which we are looking. Finally, though we may consciously work to see and understand gender schemas, the expectation of others may prove too strong (Valian, p. 175).

Preindustrial Ideas about Women

The Industrial Revolution—that economic and social transformation that first emerged in nineteenth-century England—became a defining era in human history. But what were people's lives, especially women's lives, like before this time? Anthropologists and sociologists alike often speak of changes in societies over time as *societal evolution*. According to this perspective, women's and men's roles before the Industrial Revolution were very different from what they are today. Moreover, many ideas about women and men were also different. On the other hand, some of these ideas have persisted to today—unfortunately.

For example let's look at ideas about women from a primary historical source in many Western cultures—the Bible. In the first book of the Old Testament, we find the following ideas about women: "Unto the woman he said, I will greatly multiply thy sorrow and thy conception; in sorrow thou shalt bring forth children; and the desire shall be to thy husband, and he shall rule over thee." In fact, the entire Eden story is about women's role in the downfall of humankind. It is well known that Paul the Apostle had less than positive views of women. As Agonito (1988, p. 67) notes, "As regards the status of women in the church, Paul adheres to the traditional Jewish practice of enforcing women's subordinate position, which entailed restricting her movements and influence lest she employ her sexuality to ensnare men." And the Judeo-Christian tradition was not the first expression of these kinds of ideas about women. Indeed, the ancient Greek philosopher Aristotle thought of woman as a mutilated, incomplete man (an idea later reflected by Sigmund Freud and others).

Regarding hunting-and-gathering societies, most people consider men the hunters and women the gatherers. True, women did often stay with the children—for they were the only ones who could nurse children—and gather food while men went off to hunt. But that scenario tells only one part of the story. Hunting was a risky business—it was not always successful, it could take days to accomplish, and it could result in death or injuries for the hunter. Gathering was actually the mainstay of many hunting-and-gathering cultures. Without the daily collection of berries and other rations, cultures could not have survived. Thus women's contribution was *as significant* as men's.

In early agricultural societies, women and men worked side-by-side to plant and harvest crops. Industry had not yet introduced the farm implements that would render this work less time consuming and physical. Pregnant women delivered babies and promptly went back to work in the fields. Families created products such as butter in their home and bartered or traded them with others for goods they needed or wanted. Again, women and men made equally important contributions. Indeed, in the early days of preindustrial, colonial America, women had as much value as men (Kerber & DeHart, 2000) because they helped establish and sustain the settlements.

Industrial Ideas about Women

As a sociologist, I argue that one of the most significant social movements in human history was the Industrial Revolution. Some people call the Industrial Revolution a technological movement, or simply one form of movement toward modernity. I see it as a social movement. Not only did it change the very nature of work, it also redefined how people live, how they work, how the marketplace and economics function, and what social roles people "should" play. In fact, many ideas that we now have about gender roles stem directly from the influence of the Industrial Revolution. Again, behavior patterns didn't unfold in a vacuum—something helped create the roles that women and men began to play.

Science and industrialization progressed together. Darwin nullified the Judeo-Christian tradition and put the scientific tradition in place. He believed that, because of biology and evolution, women were inferior to men. "Sexual selection purported to demonstrate a biological basis for the traditional differences between the sexes, and so it seemed that science supported the idea that women are inferior to men" (Agonito, p. 250).

After industrialization, new social ideas about women arose. Why? And how? One answer is that, as factories and central places of business cropped up, women couldn't easily enter these places with children and nurse their babies. Watching kids frolic around machinery was also frightening to mothers. So, the idea that men were more competent around machines—perhaps because they weren't chasing kids around—was born. It didn't have to happen this way, but it did.

Women, because of their physical ties to children—their unique ability to nurse—identified themselves as caretakers of kids. They had served this role in the past, but their labor was deemed more egalitarian— everyone worked the farm. Now, everyone didn't need to work the farm. Machines could do most of the labor. Why not send women away from the machinery and have them raise the children?

Such an idea proved especially applicable for "middle-class" women, who became segregated in private households. Because a status symbol of increasing prosperity was a woman in the home, middle- and upper-class men expected their wives not to sweat—particularly not in factories. Indeed, as the "new middle class" emerged with the Industrial Revolution, a whole new set of ideas took root as well. Women's worlds became defined as domestic worlds. Poor and working-class women, and those of non-European, white racial or ethnic backgrounds, were not treated as delicately. They did indeed toil and sweat in the factories—where their lives became harsh in a new way, an industrialized way.

Thus was born the idea of *separate spheres* and the *cult of true womanhood*. These ideologies did not redefine who women are—instead, they redefined the subordinate role of women. Through the cult of true womanhood, as discussed by Welter (1966), women judged themselves, and were judged by their husbands, based on their compliance with patriarchal expectations, and their ability to uphold four virtues: piety (the most important), purity, domesticity, and submissiveness. The separate-spheres ideology sanctified the belief that woman's place was in the home and man's place was in the workforce. The idea of the private world and the public world ossified; each gender had its role to play in its own social world.

It is this set of beliefs that we now often refer to as "traditional" ideas about women—but surprisingly, these beliefs are not that old. They didn't truly arise until the late 1800s. Yet they strongly influence how we think about womanhood in general, and motherhood and housework in particular. They influence the kinds of stories we read in "women's magazines" (be they *Cosmo* or *Family Circle*), the kinds of guilt trips women lay on themselves, and the myriad other aspects of contemporary life we've inherited from the Industrial Revolution.

As Belknap (1996) notes, patriarchy has used these ideas to restrict women to the private sphere, and to see them as delicate creatures in need of protection. Men have benefited from this arrangement both domestically (by being released from the responsibility of daily household chores, for example) and socially (through social ideas about "men's work" and "women's work," for example). These beliefs have also influenced social policies and laws to the point where new legislation and case decisions have reinforced these notions. On many different fronts, postindustrial attitudes toward women have limited their social participation in the United States.

Walking the Line

Throughout much of industrial history (and some of preindustrial), women have felt compelled to walk a thin line in an often uncompromising world. They live on "women's wages" and yet must care for their children. They do "women's work," yet struggle to look pretty, work hard, and not be tired. Often the choices are either/or, and neither one is good. Merlo and Pollack (1995, p. 23) call these situations "crossovers." Here are some examples of women who are "walking the line":

1. Old women with limited resources who steal cat food or cans of soup
2. Battered women who kill their batterers
3. Prostitutes
4. Battered women accused of battery themselves because their kids are also being battered
5. Women with custody of their kids who are charged with neglect (or some other crime) because they're legally required to let their children see their biological father, who then beats them
6. Women who must let their children visit their father, who then kills them because he was driving drunk; the mother gets charged with their death
7. Women who buy cosmetics to look pretty and then are told that pretty and smart don't go together

8. Pregnant female substance abusers
9. Working mothers
10. Women who have abortions

What do all of these situations have in common? They put women in a no-win situation. Either way they choose, they have to make a sacrifice, and then they are judged as bad based on that sacrifice. For example, consider the working mother. How often does a typical working mother hear, "Don't you wish you could stay home with your kids?" or, "The world is falling apart because mothers aren't with their children." Yet how does the family pay its bills without her paid labor? What if she is a single mother? If she *doesn't* "work," she will need some kind of public assistance. And if she's on public assistance, she's a "lazy welfare mother just trying to pop out more kids for more money." How can she win? When we tell women to look pretty and then tell them that pretty and smart don't equate, how can she win? If she doesn't "spend time on herself," we think she's lazy, unattractive, doesn't care, and so forth. But if she looks *too* good, how could she possibly run a Fortune 500 company (unless, of course, it is a makeup or fashion firm)?

Walking the line has a tragic end result: Society puts a deviant or criminal label on women. This label, which profoundly harms women's lives, is something that women struggle with more than men. Yes, men carry their own burdens. But these burdens are rarely so closely attached to their worth as human beings. Read the phrase above about working mothers again—then substitute working Dads in the sentence. What happens?

As we have refined and redefined women's and men's roles in the postindustrial age, we have put women in ever more problematic walking-the-line situations. We will look at these situations throughout the book.

The Essence of the Chapter

Much of what we learn from patriarchy is stereotypical and fits in with our gender schemas. Because patriarchy at its core focuses on images of maleness and femaleness, it causes society to function both consciously and unconsciously around stereotypical images. These images help us organize our world. As we will find, they also influence the decisions men *and* women make about women. And, they affect the legal and justice systems. Is the law male? Many feminist writers/scholars answer a hands-down "yes." As one writer remarks, "Women's struggle for equal rights is ultimately the struggle to destroy effectively and completely our country's belief in stereotypes" (Otten, 1993, p. 233). This author continues,

Despite the progress made, we are still light years away from giving women true equality with men. As long as laws tell women when and how they may control their bodies, but no similar laws dictate to men, there is no such thing as equality. As long as women are excluded from combat simply because they are female while men are automatically eligible simply because they are male, there is no equality. As long as laws limit women as to where and how they may work if they also want to be mothers to have no such laws for fathers and would-be fathers, there is no equality.

2 In the Beginning . . .

As I pointed out at the end of Chapter 1, the ideas that society has about women have influenced women's position with respect to justice. Whether we examine women's lives in contemporary society or in centuries past, how women were and are thought about has shaped how the justice system treats them. Law and justice do not operate in a vacuum; the people, conditions, and ideas of an era affect the rights, roles, and responsibilities of women. Likewise, how we examine the lives of criminal women is also influenced by ideas, people, and social conditions.

Comprehending the intricacies of the U.S. legal system can help us understand how justice has informed women's lives throughout time. As Otten's quote at the end of Chapter 1 points out, "We are still light years away from giving women true equality with men" (1993, p. 233). Gaining an understanding of how our legal and justice system has developed will help us understand why Otten makes this claim. We must also clarify the differences among common law, civil law, and criminal law to know what we are talking about in the legal arena. Understanding how crime is officially measured and calculated also provides insight for us; after all, crime, like justice, is a socially constructed phenomenon.

The Development of Common Law

The United States is commonly referred to as a "common-law" country, and its legal tradition is shared by only a few other nations in the world. The common-law "family" of countries is not the only legal family, or tradition, in the world; indeed, this tradition is the least common in existence these days. The civil family of law is actually the most common around the world, and is used in countries such as France, Italy, and Scotland. What distinguishes the common-law family from other families? The overriding principle is the use of precedent.

Literally translated, using precedent means "standing by decided cases." The U.S. legal system thus refers to previous decisions made in courtrooms to guide decisions currently under discussion. Some legal theorists argue that precedent is important because it provides four things: predictability, reliability, efficiency, and equality (Dworkin, 1998). *Predictability* means that decisions based on precedent are consistent, ordered, uniform, and certain. Relying on precedent gives the outcome of a legal decision a certain uniformity, an ordered sense in the legal order. *Reliability* refers to the fact that participants in the legal system expect a court to follow precedent. The notion of *efficiency* suggests that precedent allows for a timely resolution to the settling of disputes. And finally, the idea of *equality* means that similar cases are treated in a similar fashion.

Not all judges think about precedent in the same way. Dworkin distinguishes between two legal doctrines of precedent: *strict doctrine*, which obliges judges to follow earlier decisions even if they believe them to be wrong, and *relaxed doctrine*, whereby judges give some weight to past decisions and must follow those decisions unless they believe them to be sufficiently wrong. As we will see in this book, both of these doctrines, as well as the importance of the above four characteristics, have exerted a strong impact on women's lives. Indeed, the principle of precedent—the idea that it provides consistency and equality and must be followed unless it is "sufficiently wrong"—has hindered the lives of thousands of women. To this day, some legal scholars argue that following precedent is like trying to run up a hill backwards—if one is always looking back (or toward the bottom of the hill), how is one supposed to move forward (or up the hill)? It can be done, but only with difficulty.

BOX 2.1   Rousseau on Justice

I conceive of two kinds of inequality in the human species: one which I call natural or physical, because it is established by nature and consists in the difference of age, health, bodily strength, and qualities of mind or soul. The other may be called moral or political inequality, because it depends on a kind of convention and is established , or at least authorized, by the consent of men. This latter type of inequality consists in different privileges enjoyed by some at the expense of others, such as being richer, more honored, more powerful than they, or even causing themselves to be obeyed by them.

There is no point in asking what the source of natural inequality is, because the answer would be found enunciated in the simple definition of the word. There is still less of a point in asking whether there would not be some essential connections between the two inequalities. . . .

Jean-Jacques Rousseau, *The Discourse on the Origins of Inequality*

The Role of People, Conditions, and Ideas

How did common law first emerge? A change in people, conditions, and ideas started the process. After 1066, William the Conqueror, the Norman warrior who invaded England, sought to unite "his" fragmented kingdom. Up until that point, law was practiced in a piecemeal manner. Every village conducted justice in its own way, and individuals (usually religious leaders) defined right and wrong. William, wanting to establish a system that he could control, decided to send judges from town to town to hear the issues people were arguing about. Furthermore, he wanted the judges to start basing their decisions in one case on decisions that were made in the past. Why? William felt this approach would bring continuity to his legal system, and would tie all of England together. Judges would become responsible for operating the system, and would make decisions based on what one another was doing and had done in the past. This "judge-made" law is somewhat akin to what we now call precedent—the principle that defines a common-law system. The idea that the law is common to all people is another characteristic of this system.

Sir William Blackstone is credited with the actual writing of the common law in the 1700s. Like William seven centuries earlier, Blackstone believed the law should be clearly specified; penning the legal rules in use provided that specificity. In his *Commentaries on the Law* (used for over one hundred years in U.S. law-school classes), Blackstone identified the "Nature of Law in General" by discussing five key points:

1. The meaning of law
2. The law as order of the universe
3. The law as a rule of human action
4. The law of nature
5. Revealed law

Let's examine each of these points in a little more detail. Regarding the *meaning of law*, Blackstone wrote,

> Law . . . signifies a rule of action. . . . And it is that rule of action, which is prescribed by some superior, and which the inferior is bound to obey.

Law as order of the universe says,

> Thus when the Supreme Being formed the universe, and created matter out of nothing, He impressed certain principles upon that matter. . . . When He put the matter into motion, He established

certain laws of motion, to which all movable bodies must conform.

When discussing *Law as a rule of human action,* Blackstone wrote,

> This, then, is the general signification of law, a rule of action dictated by some superior being; and, in those creatures that have neither the power to think, nor to will, such laws must invariably be obeyed. . . . Man, considered as a creature, must necessarily be subject to the laws of the Creator, for he is entirely a dependent being.

"This will of his Maker is called the law of nature," Blackstone wrote. Regarding *The law of nature,*

> Considering the Creator only a Being of infinite power, He was able to unquestionably to have prescribed whatever laws He pleased to His creature, man, however unjust or severe. But He is also a Being of infinite wisdom, He has laid down only such laws as were founded in those relations of justice, that existed in the nature of things antecedent to any positive precept. These are the eternal immutable laws of good and evil, to which the Creator Himself in all His dispensations conforms; and which He has enabled human reason to discover, so far as they are necessary for the conduct of human actions.

And, finally, in *Revealed law,* Blackstone wrote,

> The doctrines thus delivered we call the revealed or divine law, and they are to be found only in the Holy Scripture. . . . Upon these two foundations, the law of nature and the law of revelation, depend all human laws; that is to say, no human laws should be suffered to contradict these. There are, it is true, a great number of indifferent points, in which both the divine law and the natural leave a man at his own liberty; but which are found necessary for the benefit of society to be restrained within certain limits.

Influenced by the ideas and social conditions of his time, Blackstone had a "traditional" view of humanity and of women. As you can likely tell from his writings above, he had strong Judeo-Christian beliefs. Many of those beliefs have specific views of women associated with them. These views were translated into the common law, primarily through the legal concept of *coverture.* Coverture is the legal relationship whereby "the husband and wife are one and that one is the husband." The legacy of coverture lasted for two centuries. Though coverture is no longer considered a valid legal concept in the United States, it still makes itself felt in the United States' legal system.

Civil and Criminal Law in a Common-Law System

Studies demonstrate that though many U.S. citizens think they know something about the law, they in fact know very little. Furthermore, what people do know is often inaccurate or it misconstrues how the legal and justice system actually operates. Why? For one thing, we get a lot of our information from television and the movies. Though often dramatic and entertaining, these two sources don't necessarily offer realistic portrayals of how the law works. The title of this section is the first place to start: *civil* and *criminal* law in a *common-law system*.

The U.S. common-law system comprises two kinds of law—civil law and criminal law. Some people would argue that this statement greatly oversimplifies the legal system, given that the system also includes constitutional law, administrative law, martial law, military law, and so on. We discuss constitutional law in Chapter 3, but in this chapter we are most concerned with the primary division of the law into criminal law and civil law. Another caution: The *division* of civil law we are talking about at this point is different from the civil-law *tradition* mentioned above. That tradition is a system, or family, of law. The division is a classification of law within a common-law system.

When people commit a crime, they are dealt with in the criminal-law division. The state (that is, the government) prosecutes that crime as a representative of "the people." Generally, criminal cases can be easily identified, because they are called something like *The People v. Smith*, or *State of Minnesota v. Smith*, or something along those lines. The state ("the people") prosecutes an individual who broke the law because it believes that person's behavior has violated the public trust. For a behavior to be considered criminal, *actus reus* ("the guilty act") and *mens rea* ("the guilty mind" intent) must be present. Many different behaviors fall under this umbrella—rape, murder, assault, prostitution, and so forth.

Civil law is basically anything that falls outside the boundaries of criminal law. Civil cases can often be identified by the use of two names in the case citation—*Smith v. Smith* or *Smith v. Jones*. In these cases, two parties (individuals, groups, corporations, or even the government) need to settle a dispute. Many different topics fall under this umbrella—divorce, custody, sexual harassment, and so on.

Some cases are tried in *both* a civil and criminal manner. For example, a person might be tried as a defendant by the state (perhaps for assault), and then tried again as a defendant by a plaintiff who is suing for damages. In this kind of scenario, the individual is being tried for two different things—the commission of a crime, and the injury inflicted by his or her behavior. The state is involved in the first trial because its purpose is to protect all citizens' rights. A plaintiff (the aggrieved person, who may have served as a witness at the first trial) is involved in the second trial to protect his or her rights and try to recover all or part of what was lost owing to the crime. Many cases involving women's justice have fallen into the civil category. They have centered on women's civil rights as opposed to crime.

Sex/Gender in the (Common) Law

Professor Katherine MacKinnon (1983) argues that "the law sees and treats women the way men see and treat women." This statement suggests a hint of patriarchy in the law. Let's talk about this.

MacKinnon and others believe the male viewpoint dominates the legal horizon, including its claim of an objective standard (1993, p. 611). Feminist analyses, in turn, consider the objective standard a myth. Feminist analysis recognizes that "patriarchal myths are projections of the male psyche" (1993, p. 96). The idea that the law is an objective, rational, and unemotional entity is itself an emotive claim. This male form of jurisprudence defines and implements a law that comes from the "male as normative" point of view. Examples of this include "standards for scope of judicial review, norms of judicial restraint, reliance on precedent, separation of powers, and the division between public and private law. Substantive doctrines like standing, justiciability, and state action adopt the same stance" (p. 611). According to this system, rules must appear to be detached decisions with an "abstract universality," meaning that the rule can be applied in all like situations. See, no attachment here.

U.S. jurisprudence is also based on what West calls the "separation thesis" (1993, p. 493). The separation thesis holds that human beings are legally separate and distinct from one another. This is not a surprising notion in the United States' legal system, especially given the ideology of individualism that permeates U.S. society. The ideology of individualism has informed much of U.S. history—ideas about Manifest Destiny, pulling ourselves up by our bootstraps, equality and justice for all.

West argues that all of this is "essentially and irretrievably masculine" (1993, p. 493). Why? Because it gives us a male vision of the world. Because it assumes that the goal in life is to be separate from one another, and to be objective in relation to one another. This vision centers on the notion that it is "man's nature" to be separate from other "men," while it overlooks what much research has come to find—that women live their lives connected to others. If, as West suggests, the law is grounded on this notion of separateness, yet women live their lives connected to others, then how does the law relate to women? Poorly. And badly. Indeed, if we look at how legal ideology assumes the world operates, and how feminist ideology assumes women's lives work, we see some stark contrasts (see Table 2.1). Law is not simply some academic discipline, Baer (1992) argues; it is a manifestation of male power and male legal ideology.

Legal ideology operates on a very different plane than women's lives do. Women have an "ethic of care, and commitment to the value of nurturance and intimacy" (West, 1993, p. 517). Moreover, this ethic is celebrated among women but abhorred by the legal world. As a matter of fact, patriarchy often operates in a manner directly opposite to those values.

There appears to be a *"fundamental contradiction"* (West, 1993, p. 520) between what the law values and what women value. The rule of law does not honor intimacy and connectedness; it emphasizes objectivity and distance. It is masculine. Women are absent in this jurisprudence because "women as human beings are absent from the law's protection: jurisprudence does not recognize us because law does not protect us" (p. 522). West maintains that the only way to find a law that truly considers women is to abolish patriarchy.

The notions of separate spheres, the "true woman," and Christian ideology define and have been defined by the law. Quadraplexation has also been defined by the law, something we can see by looking at examples of women's inequality written into the law. Laws about rape, battery, and sexual harassment define sexuality; laws about unequal pay, sexual harassment, and the "pink-collar ghetto" define production. Laws regarding custody, child support, and marital dissolution also fall within the production sphere. And laws about women's "nature" define socialization. All of these

TABLE 2.1 Legal Ideology versus Women's Reality/Feminist Ideology

	What is valued?	What is feared or harmful?	What is longed for?	What is dreaded?
Legal Ideology, or the rule of law	Autonomy, individualism, and objectivity	Frustration	Attachment and connection	Alienation
Feminist Ideology, or women's reality	Intimacy and connection	Separation	Individuation	Invasion and intrusion

(Adapted from West, 1993, p. 509.)

realities within the law point to at least one thing—that gender still plays a major role in the law.

As Belknap notes (1996, pp. 12–23), the legal arena transforms stereotypes for its own purposes; she cites several persistent themes:

1. The law views women as passive, weak, incompetent, and childlike.
2. The law assumes that women need *protection* because they are impressionable. (The law sees men as the protectors and caretakers of women.)
3. The law views women as pawns of their biology. (This creates a double standard: morality built into a law based on biological determinism.)
4. The law sees women as impulsive and nonanalytcial.
5. It also views women as masculine.
6. In the eyes of the law, the criminal woman is pure evil.

These themes influence decisions made on street corners by police personnel, in courtrooms by judges, and throughout the rest of the legal system.

Smart (1976) suggests examining the law from three perspectives: law as sexist, law as male, and law as gendered. "Law as sexist" was the first phase of recognition among feminist legal scholars. Here, the meaning and implementation of the law actively disadvantaged women. Women had fewer material (and legal) resources available to them, they were judged differently than men were, and they battled religious and stereotypical images about who they should be. This first stage has persisted throughout the life of the common law, and has emphasized a polarized view of the genders.

The second stage, "law as male," marked the beginning of a new era, one recognizing that most lawmakers, lawyers, judges, and police officers are male. This reality also strongly affects women's position in the justice system. Once maleness is embedded in the law, its "objectiveness" ceases. Why? Because the "objective" criteria used are actually male criteria and therefore male biased. This circumstance only further polarizes images and judgments about the genders.

The last stage, "law as gendered," works to abandon the polarized view of women and men in the law. Rather, the central question becomes, "How does gender work in the law, and how does the law produce gender?" This book explores this question in the hope that the answers will help people, times, and ideas change.

Challenges to the Common-Law System

Challenges to the common-law system have cropped up many times over the past several hundred years. We are not, however, talking about challenges to the operation of the system. People have not taken to the streets and tried to convert the organization of precedence. Rather, they have tried to change the documents written and the decisions made in legislative bodies and courtrooms around the country. Challenges have come in other venues as well.

For example, as early as 1776, Abigail Adams wrote letters to her husband, John Quincy Adams, asking him and his companions to "remember the ladies." She wasn't asking this because she felt women were fairly treated at the time—quite the contrary. She wanted her husband and his contemporaries to remember her and other women in this "new" country as they constructed its laws.

When the Civil War Amendments (see Chapter 3) were added to the U.S. Constitution, they grew out of the challenge to the legal system of slavery in this country. The amendments changed the system and worked to define and protect rights to those harmed by slavery.

In 1876, Mississippi became the first state in the United States to pass a Married Women's Property Act. This act chiseled away at coverture and gave women the right to own property—a formidable challenge, given the strength of the coverture legacy. When women "won" the right to vote in 1920, this event also challenged the idea that women were neither capable of choosing government leaders nor entitled to express their choice. We'll take a closer look at these examples and others as we examine the ways the common-law system has been challenged and how it has responded.

Examining Crime

The stereotypes cited by Belknap (1996) in the previous pages included references to criminal women. Up to this point in the chapter, we have mainly looked at civil law. Let's turn to the criminal aspect for a while now.

What Is Crime?

Defining and measuring crime is not easy. The most widely used and cited source of "official" crime data in the United States is the Uniform Crime Report (UCR). The Federal Bureau of Investigation (FBI) compiles the UCR by using the voluntary submission of police-report data from more than 16,000 police departments across the country. Though submission of this data is voluntary, 96 percent of departments do provide the data to the FBI. The data in the UCR are based on "crimes known to the police" or, in other words, crimes reported or observed by police that have resulted in written documentation.

The UCR reports crime by city, county, metropolitan and geographic region, age, race, and gender. It is divided into two parts: Part I crimes, or the Index crimes, and Part II crimes. These divisions have generated much discussion. The Index crimes include eight crimes—four violent crimes (murder, robbery, rape, and aggravated assault) and four property crimes (burglary, arson, larceny-theft, and motor-vehicle theft). These crimes get the most "press time," even though they make up less then 15 percent of all crimes. The remaining 85 percent or more of crime—those in Part II—include simple assault, fraud, and so forth. We hear less about these crimes, yet they are the most common. They are also the crimes women are most likely to commit. (We'll explore this more in a minute.)

Developed in 1929, the UCR is not without criticism. First, it has barely changed since it originated, although society has certainly changed. Second, some critics believe that it underestimates the extent of crime by about 50 percent. Third, because of police discretion, the UCR may be a more accurate indicator of police behavior than anything else. Officers make the decision whether to arrest or not, and as mentioned above, the UCR is based on crimes known to the police *and* reported. The voluntary submission of police data is another criticism; if this is the "official" report of data, why doesn't the FBI require all police departments to turn in their data? Yet despite these and other criticisms, we still use the UCR to calculate crime rates. Many authors (see Kappeler et al., 1996, for example) suggest that crime rates tell us virtually nothing about crime and only something about the political and social climate of the times.

Another way to identify crime came with the creation of the National Crime Victims Survey (NCVS), developed in 1972. The NCVS was developed in part to address the problems of the UCR and is meant to complement the older document. Undertaken by the Census Bureau, the NCVS collects data from 46,000 households (about 110,000 people) though interviews every six months. The NCVS is the most complex and far-reaching victimization survey in this country; it has found that only about one-third of all crimes committed are reported to the police.

To combat problems with the UCR and NCVS, the National Incident Based Reporting System (NIBRS) was developed in the 1980s. Still not in widespread use, the NIBRS restructured the crimes considered most important by identifying 22 crimes as central crimes (instead of the eight Index crimes). The NIBRS provides a more comprehensive and contemporary picture of crime in the United States. Until it is in widespread use, however, we will not fully know its benefits.

Why are these issues important to our study of women and justice? Well, not only is there some concern regarding the general collection of crime statistics, there is also some concern regarding the collection of crime statistics regarding women specifically.

What Is a "Criminal"?

The term *criminal*—believe it or not—is not so easily defined. What are we talking about? An individual under suspicion of engaging in criminal behavior? Someone who's been arrested? Only a person who has actually been convicted of a crime? Technically, suspicion does not render one anything other than being under suspicion. A person arrested may be called an "alleged offender" or some such term, but arrest does not necessarily mean guilt. The word *criminal*, then, is applicable only to individuals—male or female—who have been convicted of a crime.

Who Are Women Criminals?

If we take a closer look at crime data, we can see that women are less criminal than men. An examination of both arrest and incarceration data supports this conclusion. When women do offend, they tend to engage in minor property crimes. Yet two primary myths have emerged about women criminals. The first one goes something like this: Women are becoming more violent, serious offenders as time goes on; they are becoming more like men in the level of sophistication, seriousness, and heinousness of their offenses. In fact, there is no empirical evidence to support this. Women's reported serious crime rates have not changed significantly since the late 1700s. The second myth claims that the extent of women's crimes has changed—namely, that it has skyrocketed. Again, in reality that extent has not changed. I call this phenomenon the "2 N's," or the nature and numbers phenomenon. Let's look at some statistics to see how inaccurate these myths are.

Women's arrest statistics for 1999 are displayed in Table 2.2; the top set of crimes includes the Index crimes, the bottom set shows the Part II crimes. We can identify general patterns. The top six crimes (not including the category "all other offenses") for which women were arrested in 1999 were larceny-theft, other assaults, drug-abuse violations, driving under the influence, fraud, and disorderly conduct. Not one of these categories is a violent crime. These arrest patterns have stayed remarkably stable since the 1930s.

Women's crimes require little skill or education and yield small rewards. Indeed, one reason women engage in such crime is because they are economically marginalized (we'll discuss this more in Chapter 5). Still, these crimes usually don't lift them out of that situation, contrary to popular opinion.

True, the raw number of women arrested has risen dramatically in the last two decades. But as Steffensmeier (1995) points out, we must consider these numbers within their context. What context? Let's start by looking at proportions and comparing them. In 1980, women made up 15.7 percent of all people arrested (1,044,420/6,652,448). In 1989, women constituted 18.1 percent of arrests (1,544,336/8,495,179). In 1995, they were 20.4 percent (2,332,213/11,416,346). And in 1998, women made up 21.8 percent of all people arrested (2,245,800/10,295,129). When we consider specific crimes, we find the same thing. While the *number* of women arrested has increased, the proportion has stayed relatively the same—this is what Steffensmeier means by context.

Why have the numbers increased? We must look for answers in several places. In general, the increase stems from changes in the criminal-justice system. Specifically, U.S. society has experienced changing ideas in criminal justice about drugs and about "getting tough," changes in crime-detection methods, and new mandatory sentencing policies. New social policies, such as the shift from Aid to Families with Dependent Children (AFDC) (the "old" welfare system) to Temporary Assistance to Needy Families (TANF) (the "new" welfare system)—both discussed more fully in Chapter 7—may have also provoked more desperate actions by women. And as crime definitions change, so do the reasons behind why women are arrested. For example, some writers talk about the *"new female crimes."* They really mean behaviors either that didn't exist in the past or that we simply didn't discuss; for examples, surrogate motherhood and women's use of drugs while pregnant. *It is interesting that these crimes relate to women's bodies— surely a quadraplexation issue.* In addition to rising arrest rates, more and more women were incarcerated in the 1990s for many of the same reasons listed above. (Many women may also go to prison because they can't pay the fines required to stay out.) We will talk more about women in prison in Chapter 9.

Another striking phenomenon is what I call the *"2 M's"*—men and money. Interestingly enough, when women tell their stories of crime and criminality, often they include the two M's. They suggest that they committed crimes because they needed money (either they were poor or they had children to support, or a combination of the two). Many of them also tell stories about how the men in their lives (fathers brothers, husbands, boyfriends) victimized them or encouraged or forced them into crime. Books such as Kathryn Watterson's *Women in Prison* (1996) contain many narratives in which the 2 M's come through loud and clear. What do the theorists say about why women commit crimes?

Theories about Criminal Women

The earliest ideas about criminals did not even include discussions of women. Men have historically been defined as more deviant than women; that is true to this day. Even the earliest "scholarly" ideas about criminals—

TABLE 2.2 Arrest Statistics, 1999

Arrests by offense charged and sex, United States, 1999 (8,546 agencies; 1999 estimated population 171,831,000)

Offense charged	Total number	Persons arrested				Percent distribution of offenses charged[a]		
		Male		Female		Total	Male	Female
		Number	Percent	Number	Percent			
Total	9,141,201	7,143,931	78.2%	1,997,270	21.8%	100.0%	100.0%	100.0%
Murder and nonnegligent manslaughter	9,727	8,622	88.6	1,105	11.4	0.1	0.1	0.1
Forcible rape	18,759	18,521	98.7	238	1.3	0.2	0.3	(b)
Robbery	73,619	66,214	89.9	7,405	10.1	0.8	0.9	0.4
Aggravated assault	318,051	255,331	80.3	62,720	19.7	3.5	3.6	3.1
Burglary	192,570	167,661	87.1	24,909	12.9	2.1	2.3	1.2
Larceny-theft	794,201	512,227	64.5	281,974	35.5	8.7	7.2	14.1
Motor vehicle theft	94,335	79,660	84.4	14,675	15.6	1.0	1.1	0.7
Arson	10,811	9,251	85.6	1,560	14.4	0.1	0.1	0.1
Violent crime[c]	420,156	348,688	83.0	71,468	17.0	4.6	4.9	3.6
Property crime[d]	1,091,917	768,799	70.4	323,118	29.6	11.9	10.8	16.2
Total Crime Index[e]	1,512,073	1,117,487	73.9	394,586	26.1	16.5	15.6	19.8
Other assaults	844,728	654,386	77.5	190,342	22.5	9.2	9.2	9.5
Forgery and counterfeiting	69,853	43,033	61.6	26,820	38.4	0.8	0.6	1.3
Fraud	225,934	127,521	56.4	98,413	43.6	2.5	1.8	4.9
Embezzlement	11,208	5,690	50.8	5,518	49.2	0.1	0.1	0.3
Stolen property: buying, receiving, possessing	80,426	67,831	84.3	12,595	15.7	0.9	0.9	0.6
Vandalism	182,043	154,155	84.7	27,888	15.3	2.0	2.2	1.4
Weapons: carrying, possessing, etc.	113,880	104,953	92.2	8,927	7.8	1.2	1.5	0.4

Offense charged	Total	Male number	Male %	Female number	Female %			
Prostitution and commercialized vice	63,927	25,078	39.2	38,849	60.8	0.7	0.4	1.9
Sex offenses (except forcible rape and prostitution)	60,120	55,857	92.9	4,263	7.1	0.7	0.8	0.2
Drug abuse violations	1,007,002	829,460	82.4	177,542	17.6	11.0	11.6	8.9
Gambling	7,023	6,151	87.6	872	12.4	0.1	0.1	(b)
Offenses against family and children	92,849	72,365	77.9	20,484	22.1	1.0	1.0	1.0
Driving under the influence	931,235	782,745	84.1	148,490	15.9	10.2	11.0	7.4
Liquor laws	427,873	333,530	78.0	94,343	22.0	4.7	4.7	4.7
Drunkenness	437,153	381,806	87.3	55,347	12.7	4.8	5.3	2.8
Disorderly conduct	421,662	324,691	77.0	96,971	23.0	4.6	4.5	4.9
Vagrancy	20,213	16,498	81.6	3,715	18.4	0.2	0.2	0.2
All other offenses (except traffic)	2,416,544	1,918,033	79.4	498,511	20.6	26.4	26.8	25.0
Suspicion	4,907	3,888	79.2	1,019	20.8	0.1	0.1	0.1
Curfew and loitering law violations	114,220	79,433	69.5	34,787	30.5	1.2	1.1	1.7
Runaways	96,328	39,340	40.8	56,988	59.2	1.1	0.6	2.9

Note: Estimates by the U.S. Census Bureau indicate that on July 1, 1999, males comprised 48.9% and females 51.1% of the total U.S. resident population (U.S. Department of Commerce, Bureau of the Census, "Resident Population Estimates of the United States by Sex, Race, and Hispanic Origin: April 1, 1990 to July 1, 1999, with Short-term Projection to November 1, 2000" [Online]. Available: http://www.census.gov/population/estimates/nation/intfile3-1.txt [Jan. 8, 2001].)

aBecause of rounding, percents may not add to total.

bLess than 0.1%.

cViolent crimes are offenses of murder and nonnegligent manslaughter, forcible rape, robbery, and aggravated assault.

dProperty crimes are offenses of burglary, larceny-theft, motor vehicle theft, and arson.

eIncludes arson.

Source: U.S. Department of Justice, Federal Bureau of Investigation, *Crime in the United States, 1999* (Washington, DC: USGPO,2000), p. 229. Table adapted by SOURCEBOOK staff.

those put forth by Cesare Lombroso, often identified as the "founder" of criminology—were about men only and were couched in the ideas of Lombroso's time. As with everything human, social conditions, people, and ideas have influenced how we think about criminal women versus non-criminal women. As a result, criminology as a discipline, as well as theorists, have until recently largely ignored women criminals. Belknap (1996) suggests two primary reasons for this: One, women make up a small percent of all criminals, and two, they thus are considered an insignificant topic. Contemporary theorists often want to ask the question, why are people criminal? But a much more important question is, why are women so much less criminal than men? It would seem that society could truly learn something valuable if it could answer that question. Thus women's role in crime is hardly insignificant. It is widely recognized today that gender is a primary determinant of crime; to some criminologists, it has more significance than race, social class, or even age—the variables traditionally scrutinized within the discipline.

Belknap suggests the older, mainstream theorists created an "armchair tradition" by grounding their theories in a set of assumptions linked to women's "nature" and the quadraplexation stereotypes that confirmed the notions of separate spheres and true womanhood. What are these assumptions?

1. Criminality is the result of *individual characteristics* that are only peripherally affected by social, economic, and political forces.
2. These individual characteristics are of a *physiological or psychological nature.*
3. The *biological and psychological characteristics* of women define their role in crime.
4. The basic way to *rehabilitate* criminal women is through *individual adjustment*, not through addressing the plight of women in society.
5. *Sexuality* is the key root of all female behavior and the problem behind crime.

Notice the primary role that sexuality plays in these assumptions. The following discussion of theories about female criminality demonstrates just how important this quadraplexation variable is.

The Early Theories

In 1895, Lombroso published *The Female Offender*, in which he argued that criminals are born criminals and possess atavistic (crude, apelike) characteristics. Though he found fewer instances of born female criminals than born male criminals, he nevertheless maintained that women are less evolved than men and more biologically primitive. Lombroso saw women as more childlike, less sensitive, and less intelligent than men, as well as more menacing and immoral. According to Lombroso, the atavistic characteristics possessed by women offenders included excessive body hair, wrinkles and "crow's feet," and abnormal craniums. He felt that while "normal" women are feminine, criminal women are masculine. And, he considered prostitutes the lowliest of all female criminals. These attitudes reflected his era. At the time he was researching and writing (the Victorian era), the ideas of separate spheres and true womanhood were flourishing. Prostitutes were anything but dedicated to hearth, home, and family (at least in Lombroso's mind); thus they lacked the most important quality—piety.

W. I. Thomas published *Sex and Society* (1907) and *The Unadjusted Girl* (1923) a few years after Lombroso's work. Initially, Thomas stated in *Sex and Society* that the differences between men and women are socially determined. However, he then suggested that women are passive wells of energy (*anabolic*) and men are consumptive wells of energy (*katabolic*). In the end, he argued a biological predisposition to the roles of women and men. In *The Unadjusted Girl*, Thomas discussed the interplay between the social environment and biology. He claimed that women's criminality is largely influenced by the desire to have new experiences. Therefore, women become criminals (especially prostitutes), because crime offers exciting new experiences. Wanting excitement and change was a whole new way to think about women criminals, although it still described a deviant "way" to be a woman.

Even Freud had something to say about women's deviant (or criminal) behavior. He regarded women as biologically deficient, passive, narcissistic, and masochistic. He attributed these qualities to their lack of a penis. Because Freud believed that the world centers on maleness, and therefore that maleness is the norm, he said that women believe their sex organs to be incomplete. This sense of "anatomical deficiency" inclines women toward amorality. The deviant woman is one who is attempting to be a man. Why? So she can have a penis. Thus she engages in male behaviors—such as become a criminal. Writers through the years, among them Karen Horney, have worked with Freud's theories. Some have postulated that although women might have penis envy but that men's womb envy was more severe—men, unable to bear children, must prove their worthiness to society and do so by acting out in macho ways.

Eleanor and Sheldon Glueck wrote *Five Hundred Delinquent Women* (1934) with the objective of finding out what factors led to delinquency in women. The Gluecks determined that female delinquency stemmed from a combination of biological and economic factors. In their sample, many delinquent women came from abnormally large families that had a history of criminality, and the women tended to be "sexually loose" and "mentally defective." The researchers also found a connection between low socio-economic status and delinquency. In the Gluecks' view, the best way to solve the problem of female delinquency was to implement an eugenics program, or a policy of enforced sterilization. Because criminality seemed to be at least partly genetic, one way to stop it would be to breed it out.

Perhaps one of the best-known and most frequently cited works on women and crime is Otto Pollak's _The Criminality of Women_ (1950). In this work, Pollak suggested three things:

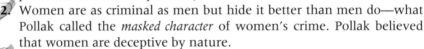

1. Women's crimes are sexually motivated. (Here we *again* see quadra-plexation and sexuality issues.)
2. Women are as criminal as men but hide it better than men do—what Pollak called the *masked character* of women's crime. Pollak believed that women are deceptive by nature.
3. Women are given preferential treatment in the criminal-justice system—the *chivalry hypothesis* notion. He argued that because women are women and are not supposed to be criminal, the criminal-justice system treats them more leniently that it does men.

Pollak's work introduced a whole new area of discussion concerning women and the criminal-justice system. Scholars now discuss the chivalry hypothesis alongside two other hypotheses concerning gender disparities in the criminal-justice system: the "equal-treatment" hypothesis and the "evil-women" hypothesis. The equal-treatment hypothesis suggests that the system treats women and men equally; current research supports this idea. The evil-women hypothesis suggests that women are treated more harshly because they are considered bad by nature—that traditional idea about deviant women. The chivalry hypothesis comes directly from Pollak's work. Though some research finds support for this notion, most studies suggest that chivalry may exist only for certain women. Who might feel the effects of chivalry? Women who act in *expected* criminal ways seem to be treated more leniently than women who act in ways considered too heinous for a woman; for example, committing murder. Furthermore, white women are more likely to feel the effects of chivalry, as are middle-class, heterosexual women. One thing is certain: *If* the system treats women with chivalry, they have paid a high price for that chivalry.

From the 1960s Onward

In the 1960s, a handful of sociological studies of women offenders began to appear. Criminology texts started including a few pages on women. In 1968, Cavan and Cavan introduced a short chapter on delinquency in girls in their juvenile-delinquency book. Studies of women's prisons also began to emerge, such as Giallombardo's *Society of Women* (1966). In the 1970s, two authors advanced similar but not identical ideas. Adler (1975) claimed that the women's-liberation movement was producing a "new breed of female criminal." This new offender, Adler maintained, was moving into the world of robbery and burglary—traditionally male crimes—because of changing gender roles. Simon (1977) suggested that women's criminality would catch up with men because of increased social opportunities, particularly in the labor force. These ideas are known collectively as the "liberation theses." They have not held up as time has passed. The assumption behind these theses is that "liberation changes women." But does it? Research has found that women criminals tend to have traditional ideas; thus they are not likely to respond to ideologies of sex-role equality.

Numerous economic theories have pointed to women's secondary economic position as a motivating force in their criminality. If women's economic status is the motivator, that may explain why many of the crimes women commit are property rather than violent crimes. Consider the economic pressures women face: job segregation, the wage gap, feminization of poverty, the need to support children, and the combined economic effects of gender and race. Perhaps women turn to crime primarily to support themselves, and to support their children.

Feminist Explanations for Women's Criminality

There are numerous ways to discuss feminist theory and to group such theories. In this chapter, I talk about four "kinds" of feminist theory, although others may break the distinctions down differently. These four kinds of theories are (1) liberal feminism, (2) radical feminism, (3) Marxist feminism, and (4) socialist feminism. Though these theories identify different sources of oppression of women, they concur that all women, along with other groups, are oppressed.

Liberal feminism believes that women are oppressed because of a lack of equal opportunity. This lack of opportunity denies women the educational, employment, political, and social opportunities that men enjoy. Liberal feminism argues that women's criminality derives directly from this lack of equal opportunity. Indeed, the theses of Adler and Simon mentioned above are liberal-feminist theories, though they each suggest that as women gain opportunity, their crimes will *increase*. Liberal feminism today suggests that as women's opportunities increase, their crime rate will fall. They will not need to engage in property crimes such as fraud to get money for food; they will be making the money themselves.

Radical feminism claims that women are oppressed because of patriarchy. Patriarchy, as we've seen, defines women's lives for them. It also forces them into subservient roles, marginal jobs, and unpaid labor.

Patriarchy thus drives women to crime. Furthermore, patriarchy defines women's roles in crimes such as prostitution as evil because of these crimes' sexuality component. Yet patriarchy also wants women to be sexual. Radical feminism is best known for its analysis of the patriarchal crimes of rape, sexual harassment, and domestic violence. Only within patriarchy can such crimes exist.

Marxist feminism says that women are oppressed because of the capitalist/class system. Women become secondary in this analysis, because Marxist feminists see capitalism as the primary evil in society. Once the capitalist system is overthrown, women too will be free of their oppression. The capitalist system creates the subservient employment traps facing women; it is these traps that force women into crime.

Finally, **socialist feminism** argues that both patriarchy *and* capitalism oppress women. This form of feminism serves as the framework of Juliet Mitchell, the author of the quadraplexation variables discussed in this book. Some socialist feminists believe that either patriarchy or capitalism is the more powerful and oppressive force. Others contend that they are intertwining evils that we cannot separate. Within this analysis, it is the combined effect of patriarchy and capitalism that forces women into crime.

Mainstream Criminology Theories

There are numerous criminology theories that we would describe as "mainstream." Often they are divided into different groups—classical or neoclassical theory, structural theories, social-process theories, labeling theory, and radical or critical theories. The feminist theories discussed above most often fall under the latter group. That leaves four other categories. Let's look at them.

Classical Ideas

The classical theories focus on the work of Ceasare Beccaria and Jeremy Bentham. These early writers believed that society could control crime if it just found a way to deter individuals from engaging in it; crime was something people did because it brought them some kind of pleasure. Beccaria (1963) argued that deterrence worked best if it was swift, certain, and severe; in other words, people don't stop engaging in crime unless they are punished for it. Bentham (1789) felt that social-control institutions (prisons) would scare people away from crime. These authors focused solely on male criminals, however. Classical theory, and today's neoclassical theory of deterrence, deemphasize *why* people commit crime and instead stress how to deal with people who commit crime and how to deter crime. And because the majority of people arrested and jailed are men, these theories are directed at male criminals.

Social-Structural Ideas

Social-structural theories of crime focus on the role that social structure plays in crime. Generally, such theories look particularly at people on the lower end of the social-class system. Why? Because the social structures facing many poor and working-class people are different from those that characterize the lives of middle- and upper-class people. These more priviliged folks have many more opportunities available to them—such as college and "white collar," well paying jobs—than those in the lower classes have. The structural barriers, then, that lower-class members must overcome can be overwhelming.

Strain theory (or anomie theory), the work of Robert K. Merton (1938), applies both inside and outside criminology. Indeed, Merton asks why people are deviant. Within criminology, his thinking is considered a social-structural theory, for it looks at the opportunities that social structures do or do not present to people. The term *anomie* refers to what sociologists call a state of "normlessness," or when the collective order of society has unraveled and life's usual norms and goals seem unattainable. Such chaos causes stress and strain in people's lives, and these strains can lead people to commit crime. Merton argues that we emphasize certain "acceptable" goals in the United States; namely, to gain wealth and have monetary success. Indeed, most U.S. citizens believe strongly in this set of goals. Merton also explains that people use different methods to achieve these goals, and that not everyone uses methods that society considers acceptable.

Merton sees five "adaptations" in society, or five ways in which people put methods into practice to achieve a set of goals. The most common adaptation is the *conformist* adaptation. The conformist uses commonly accepted means to achieve goals; for instance, going to college and earning a degree so as to achieve wealth and material success. However, some individuals do not have access to these commonly accepted means. For example, they cannot afford to go to college. These folks engage in the *innovation* adaptation; through innovation, they find other ways to achieve success and money. What is the innovation? Maybe it is selling drugs, robbing a store, or engaging in the underground economy. Because these people do not have access to accepted means, they come under enormous strain. These are the people Merton was most interested in studying.

Ritualists don't necessarily value the wealth and money goals of society, but they do engage in socially acceptable behavior in their day-to-day lives. These are people who go to work day in and day out but who do not care whether they have a 401(k) retirement fund. *Retreatists* basically check out of society; they do not believe in the societal goals, nor do they use socially acceptable means to attain those goals. Indeed, they may go off to live on a mountaintop somewhere. This is the least common adaptation. Finally, *rebels* may or may not use acceptable means and may or may not believe in societally important goals. They are rebels precisely because they act depending on how they are feeling.

All of these last three adaptations are considered deviant. Yet they are of less consequence to Merton's discussion. This is largely because they are uncommon. Merton believes that some people, in order to achieve the goals of society, must engage in criminal behavior because they have no other way to achieve those goals. And because social structure limits who has access to acceptable means, it in part causes crime. Since Merton first wrote this analysis, researchers have spent many hours reworking his ideas. Many writers have redefined Merton's goals to mean practically anything— foregoing his early analysis focusing on wealth and monetary success.

How does Merton's thinking apply to women? In essence, it doesn't, at least in its original formulation. Most researchers today believe that the real goals of women are not success and money, but rather strong relation-ships. Women in U.S. society are taught (socialized) to value relationships over money and success. Even though women are moving away from this teaching to some extent, most gender scholars argue that it remains impor-tant in many women's lives. Often women define success as healthy chil-dren and a happy family. This definition of goals falls outside Merton's original analysis. If women's most important goals are marriage and chil-dren, then it's no wonder they are less criminal than men are. Attaining these goals is often not nearly as difficult as achieving success and wealth. On the other hand, some women do try to achieve wealth and success, but because the avenues to these ends are not open to them, they resort to crime.

When women's goals shift, as they are doing currently, then we might expect to see more strain in women's lives and, hence, an increase in female criminality. So, although Merton's theory did not originally address women, we can use it to understand female crime. Merton's theory has some problems. Among them, he ignored women's lives when trying to analyze crime and deviance. Moreover, his ideas cannot explain deviant be-havior among people who accept *both* the goals and the means—deviant behavior such as smoking dope. Why would someone who can and has achieved monetary success smoke marijuana? His or her strivings are not limited by structural roadblocks yet the behavior is criminalized.

Social-Process Ideas

Social-process theories in criminology examine how social processes such as family life, community, and school influence criminal behavior. Process theories argue that the relationship dynamics in these processes affect how people relate to the world around them, and may propel people into crime.

Sutherland's (1947) *differential association* theory is one example of this kind of theory. Sutherland identifies nine principles that can be summarized as follows: Crime is learned within intimate personal groups. Such groups—meaning personal relationships, not television or movies—teach people how to rationalize crime and use the tools of the trade. Learning about crime is no different from any other kind of learning—crime is indeed a social-learning process. In this theory, crime does not stem from lack of opportunity; rather, it comes from the relationships we form with other people and what those relationships teach us. Sutherland's ideas could apply easily to women. And though Sutherland mentioned that this theory might explain why males are more delinquent than females, he never pursued that hypothesis.

The bottom line is this: If people learn criminal behavior by associating with criminal people, then differential socialization—the differences in the male and female socialization patterns—could indeed explain women's lower crime rates. Sutherland claims that the social-learning process takes place in small, intimate groups. The intimate group that women most associate with is the family. Generally, families do not explicitly teach criminal behavior. Women thus are shielded from criminal learning experiences, whereas men, through their association with male deviant companions are more likely to come into contact with criminal behavior. Of course, this assumes that all women are tied to traditional roles in the family. Perhaps as women's social roles change, their crime rates will as well.

Labeling Ideas

Labeling theory, which reached its zenith in the 1960s and 1970s, is associated with the work of scholars such as Lemert (1951), Becker (1963), and Chambliss (1973). This theory argues that deviant behavior is not deviant behavior until someone labels it so. A central question is, who has the power to apply the label? Individuals with power and status, such as police officers, legislators, and judges, define incorrect and correct behavior and decide which sanctions behavior will earn.

When people are labeled as deviant, they consciously or unconsciously are affected by that label. If they begin to believe the label, they can become more deviant. Labeled individuals start to see themselves as criminal or delinquent—"Gee, if I'm a delinquent like everyone thinks, I might as well engage in delinquent behavior." Thus a self-fulfilling prophecy emerges—they weren't really deviant until someone labeled them that way. It's analogous to someone saying, "You'll never amount to anything," and then you don't. Labeling theory is a *micro* theory because it focuses on the face-to-face relationships and reactions between people.

How can this theory explain women's crime rates and increasing crime? Labeling theory points out that people in certain groups, such as the middle and upper classes, are less likely to be labeled. That's because middle- and upper-class people are not generally associated with criminal behavior. Women also fit this bill. Such preconceptions about women's behavior might prompt the criminal-justice system to take women's crimes less seriously. Women, then, can avoid being labeled.

On the other hand, when women do step out of line, someone in power may label them specifically to get them back in line. Recall our discussion in Chapter 1 about women and witchcraft; the label "witch" was a powerful control mechanism. Poor and working-class women, women of color, and women who do not fit stereotypical notions of femininity, may be labeled deviant easily. Indeed, women of color may find this especially true, because in U.S. society, color is often associated with crime.

In considering labeling theory, we should not forget the question of who has the power to apply labels. Perhaps one of the most important points we can take from labeling theory is that most women neither apply labels nor get labeled as deviant.

We can use each of these mainstream theories to explain women's criminality; some of them apply better than others. Although the above discussion offers just a smattering of the theories that are out there, keep one thing in mind: For the most part, these theories were not intended to be applied to women.

The Essence of the Chapter

In defining women as sexual beings who are less important than men, the law has struggled with its treatment of women. Whether in common law, civil law, or criminal law, we find the same thing—an inequality has been ingrained in the system and persists. Some folks have claimed that the law has become more gender neutral over time—a development that some people deem good and others deem not so good. In the next chapter, we discuss issues of equality between women and men. We also examine the role of the Constitution in defining women's legal status. As we do these things, let's consider the following provocative questions raised by Otten (1993, p. 9):

1. Has protecting the interests of the powerful (men) from the powerless (women) been one of the law's functions?
2. The "primary thrust of our law is the promise to protect each person. . . ." Has U.S. law kept this promise to women?
3. How effective is the law as a tool of redress for women?

3 The U.S. Constitution and the Notion of Equality

"Feminists have always considered the law a key factor in reproducing, and obscuring gender inequality. Feminists have also relied on law to relieve women's oppression and to improve women's social and economic positions."

—Baron

Can the law serve as a tool to redress women's inequitable treatment? Has it watched over women and kept them from harm? Or has the law been more apt to protect men than women? Such questions bring us to the issues raised in this chapter. Here we examine ideas about equality and about how men and women should be treated by the law.

Let's start with another question: What is "equality"? How do we define that idea? Does equality have something to do with justice? With law? Is the common law just and equal? Are criminal and civil law just and equal? How have the documents of the United States—the Bill of Rights and amendments to the U.S. Constitution, for instance—carried out these ideas of justice and equality? How have these foundational documents defined the roles and lives of women? We already know that justice is not an easily defined concept. But what is the relationship between the U.S. Constitution and equality? This chapter examines the role of the U.S. Constitution in U.S. society, and its effect on equality.

A Few Notes Here . . .

Belknap (1996) believes that women in the United States must obtain the following in order to gain true equality: equal treatment under the law, protection from discrimination, and physical self-determination (control over their own bodies). This chapter examines the first two issues. Chapter 8 explores the third.

Ava Baron (1987) points out three critical questions that have emerged in feminist debates about the role of law in women's lives. First, "feminists [must] seek to assess whether, and in what ways, women have benefited from legal changes over the past two centuries. Has legal reform reduced gender inequality?" Second, "feminists need to decide whether the legal goals of freedom and protection are mutually exclusive. For example, can women obtain state protection against male sexual violence without this becoming paternalistic and resulting in further restrictions on women?" Finally, "feminists must evaluate whether formal (legal) equality contradicts substantive (actual) equality. How should the law handle actual sex differences of sexuality and reproduction?" "Most [feminists] concur that the legal system is patriarchal—that is, law operates to reinforce male privilege and power—but disagree about what that means for feminist political action" (Baron, 1987, p. 475).

There is an irony at work here: In a system that "guarantees" equality but that is built around men's ideas, women are not always equal. Nor are they always protected from inequality. As Kerber and Dehart note, when men's needs are the norm, society can't achieve gender neutrality. Even when so-called gender neutrality is facially produced, the underlying reality does not necessarily reflect the surface-level pictures. "Although the standard appears to be gender-neutral, it presents women with excruciating choices that do not confront their male peers" (Kerber & Dehart, 2000, p. 19). This statement echoes our earlier point about walking the line. Goldstein makes a similar comment when she writes, "Not only did government originate as a protection racket, but it originated as a male protection racket, set up by men for men. . . . The overwhelming male bias of these systems [of law] puts feminist lawyers and law professors in a difficult position. They are trying to fix a rigged system by means of the processes provided by that system" (Goldstein, 1992, p. 12).

The U.S. Declaration of Independence

Perhaps the best way to start a discussion of the Constitution and "equality" is to place early U.S. history in context. After European peoples landed on the shores of the North American continent, they established colonies and spent several decades figuring out how to survive. They gained some survival skills by making friends (and enemies) with indigenous peoples, even while growing ever more distraught over their troubled relationships with the governments they had left behind, particularly in England. Tensions reached a climax, and on July 4, 1776, the U.S. Congress wrote the

Declaration of Independence. This became the first official document of the "new" nation—the first of three "Charters of Freedom"—and the first to use the phrase "all men are created equal." (Of course, the statement "all men are created equal," referred only to white, propertied men.) U.S. citizens toss around several other phrases as well that originated in this document; for instance, "unalienable rights" and "life, liberty, and the pursuit of happiness." The Declaration of Independence lists the repeated offenses and oppressive actions of the British crown, and states that the American people will no longer stand for such treatment. For the next decade, the Declaration served as the guiding document of the colonies. Then, in 1787, the fledgling nation adopted its Constitution.

The U.S. Constitution

The United States Constitution is the "law of the land"; it guides all other legal decisions in this country. That said, there is also an enormous amount of discussion and debate about the original intent of the framers of the Constitution. Did they envision that it would be strictly followed indefinitely, or did they recognize the changing face of society? Most people don't take time to examine the Constitution these days. Thus many of us have little understanding of either the historical or contemporary debates surrounding the Constitution. (This is evidenced by the number of people who claim that abortion is a constitutional right; it is not.) The U.S. Constitution has survived as long as it has because it was written in general terms; this breadth has allowed generations of U.S. citizens to modify the document to reflect shifting times and ideas.

The Constitution itself was not written in an evening over a nice, quiet dinner. The Constitutional Convention, held in 1787, proved divisive and turbulent. The framers could not agree on what to say in the document, how to say it, or which ideas the document should emphasize. The passage of the Bill of Rights one year after the Constitution was written was an attempt to ensure that government didn't trample on the people's rights. Indeed, U.S. citizens at the time still feared the government would grow too powerful and would willfully deny them the ability to make their own choices in life.

The Constitution was written by white, propertied men. In fact, only they could vote in that era. These men defined issues as "constitutional," and they set up the legal system in a way that protected their own interests. For example, they did not let women or people of color vote, they considered a black person as three-fifths of a white person, and they did not consider indigenous persons citizens. It was Abigail Adams, wife of John Adams, who pleaded with her husband to "remember the ladies" as his *fellow* framers worked on the Constitution.

Some Biographies

The signers of the U.S. Constitution generally came from well-to-do or well-known families. Most were well educated and prominent in community and state affairs. Many had long involved themselves in public service. The majority had been born in the colonies but had moved around during their lives. The following short biographies, from the National Archives and Records Administration, shed light on who some of these men were.

Richard Bassett (Delaware) was born in Cecil County, Maryland, in April 1745. Reared by a relative, Peter Lawson, he received a license to practice law in 1770. He prospered as a lawyer and planter, and eventually came to own not only Mr. Lawson's estate but also homes in the nearby towns of Dover and Wilmington.

Daniel Carroll (Maryland) was born in 1730 in Upper Marlboro, Maryland, to a prominent family. The son of wealthy Irish Roman Catholic parents, he studied for six years at St. Omer's in Flanders. (His older brother, John, was the first Roman Catholic bishop in the United States.) Though little is known of Carroll's life until 1781, we do know he entered the political arena that year and was elected to the Continental Congress. A good friend of George Washington's, he supported the establishment of the District of Columbia and was named to survey the land and define the area we now know as Washington, D.C.

William Samuel Johnson (Connecticut) was born in Stratford, Connecticut, in 1727. His father was Samuel Johnson, the first president of King's College (later Columbia College and University). Graduating from Yale in 1744, Johnson later earned a master of arts degree from his alma mater and an honorary master's from Harvard College. He became a wealthy lawyer and civil servant.

Robert Morris (Pennsylvania) was born in Liverpool, England, in 1734. When he was 13 years old, he traveled to Maryland to join his father, a tobacco exporter living in Oxford. As a young man, Morris started working at a prominent banking firm in Philadelphia and in 1754 became a partner in the firm. For four decades, he was one of the company's directors as well as an influential Philadelphia citizen. Throughout the rest of his life, he was involved in business dealings between his firm and the government, often sparking criticism for his apparent conflict of interests. However, he served the country faithfully and, along with Roger Sherman (below), signed all three U.S. freedom documents.

Roger Sherman (Connecticut) was born in 1721 in Newton, Massachusetts. As a young man, he became a store owner and county surveyor. He prospered and assumed leadership in the community. Admitted to the bar in 1754, he then embarked on a distinguished judicial and political career. In 1761, Sherman left the law and once again went into business. He managed two stores in New Haven, Connecticut, one of which primarily served

Yale College students. He became a friend and benefactor of the college, and served for many years as its treasurer. Sherman and Robert Morris were the only two men to sign the Declaration of Independence, the U.S. Constitution, and the Bill of Rights.

These men were just five of the Constitutional Convention attendees. In all, 55 delegates attended the convention and wrote the document. How should we interpret their words?

Constitutional Interpretation

Let's take a minute here to discuss constitutional interpretation. How do jurists decide what the Constitution is saying? If you've taken a class in constitutional law, you've probably found that different texts answer this question in different ways. As Baer (1992, p. 159) points out, there are discussions of "modes of, methods of, techniques of, and approaches to constitutional interpretation." If there are this many facets to interpreting the Constitution, then there must be at least that many ways to think about it. Some interpreters take the Constitution at face value. They argue that we should examine it based on what it says—for example, "man" means "man." This argument suggests that the original intent of the framers meant what they wrote—exactly.

Other interpreters contend that all constitutions are fluid documents; thus we should interpret them as such. For most feminists, the idea that the U.S. Constitution should be read as fluid is essential. Strict interpretations generally harm women, because the law then applies only to men. Feminists argue that the text of any constitution must be considered in light of the peoples, conditions, and ideas that defined the values and thinking of the time in which the document was created. Values change, ideas change—interpretations of the Constitution should recognize those changes. Of course, this argument also has its own problems.

Is the Constitution Male?

In Chapter 2, we considered the idea of the law's being male. Let's talk more specifically about the U.S. Constitution. The Constitution, as we saw, is the "law of the land." But is it the *male* law of the land? We *know* that it was written and ratified by white men of property. And over time, it has primarily been male judges who have used the Constitution to make decisions, and male lawyers who have argued cases on constitutional grounds.

Baer notes,

> [I]nterpreters who look to original intent for guidance rather than for mandates must still be aware that reference to sources

of original meaning is, inevitably, reference to male words, male values, and male purposes. This male monopoly applies to text, doctrine, and precedent. Women did not participate either in the drafting or in the adoption of the original Constitution; throughout most of American history, women were excluded from participation in amending the Constitution or applying cases to it (1992, p. 160).

U.S. history is rife with examples of men using the Constitution to protect their own interests and to limit women. The Constitution has a male bias which influences all decisions about women's lives. U.S. citizens have argued since the birth of this country whether the original drafters meant *men/man* when they said *men/man*, or whether they meant people in general. We can look to any number of cases decided on constitutional grounds and find evidence of male bias. But does all of this make the Constitution *male*? As Baer points out, legal—and thus constitutional—thinking has a certain set of priorities: rational over emotional thought, general thought over particular thought, abstractness over concreteness (p. 151). Note that these dichotomies reflect patriarchal society itself. (Recall the discussion of patriarchy from Chapter 1.) These priorities may not necessarily be bad. But when they are used in cases and legal decisions "by men against women," they can create problems.

First, the men have the power to refuse to change their behavior, whether the context is personal or public. Second, the men have preset the agenda; the concept of equality . . . and the constitutional agenda . . . result from the priorities that men have chosen in activities on which they have had a monopoly. It is the uses to which reasoning is put—not the reasoning itself—that is coercive (p. 153).

Most of us assume that law is objective, rational, and unemotional (see Chapter 2). Not so. Though those who create the law claim it has these qualities, *their very claims* are filled with emotion. Thus, they unconsciously find themselves in a Catch-22; they argue *with emotion* about the unemotional and objective nature of the law. Such passion about the law's nature can certainly only suggest something about the passion of the law's content. Since passion is about excitement, intensity, and fervor, we are back at the beginning of the argument. When lawyers, legislators, and judges go on and on about how this needs to be done or that needs to be done *because it is the rational thing to do* (emphasis mine), they are emoting. There are many issues in law—abortion, family, children, women, work, and so on. Often lawmakers view these issues through the "lens" of traditional stereotypes of

---

B O X **3.1**   Mill on Justice

In the first place, it is mostly considered unjust to deprive anyone of [*his*] personal liberty, [*his*] property, or any other thing which belongs to [*him*] by law. Here, therefore, this one instance of the applications of the terms "just" and "unjust" in a perfectly definite sense, namely, that it is to respect, unjust to violate, the legal rights of anyone. . . .

Secondly, the legal rights of which [*he*] is deprived may be rights which ought not have belonged to [*him*]; in other words, the law which confers on [*him*] these rights may be a bad law. . . .

John Stuart Mill, *Utilitarianism* [emphasis mine]

"the true woman" and the "separate spheres." When lawmakers emote, they negate their arguments about the rational, unemotional, and objective nature of the law, yet hide behind such claims by saying things such as "it is women's nature to clean, and this is the objective truth." Feminist thought seeks to analyze and discredit such "objective" thought because it has been used against women over time.

Equality and the Constitution

The body of the Constitution lays out the government of the United States. If you read through the document's different articles, you find what amounts to a description of congressional power, executive power, judicial power, procedures for amending the document, and so forth. Not until you start reading the amendments to the Constitution will you see references to many of the "issues" we discuss today. The Bill of Rights, the first ten amendments, was ratified in 1791. The first amendments dealing with equality are commonly referred to as the "Civil War amendments"—the Thirteenth, Fourteenth, and Fifteenth (ratified in 1865, 1868, and 1870, respectively). These amendments abolish slavery, provide for due process and equal protection, and grant voting rights to people of all colors, but not both genders.

The Fourteenth Amendment, in particular, has played a central role in the movement to "give" women rights. The Equal Protection Clause—a section of the amendment—says: "No state shall deny to any person the equal protection of the laws." Sounds pretty simple, doesn't it? We'll take a closer look at this clause later.

BOX **3.2**   **Equal Protection Clause**

All persons born or naturalized in the United States and subject to the jurisdiction thereof, are citizens of the United States and of the State wherein they reside. No State shall make or enforce any law which shall abridge the privileges or immunities of citizens of the United States; nor shall any State deprive any person of life, liberty, or property, without due process of law; nor deny to any person within its jurisdiction the equal protection of the laws.

Fourteenth Amendment, Section 1, U.S. Constitution

Women did not attain the right to vote (the Nineteenth Amendment) in the United States until as late as *1920.* To understand the magnitude of this event, think about what voting lets you do. The right to vote gave women, for the first time, a say in who runs this country, and how they run it. Once women had the ability to speak through the vote, politicians soon learned that they must listen to women if they wished to be elected and reelected. Certainly some political figures heed women's voices less than others, but women as a voting block still wield power.

All of these changes—the Civil War Amendments (and the Fourteenth Amendment particularly), the Nineteenth Amendment, and court cases we haven't yet discussed—are all about equality; that is, freedom from tyranny and oppressive control, justice and self determination, and the ability to participate in a society that prides itself on fairness.

The Equality Debate

What is equality, really? Did we answer this question above? Is equality about attaching amendments to the guiding document of a country? Or is it about more than that? Does it mean that all people are the same? Can equality also be about acknowledging people's differences? In Chapter 1, I promised we'd come back to this issue—so here we are.

It is relatively easy to say, "I think all people should be equal." Most of us have said that kind of thing at one time or another, or have heard others say it. We often argue that people should have equal opportunities, equal rights, equal treatment, equal protection, and so forth. Yet we're not always clear what we mean by "equal" and "equality." Those of us interested in changing the status of women in U.S. society have worked hard to define what equality really means. Legally, equality has been defined as treating everyone the same. But this definition raises a question: What does it mean to treat everyone the same? Is there one standard of equality? Many scholars these days say "no," because they believe that not all situations are the same, nor are women and men the same. Clearly, we have a debate.

This is commonly referred to as the "sameness/difference" debate or, as some writers refer to it, the "symmetry/asymmetry" debate. In the simplest of examples, we can ask, "Okay, we want all people to be treated equally, *but* what happens when women get pregnant?" Men do not take time from paid labor because they have to deliver a baby—only women give birth. To be sure, in some companies, men can take paternity leave. However, this differs from women's situation because men can choose to take time off but women *must* take at least a day off. Someone on the sameness or symmetry side of the argument would say that men and women should have the same expectations and opportunities surrounding a pregnancy. Someone on the differences or asymmetry side of the argument would say that because only women have babies, they face a unique situation, and that employment law must take that uniqueness into account. Pregnancy is a good example of why some people suggest that we must have asymmetrical law at times.

Are women better served when the law treats them in the same way it treats men? Or are they better served when the law acknowledges the unavoidable differences between women and men? Many women respond to these questions with "Of course I want to be treated just as men are treated!" This response assumes that the law is unbiased and actually treats everyone equally. Indeed, some feminists have found this model preferable because it turns the focus on women away from the separate-spheres ideology.

According to Littleton (1993), there are two models of sameness or symmetry. The *assimilation model* is the one most accepted by the courts, because it is based on the idea that women can be or really are just like men. Women can assimilate into the world and, in effect, be men. Therefore the law should require society and its institutions to treat women exactly as it treats men. The second sameness model is the *androgyny model*, which argues that women and men are more alike than they are different, and that the law should define and apply to a mean between the two.

The sameness idea, particularly the assimilation model, has benefited women to some extent by eliminating certain kinds of discrimination. However, as with most things, this argument has a problem.

> The problem with equal treatment arguments is that they adopt an unspoken and often unacknowledged male standard under the guise of neutrality. While the demand for equal treatment can effectively knock down employment barriers based on sex, it gains for women only what men already have, and only for

those women whose life situations match that male standard. . . . Strict equal treatment arguments are therefore not particularly helpful when female workers seek to protect their income or jobs when they become mothers, since men do not interrupt their work to become parents, and employers are reticent to expand their leave policies in sex-neutral ways (Shanley & Battistoni, 1992, p. 265).

What about the difference, or asymmetrical, approach? Littleton (1993) argues there are several models here as well. We will discuss four of them. The *special-rights approach* affirms that women and men are indeed different—that cultural roles are rooted in biology. Therefore, society must take these differences into account and make sure that women are not punished for what they can't control. Also called the *bivalent approach,* this argument suggests that women need special rights.

Accommodation is the second asymmetrical approach. It suggests different treatment for biological differences (such as pregnancy) but equal treatment for cultural differences (for example, career choices).

The third approach is *acceptance,* or acknowledging that biological *and* cultural differences exist between women and men. This argument focuses on the ways in which biological and cultural differences are used to justify differential treatment and inequality. It asserts that eliminating the actual inequality is much more important than debating the issue of whether the differences are "real."

Finally, Littleton speaks of the *empowerment approach,* which rejects the notion of difference altogether and claims that men's subordination of women is what has constructed the sexes' differences. In essence, a social-constructionist approach, this perspective argues that the only issue at hand is the domination and subordination of women in society.

What kinds of laws are most relevant to discussions of women's differences from men? Laws pertaining to rape, sexual harassment, maternity, affirmative action—in other words, laws intricately tied to what's unique about women's lives—are most relevant and therefore merit the most attention. Such laws can benefit women "because they do not require that women be regarded as or act like men in order to receive legal protections or benefits. 'Special treatment' accommodates gender difference where appropriate and thereby gives voice to women's specific experience and needs" (Goldstein, 1992, p. 265).

But if we argue that women need to be treated specially because of such and such, we risk falling into a situation in which patriarchy defines some differences as superior or desirable and others as inferior or undesirable. For example, in a courtroom, patriarchal judges (consciously or not) may conclude that women *do* fit the "true-woman" and "separate-spheres" stereotypes. Feminist scholars have long grappled with this side of the difference debate. It is an arduous task because the stakes are high.

Perhaps the answer is as Williams (1991) and Goldstein (1992) argue it: we need laws that move away from attributing something to either one gender or the other. Instead, we need laws written in truly gender-neutral tones. Parent leave, not maternity or paternity leave; primary-caretaker policies, not maternal preference, are the kinds of policies that may create true gender neutrality.

Belknap (1996) suggests that U.S. law uses two strategies in an effort to achieve equality—*formal equality laws*, as mentioned above, by which everyone is treated equally, and *compensating equality laws*, by which people are compensated for social inequalities in some way.

Formal Equality

Let's look at formal equality—or treating everyone the same. Much of the following discussion comes from Becker's (1992) analysis. As Becker sees it, the idea of formal equality has several problems. First, it relies on a standard that is also up for discussion—the standard of objectivity. Formal equality assumes that objectivity in the law and legal decision making is best. But it is difficult to objectively decide whether people are in similar or different situations. When we examine equal-protection analysis later in this chapter, the notion of individuals' being "similarly situated" comes to the forefront. Similarly situated means being in a similar kind of situation. Judges are required to decide, based on their "objective standards," whether two parties are in similarly situated circumstances. But how do they decide?

Second, formal equality also assumes that if women are to be thought of as just like men, then they are entitled to be treated like men. The problem with this view is that it is androcentric; it assumes that men are the standard against which women should be compared. This is not a neutral way to think about gender and the law.

Third, "formal equality assumes it is possible to ignore an individual's sex" (p. 104). However, we all know that sex cannot be ignored.

It appears that formal equality is most likely to help certain kinds of women—those in privileged positions in society whose voices are most likely to be heard anyway. Why? Because privileged women generally have the educational resources, career resources, and networking advantages which allow their voices to be heard. Given the above three realities, it would seem that this perspective cannot help us equalize society.

But as Becker points out, formal equality has its good points. Sameness arguments have been used to challenge barriers to women's entrance into certain occupations. It has flung doors open that were previously closed to women, because we have been able to argue that women and men are no different. The rising number of women in law school, on police forces, in colleges, on sports teams—much of that comes from the formal-equality argument. Furthermore, some scholars suggest that arguing for anything *but* formal equality in a courtroom will only hurt women, for several reasons. First, if one doesn't argue that men and women are the same, then one risks arguing that women need special treatment. Special-treatment arguments often reinforce stereotypes about women. Special treatment "has been used to burden as well as to benefit" (p. 107). Second, those in favor of keeping formal-equality arguments suggest that it is better for women to equate a pregnant worker with other workers who may need time off for medical reasons. (For example, someone having surgery) to demonstrate that all workers need to take time off for some reason.

Many U.S. citizens believe the Constitution, as the law of the land, protects them from harm and treats everyone the same. The Constitution, then, is often viewed as supporting the sameness argument. It protects citizens by arguing that we are all created equal and, therefore, are the same. But, how does it put that idea into practice? And how does it provide justice for women?

The Dilemma of Difference

Minow (1993) argues that there are three versions of difference—each of which poses a dilemma adding to this discussion. The first version of difference suggests that we may *re-create difference* by either ignoring it or noticing it. When we talk about women and men, do we make the differences between them seem even bigger than they are? If we don't talk about differences, do they seem even bigger because we have not dealt with them?

What about the *dilemma of neutrality?* Does neutrality mean presenting both sides of an argument or not presenting either side blatantly? If the answer is the latter, does that then reinforce the fact that the topic is not being presented—and thus work against the neutrality position in the first place? If the public schools must teach about sexuality does that mean they should "balance" their discussions with teachings about both heterosexuality and homosexuality? And if they don't discuss homosexuality, are they symbolically reinforcing the differences between the two?

What about the dilemma of *broad discretion*, which permits individual decisions, and *tight formal rules*, which specify how decisions will be made for individuals? Do we leave the rule broadly open so that individuals can make decisions for themselves—and then risk their defining things to their own liking? For example, judges using their own biases to strictly determine case outcomes. Or do we narrowly define the rules so everyone operates within them—and then risk disaster when judges must hand down the same case outcome for all similar offenders?

I don't have the answers. I just want to bring the questions to your attention and encourage you to think about them.

Constitutional Protection, Precedent and People, Conditions and Ideas

What does "law of the land" really mean? Technically, it means that all laws written, and cases decided, must not violate the U.S. Constitution. But how do we decide what's unconstitutional? Some laws were originally considered constitutional but later were deemed unconstitutional. How are these changes decided? There are a number of answers to that question. Perhaps a court decision was downright sexist (at least according to our current views) but did not strike the judge or legislators as sexist at the time. Perhaps those who sat on the appellate bench interpreted the Constitution differently than did those who made the law or decisions. Most likely, people, conditions, and ideas have changed. Let's now examine the Equal Protection Clause to see how the purpose of and protection offered by the Constitution have shifted over time.

The Equal Protection Clause

As we saw, the Equal Protection Clause, which is one section of the Fourteenth Amendment, was part of a set of amendments promulgated after the Civil War. It argued that people could not be denied equal protection of the law based on a variety of statutes (see Box 3.2). The clause has come to mean that states cannot pass laws that single out a specific group for favored or disfavored treatment or status over any other group. Technically, if this singling out happens, the courts must rectify the situation by declaring that law unconstitutional and requiring the state to address the inequity. The U.S. Constitution serves as a guide for state constitutions and laws. States must use it to justify any legal decisions they make that treat people differently.

There are a few key issues here to keep in mind. For example, consider the role of states. The Fourteenth Amendment specifies that equal protection is each state's responsibility. It doesn't require private employers (whether companies or individuals) to provide equal protection. Only state laws (meaning the federal, as well as state and local governments) cannot legally discriminate against people by treating them differently. In this sense, we are talking here about specific circumstances. For example, state laws about drinking age limits and estate representation have been implemented using gender as the basis for distinction. Such distinctions have been found unconsitutional but they were originally considered acceptable. States do write laws that categorize people (for example, driver's license laws), and they are rarely challenged for it. Such laws seem acceptable because they emphasize *relevant* differences among individuals. (We certainly wouldn't want a 12-year-old driving a car!)

The concept of state is important. First of all, if we see or experience discrimination that is *not* stemming from an unconstitutional state law, then the victims of that discrimination must look to other laws and case decisions for protection. Second, if discrimination has resulted from a state action, such as the examples just mentioned regarding drinking age limits or estate issues, its victims can legally challenge that action even though such a law has not yet been challenged or identified as unlawful.

The notion of "similarly situated" is also important. Equal-protection analysis applies to situations in which one person says that she or he is in a similar situation as another person but is being treated differently. For example, women and men are being hired for the same job but the women are told they can't work past 8 P.M. because of a legislative mandate. These two groups—women and men—are in a similar situation; they are applying for a job. However, the women are being told they can only work until 8 P.M. Are they being treated differently? That is up for challenge in a courtroom.

With virtually all legal issues, such a challenge sounds simple. However, Smith (1993) points out three considerations. First, the court must identify what is meant by *like cases.* Are men and women similar or different? Second, if we decide that the cases are similar, then what does it mean to *treat them alike?* In the case of men and women, does like treatment mean giving them the same opportunities, the same treatment, the same protection, or what? Third, if people can be *different but equal,* what does that mean? And how do we treat them? These kinds of questions lie at the core of an equal-protection analysis.

TABLE 3.1 Equal Protection Standards

Constitutional Standard	Classification	Scrutiny	Burden of Proof	Objective of Law must be:	Classification must be:
Rational basis	Nonsuspect	Minimal	Challenger	Legitimate	Rationally related
Intermediate	Semisuspect	Heightened	Government	Important	Substantially related
Strict scrutiny	Suspect	Strict	Government	Compelling	Necessarily related

This discussion of the importance of equal protection for justice in women's lives, and in the lives of other discrimination victims, did not have import until the 1950s, when the *Brown v. Topeka Board of Education* (347 U.S. 483) case was decided. The Brown decision, which said that separate but equal was not equal was argued as an equal-protection case. It represented the defining moment in the U.S. Civil Rights Movement of the twentieth century. From that point on, U.S. courts started paying more attention to the Equal Protection Clause and its effect on society.

From 1954 Forward

After the Brown decision, numerous people started challenging state laws under the auspices of the Equal Protection Clause. Under the guidance of Chief Justice Earl Warren (1953–1969), the U.S. Supreme Court formulated a two-tier system of analysis by which courts (state and federal) can examine the constitutionality of state laws. This system used two levels of scrutiny—strict and minimal—to evaluate laws. The Court argued that judges should use minimal scrutiny to examine laws where the alleged differential treatment is based on classifications that are changeable or related to ability, such as age. By contrast, strict scrutiny should be used to examine laws whose classifications are based on the belief or suspicion that discrimination is at work, such as with race. These tests are not set in stone, nor are they precise in their application. Each examines two things: the government's reason for passing the law in question, and the relationship between the law and the classification it uses. In other words, the Court asks: Does the government have a sound reason for passing the law, and does the fact that the law specifices men over women (or blacks over whites, etc.) have a basis? As we'll see, a court's choice of a test has important ramifications for the outcome of a case.

Courts have used the rationality test (also referred to as the reasonable test) most often to evaluate laws. Basically, the test asks whether the state's law is rational or reasonable? Simply put, did the state have a reasonable idea in mind when it passed this legislation? Also, does the classification of different treatment make sense? If a court answers yes to both of these questions, then it finds the law valid and thus constitutional. Many critics argue this test is nothing more than show; it lets a court make a ruling without taking much responsibility for truly examining differential treatment. The test, critics maintain, is not a critical examination of the behavior at hand; virtually all state laws examined using this "soft" test are found valid. (See Table 3.1.)

The strict-scrutiny test falls on the other end of the continuum from the rationality test. This test almost always finds laws that are indeed invalid and unconstitutional. This much more stringent test sets up the notion of a *suspect classification*, or the belief that some groups probably are being discriminated against simply because of historical attitudes toward them. With the strict-scrutiny test, a court examines the law very closely, asking whether a state has a compelling purpose for writing the law. And if so, is the law then necessary for the state to accomplish that purpose? For example, is it necessary to hire a man, or a white Anglo person, into a particular position for the state to fulfill its purpose of the position?

How is a "suspect class" defined? Courts ask four questions to answer this, and base their answers on the treatment of this class, or group, as a whole over the course of history.

1. What kinds of *stereotypes* has this group faced, and does it still face them? If the stereotypes have harmed the group, then its members are probably being discriminated against.
2. What is the *immutability* of the group? Because immutable characteristics such as race or national origin (those that cannot be changed) bear no relationship to a person's ability or a set of legislative goals, they strongly suggest discrimination.
3. Has the group faced a *history of discrimination*? If discriminatory behavior has happened in the past, it may well still be occurring.
4. Has the group historically *lacked political power?* If so, then that powerlessness is probably having repercussions (including discrimination) to this day.

If a group fits the above four criteria, then courts deem it a suspect class; that is, the group, it is suspected, is being discriminated against. Courts have yet to declare gender a suspect class, which means, for women, there is not judicial acknowledgment of their discriminated past.

In 1976, the Supreme Court identified a third test, which it called *intermediate.* This test came about for several reasons, including the state courts' increasing use as a forum for the gender-equality debate. Chief Justice Warren Burger's (1969–1986) court developed a doctrine that

TABLE 3.2   Equal Protection Case Citations

Goesaert v. Cleary 335 U.S. 464 (1948)
Hoyt v. Florida 368 U.S. 57 (1961)
Reed v. Reed 404 U.S. 71 (1971)
Frontiero v. Richardson 411 U.S. 677 (1973)
Geduldig v. Aiello 417 U.S. 417 (1974)
Craig v. Boren 429 U.S. 190 (1976)
Califano v. Goldfarb 430 U.S. 199 (1977)
Orr v. Orr 440 U.S. 268 (1979)
Mississippi v. Hogan 458 U.S. 718 (1982)

courts have used primarily to examine gender-discrimination claims. The Court did not want to go so far as to say that female gender constitutes a suspect class. However, some critics argued that using the reasonable test to argue all gender cases was inadequate because laws were never found invalid and unconstitutional. Specifically, courts that use only the rational test rarely declare a law invalid. If courts continued to use the rational test in cases brought by women, the laws in question would remain on the books. The intermediate test asks the following questions: Does classification by sex serve an important governmental function, and is classification by sex *closely and substantially related to* the achievement of the government's functions? If the anwer to both questions is yes, then the law stands; if no, then the law is deemed unconstitutional and invalid.

The Equal Rights Amendment

In 1923, Senator Charles Curtis (R-KS) and Rep. Daniel Anthony (R-KS) proposed a new amendment to the Constitution. Named the Equal Rights Amendment, it was authored by Alice Paul and it stipulated the following:

- *Section 1.* Equality of rights under the law shall not be denied or abridged by the United States or by any State on account of sex.
- *Section 2.* The Congress shall have the power to enforce, by appropriate legislation, the provisions of this article.
- *Section 3.* This amendment shall take effect two years after the date of ratification.

In 1971, the House of Representatives approved the amendment with a vote of 354 to 24. The next year, the U.S. Senate approved it with a vote of 84 to 8. The amendment had seven years (that is, by March 22, 1979) to be ratified by 38 states. In 1972, Phyllis Schafley, the conservative founder of the *Eagle Forum,* launched the National Committee to Stop ERA. The National Education Association, the AFL-CIO, the United Auto Workers, and the League of Women Voters had all endorsed the amendment, but it was about to enter a rocky point. As the ratification deadline approached, supporters began worrying that not enough states would be willing to ratify the ERA. In 1978, the deadline was extended to June 30, 1982. At the 1980 Republican Convention, the Republican party voided 40 years of support for the amendment and took it off its platform. The party's leading voice, Ronald Reagan, as well as several others, strongly opposed the ERA's wording, fearful that women would be given special privileges, or the family would fall apart, and other such ideas. In June 1982, only 35 states had voted to ratify the amendment (some states that had initially voted for ratification withdrew their support). The push for the ERA ended. Supporters continue to introduce the amendment into Congress every year, but it has not moved forward in any meaningful way.

The ability of the Republican party and opponents such as Phyllis Schafley to engineer the ERA's demise is an apt example of how people, conditions, and ideas can "work" an issue. Based on the votes in the House and Senate in 1971 and 1972, strong support existed for the amendment. During that era—the 1960s and early 1970s—reform movements and new ideas of all kinds were percolating. But the ebb and flow of thinking changes. By the time the 1980s dawned, the tide had turned conservative. Schafley's and others' work of eight years gave voice to the opposition. Conservatives throughout the country saw the amendment as a ticket to "special treatment" and ultimately turned people against it.

Several states have passed ERAs to their own constitutions. However, a federal ERA is the only way to escape the drawn-out piecemeal process of passing statutes or creating new precedent to establish laws of equality for women and others. The Equal Rights Amendment is essential because, without it, sex discrimination remains constitutional. Women looking for redress under existing sex-discrimination laws or precedent walk a shaky ground; such laws and cases can be fully enforced, or not. Furthermore, most defendants must first convince a court that their case matters. A *constitutional* guarantee of equality would shift the burden away from those fighting discrimination and place it on those who do the discriminating, where it belongs.

To that end, a "new" ERA is in the works. The Constitution Equality Amendment (CEA), adopted in July 1995 at the National Organization for Women's annual conference, is a document in progress. It currently states:

- *Section 1*. Women and men shall have equal rights throughout the United States and every place and entity subject to its jurisdiction; through this article, the subordination of women to men is abolished;
- *Section 2*. All persons shall have equal rights and privileges without discrimination on account of sex, race, sexual orientation, marital status, ethnicity, national origin, color or indigence;
- *Section 3*. This article prohibits pregnancy discrimination and guarantees the absolute right of a woman to make her own reproductive decisions including the termination of pregnancy;
- *Section 4*. This article prohibits discrimination based upon characteristics unique to or stereotypes about any class protected under this article. This article also prohibits discrimination through the use of any facially neutral criteria which have a disparate impact based on membership in a class protected under this article.
- *Section 5*. This article does not preclude any law, program or activity that would remedy the effects of discrimination and that is closely related to achieving such remedial purposes;

- *Section 6*. This article shall be interpreted under the highest standard of judicial review;
- *Section 7*. The United States and the several states shall guarantee the implementation and enforcement of this article.

Such an amendment would broaden the language of the ERA by including statements about sexual orientation, indigence, and pregnancy discrimination. It would also require courts to use the highest standard of review for cases (thereby designating sex as a suspect class). Finally, it would make abortion a constitutional "right." For the first time, the CEA would insert the word *women* into the Constitution. This amendment has not yet been put forward in Congress.

Feminist Alternatives

If equal-protection analyses and decisions are marred, if the sameness/difference debate is unanswerable, and if notions of formal equality rage on, what can we do? Here are some suggestions:

MacKinnon (1979) suggests using the *inequality approach*, a model that severely criticizes formal equality. This model suggests that discrimination is the "systematic disadvantagement of social groups" and that this systematic disadvantage has worked against women and for men. She suggests the only true question in a courtroom is how much a particular practice perpetuates the subordination of the underclass. According to MacKinnon, there are any reasonable explanations for why discrimination and inequality exist. She argues that we must challenge the system to uproot itself and rid itself of such realities.

Littleton (1987) offers the *acceptance standard*—or the application of equality in terms of equalizing resources between women and men. Her model resembles a comparable-worth standard (which we discuss in Chapter 5). Littleton argues that women and men should be compensated by the courts for the things they do that are comparable. For example, when women have the choice to stay home and raise children, their contributions to society should be recognized as significantly important. She is not "just a housewife," but an important player raising the next generation of citizens. She highlights the notion of *gender complements*—the things that men and women do that are not identical but are complementary; for instance, if the wife cleans the exterior of the house and the husband paints it, their activities are both contributing to the household. The law should recognize *each* contribution as important and one which should be equitably compensated.

Finally, we have Becker's notion of *formal equality with limited special treatment* (1992). Though we've emphasized the idea of formal equality in this discussion, according to Becker, some policies would treat women and men differently in limited situations. To illustrate, pregnancy is different for women and men; shouldn't women receive special treatment in this instance? The problem, of course, remains—what limited situations?

The Essence of the Chapter

Can the law serve as a tool for redress for women? Does it watch over women and keep them from harm? Or has the law been more apt to protect men than women? We started this chapter with these questions—how would you answer them now? Indeed, the law has often been used against women; for instance, to keep them out of certain kinds of jobs or training. Through equal-protection analysis, women have struggled to use the law as a form of redress. Certainly early equal-protection cases did not concern themselves with protecting women from such differential treatment or keeping them from harm. Though the courts have responded to some degree to women's demands for equality and equal protection since the 1970s, the justice system remains unwilling to acknowledge and respond to women's persistent marginal social, legal, economic, and political status. Battles over the ERA, for example, would have been fought, won, and considered "old hat" if the system were truly concerned about equality and justice. In the next chapter, we examine how notions of justice, equality, and quadraplexation have affected women's lives in the United States.

4 Unmarried, Married, and Coupled Women's Lives

While it may seem that a segue from the discussion of equality and constitutional issues to one of marriage and partnership does not fit together, it actually does. Women's roles in family matters often focus around issues of what's fair and equal. Even if we don't specifically raise the issues in that language, when we are talking about the responsibilities of women and men in the family home or with the children, often we are addressing things such as who is doing their fair share. Furthermore, when families dissolve, deciding who is responsible for what becomes an issue which must be addressed. Such questions continue to focus around fairness and equality for both genders. The roles of men and women in families are defined by people, conditions, and ideas, because the family is another one of those socially constructed societal creations.

"Family"

In discussing feminist perspectives on the family, Andersen (2000) makes several key points:

- *The family is a social unit, not a natural unit.* "Family" is created by the social merging of at least two people, who may or may not be legally married. Many people refer to someone as "family" who is not related to them by blood. In these cases, "family" means "close." In Westernized cultures, people tend to think of a family as a biological entity, but that notion doesn't capture what family really is.
- *Emotional ties occur inside and outside of families.* Though we may have strong family ties, many of us also have strong ties outside of our families. For some people, nonfamilial ties are the strongest and most important ties in their lives. In such cases, the people on the other end of those ties are more like family than blood relatives. All social life is associated with emotion, not just life within one's family of origin.

- *Families are economic units.* The family car, the family house, the family vacation, the family restaurant, the family movie—all families function as producers and consumers. Thus, they are economic units.
- *The family ideal is ideological.* The family ideal that still reigns in the United States—the white picket fence, 1.1 kids, Mom who bakes cookies at home, Dad who goes to the office, etc.—is based on an ideology, often associated with "Donna Reed" and the 1950s, not reality. In real life, these ideas and images do not reflect everyone's vision of the family, or everyone's actual family life. Many people have not grown up with this ideal. Some people grow up with one parent or a step-parent. Some grow up in the city rather than the suburbs. Some have many siblings. Some were adopted. Indeed, even as far back as colonial times, when many women died in childbirth and people fell victim to fatal diseases early in life, numerous adults remarried several times and created step-families with complex ties.
- *Women and men experience family life differently.* Because of quadra-plexation (that is, issues of sexuality, socialization, reproduction, and production), family is a different experience for women and men. Experiences of battering and harassment by men, expectations about motherhood and wifeliness presented by the media, all of these things put women and men in different places within the family.

To understand the status and rights of women in the United States, we have to understand ideas about marriage and family and family law. The U.S. Constitution places the responsibility for family law clearly on the states. State legislative bodies write family law that defines, for example, legal age at marriage, divorce, and custody. The laws are then carried out in courtrooms. There is little uniformity in statutes across states. In addition, for the most part, the family is considered private; states thus take little interest in families and their behavior, except in terms of certain issues.

The case of *McGuire v. McGuire* (157 Neb. 226, 59 N.W.2d 336 (1953)) is a good illustration of this point. Lydia McGuire argued that her husband had not adequately provided her with financial support during their marriage. He was stingy with the resources he had, and she lived with just the barest of necessities provided. A district court agreed but upon review by the Nebraska Supreme Court, the lower court's decision was overturned. Why? Because she had lived with these circumstances for over three decades and found them adequate, and because she did have what she needed. The court saw her argument, then, as basically moot and not a court issue. This case highlights the reluctance of the courts to get involved in family matters. It also reinforces the notion that men support families while women serve families. Mr. McGuire had supported his wife financially, and she had engaged in her domestic duties; both parties did what they were supposed to do. Though an old case decision, it was supported in its basic ideas in *Glover v. Glover* (64 Misc.2d 374, 314 N.Y.S.2d 873 (1970)), 17 years later. In this later case, Mrs. Glover sued Mr. Glover for divorce and alimony. Mr. Glover argued that his wife hadn't served him appropriately because she didn't entertain his business partners, said nasty things about him, kept a dirty house, and so forth. Thus, he argued, she didn't deserve alimony. The court agreed. Such case decisions were influenced by the legacy of coverture.

Given the effect of coverture on women's lives through the mid-1800s (with Mississippi's passage of its Married Women's Property Act), women were often better off single than married. Why? Once a woman married, she faced a "civil death." Recognizing this, some women chose not to marry. She could no longer own property, sign contracts in her own name, run her own business, and so forth. The common-law system saw her as an extension of her husband—anything she did reflected on him. Children, also considered property, belonged to their father, not their mother and women were expected to have children as part of the marital relationship. In the case of divorce, men were granted custody. (We'll look at this in more detail below.) It was not until 1960 in *U.S. v. Dege* (364 U.S. 51 (1960)) that spouses were legally deemed two separate persons.

In Western society, people have generally valued adult women's married status more than any other status. Adult women who are unmarried have been given various labels—"old maid" is one of the nicest. And the questions surface—Why isn't she married? What's wrong with her? It wasn't until relatively recently that a viable answer to these questions was that perhaps she didn't want to be married, or couldn't legally marry (as in the case of a lesbian). Given the patriarchal nature of society,

---

BOX 4.1   Sandel on Justice

What goes on in the original position is first of all a choice, or more precisely, a choosing together, an agreement among parties. What the parties agree to are the principles of justice. Unlike most actual contracts, which cannot justify, the hypothetical contract the parties agree to does justify; the principles they choose are just in virtue of their choosing them. As the voluntarist account of justification would suggest, the principles of justice are the products of choice. . . .

Justice as fairness differs from traditional contract theories in that "the relevant agreement is not to enter a given society or to adopt a given form of government, but to accept certain moral principles. . . ."

Michael Sandel, *Liberalism and the Limits of Justice*

the expectation has been that a woman would *want* to marry—after all, that "completed" her and brought her children, domesticity, economic security, and so forth.

Marriage

Marriage is a socially constructed legal union between two people; it is different from "family." Marriage is a legal union, although for some couples it may also be a religious union. Aries (1962) wrote that marriages were not considered religious unions until approximately the 1400s, when the Catholic church decided to step in and bless this convergence of two people. When we discuss marriage in this book, we are talking only about the legal union between a man and a woman. We will discuss the (generally) non-legal union between two women a bit later in the chapter.

As a legal union, marriage brings with it many rights. For example, married individuals can file joint tax returns, receive spousal benefits (social security, unemployment, disability, and so forth), receive "family" rates on insurance, and not be forced to testify against their spouse. One's legal rights and responsibilities toward one's legal mate are defined by the state. This legal union can be terminated only through the formal process of divorce.

States clearly define who can marry whom. For instance, all states prohibit marrying one's sibling, parent, and so forth. Newlyweds must also be the age of majority (which varies by state). One can't be married to more than one person at a time, and one needs to obtain a license (and its prequisites) to marry. In some states, one can become legally married through the process of "common-law marriage." Common-law marriage is recognized in fewer than 20 states and arises only when a man and woman have been together for a long time, when they think of themselves as spouses—and tell others such—and when their intention is to marry at some point. Common-law marriage affords one all the same rights as civilly sanctioned marriage.

As a social construction, this relationship is defined by law and society—both of which, we know, changes over time. Because Western societies have a way of sneaking "nature" into explanations of why we do certain things, many people proclaim that marriage is a natural union between a couple. That sounds nice, but it's actually *part of* the social construction. In making this social construction, we have decided what roles people are to play in families. Sociological and anthropological research suggests that since the earliest human societies, men have been identified as the higher status individuals in the union. Even history books suggest that as far back as the era of hunting and gathering societies, men were more important than women. Why? Because they were the hunters—they felled large, dangerous animals and brought meat home. And meat was considered special because, in part, it was so rare. This historical bias overlooks the fact that women—the gatherers—fed families and communities on a daily basis. The men might bring home meat just once every few weeks; women picked berries and prepared food daily.

Not only has patriarchy defined the historical division of labor in marriage and families, it has also defined other relationships in the marriage. For example, many women take their husband's last name as their own when they marry. Children, also, are given their father's name. Indeed, in some countries, the children's last name is defined by their father; for example, David*son* or Jons*dottir*. Historically in patriarchal societies, possessions and wealth have passed through the male heir(s) in the family line. Patriarchy, then, has played a strong role in how we socially construct our marriages and families.

Gender schemas also strongly inform the construction of marriage, as does quadraplexation. Within marriage, spouses have to negotiate and make decisions about production and reproduction. Ideas learned from the socialization process inform such decisions, and further influence future decisions. Notions of sexuality must be agreed upon with the relationship. The social realities affecting our lives—changes in ideas, people, and conditions—also affect our marriages and our ideas about marriage. What was considered acceptable marital behavior in the 1890s was probably thought of differently in the 1990s.

According to Stetson (1997), there are three theories of gender-role relationships in marriages: *the unity model*, which says that husband and wife are one, as defined by the husband; the *separate but equal model*; and the *shared equal-partnership model*. The *separate but equal* model dominated people's image of marriage in the United States from the early 1900s until the 1960s. This model assumed that each partner in a marriage was responsible for certain tasks, depending on her or his gender. For example, wives did the housework while husbands took out the trash and changed the oil in the car. Ideally, the partners would carry out those tasks as equal members of the partnership. This may be a nice idea, but in reality it doesn't work so well. "Women's work" tends to be seen as less important or significant, and men's work is often less frequent and less time-consuming. The *shared equal-partnership* model is the most contemporary model and emerged in the late 1960s. To some advocates of this model, the two partners create a new unit together, while to others the two individuals have many common interests and forge an alliance. Ideally, the marital partners share housework, economic support, child care, and so forth. In our "modern" notion of married households, this idea is the most popular and often espoused. However, research finds that it doesn't play out in reality for many couples. As one example, many couples still tend to fall into the roles mentioned above. Old ways are difficult to change; the first two models describe most actual contemporary households far more accurately than the third one does.

Research findings about marriage vary significantly depending on which variables are under discussion. Many U.S. citizens today believe that gender relationships have become far more fair than before; for example, that men and women do equal amounts of housework, that marriage is a shared endeavor, that childrearing is a "we" task. In reality, even couples who start out with egalitarian ideas settle into much more traditional gender schemas, especially after having children. Undoubtedly, you may know couples who do not fit this pattern; perhaps you were even raised in such a family. However, most marriages fit this larger societal pattern.

Formal education modifies this—a bit. People who have more formal education tend to share household tasks more frequently. After a point, however, formal education plays little role in the gender dynamics between a couple, and many women remain the primary child caretakers. These dynamics have major implications for families and society. For example, if the couple expects the woman in an heterosexual partnership to be the primary caretaker of children (whether this expectation is conscious *or* unconscious), this role will affect her work life, her sense of self, and her energy levels. In the next chapter, we talk about the pay gap between women and men; a leisure gap also exists. Unfortunately, many women are exhausted. They're responsible for kids and the household 24 hours a day—and many of them hold down a full-time job outside the home as well so their families can "make ends meet" financially.

Ideas about marriage do vary by gender, race/ethnicity, and social class. What women think makes a good marriage isn't necessarily what men think is important. Married black couples construct their life around cultural models that may vary significantly from Latin/Chicano/Hispanic couples. Working-class families and well-to-do or middle-class families see marriage in very different terms (numerous authors discuss such differences).

Finally, let's not forget that contemporary marriage is strongly shaped by the legacies of the common law. Examples? I've already mentioned that many wives take their husband's surname—a perfect example of the coverture legacy. Another prime example is that women must work *consciously* to establish credit *in their own name* after they marry, because adult women often lack their own credit. Evidence of this is when credit checks are run under the primary name of the husband—the credit is *his* credit.

Marital Dissolution, Property, and Support

Unfortunately, not all marriages last until "death do us part." In some marriages, partners live apart for awhile to allow time to investigate their issues and problems. If this arrangement is formalized by a court order, it is called a "legal separation." After time has lapsed, some couples reunite. Others, however, do not reunite. In such cases, divorce, or marital dissolution, becomes the life experience of those partners. Numerous issues arise—how can the couple socially and legally dissolve the union, what does the couple do with their "stuff," should one soon-to-be ex-partner help support the other partner financially? Let's discuss the dissolution process first.

Dissolution

For many decades, the only way out of a marriage in Western societies was through abandonment or death. This has not always been the case. In ancient Babylon, a woman could divorce her husband if he had degraded her; she even retained custody of the children. However, in most places and eras, divorce has been a man's option only.

In sixteenth-century England, divorce was impossible. Once Henry VIII (1491–1547) established the Church of England and divorced Catherine of Aragon, Parliament stood up and said, "No more." For several hundred years afterward, the only way to divorce in England was through an act of Parliament. However, in the North American colonies, rules of marriage and divorce were left to each colony. Connecticut passed the first law allowing divorce in 1667 but allowed it only in specific cases, such as adultery or seven years' desertion. Divorce generally was possible only in New England, at least until the late 1700s. Divorce was rare, at least until the mid-1900s when women entered the labor force in large numbers to help with the "war effort." There they met new people and ideas. They also earned more of their own money, as well as gained a sense of confidence and professional skills. After this era, divorce became more commonplace than it had been.

Originally, divorce was allowed only if one of the partners could be deemed as "at fault." "Fault" was often identified as something like adultery, cruelty, or desertion and the "faulted" partner was often labeled "the bad person." Spouses could prevent a fault divorce by demonstrating to the court that they were *not* at fault. This would create a "contested" divorce, or a divorce where someone contested the issues at hand (which could also include property division, child custody, alimony, and so forth).

In 1970, California put into place the idea of "no-fault" divorce, whereby one spouse does not have to prove that the other spouse is at fault for the failure of the marriage. The original intent of no-fault was to give people a modern way to end their domestic relationships. People hailed it as an opportunity for individuals to watch out for themselves, make their own decisions, end unhappy unions with less emotion—in short, a revolution in marital dissolution. To get a no-fault divorce, all you needed to do was claim that you and your spouse were "incompatible," or that the marriage had been "irretrievably broken." If your spouse didn't challenge this claim, then you received an uncontested divorce.

Uncontested divorces are of two types—*mutual-consent,* in which the parties agree on everything, or *default cases,* in which one partner doesn't appear in court to contest the divorce. In some states, partners must live apart for a period of time to prove this incompatibility. Neither spouse can stop a no-fault divorce from proceeding.

Today, all states have a no-fault divorce option; many let individuals select either a fault or no-fault option. No-fault divorces are generally cheaper and less emotionally taxing than fault divorces. They lack the courtroom brawling that often erupts between two people who do not want to be together any more. In fault divorces, one partner needs to "prove" something, and that requires experts, witnesses, and lawyers. In a courtroom, those things can become pricey.

Critics of no-fault divorce argue that it has caused divorce rates to skyrocket. With "easy divorces," critics say, people don't have to think about marriage as a long-term commitment; if you don't like it, get out. Researchers disagree on whether a relationship exists between divorce rates and no-fault divorce. Glenn (1999) argues that no-fault divorce laws were actually a redundancy in the legal world; many states had already liberalized their divorce laws before no-fault divorce became a nationwide phenomenon. Whether we look to the work of Peters in 1986, which suggested that no-fault laws did not affect the divorce rate, or Allen's work in 1992, which said it does, or Rodgers' *et al.* in 1999, which claims that a case can be made on both sides, we find that the debate keeps going. Gatland (1997) points out that lawyers—those who deal with these issues directly—largely support no-fault divorce and do not see it as raising divorce rates overall.

What impact has no-fault divorce had on women? These answers, too, are mixed. Weitzman (1985) suggests that no-fault divorce has made women's and children's lives more difficult, particularly in terms of economics. When "fault" was taken out of divorce, women were left without a "bargaining chip"—no husband, no money, and lots of bills. At least when men could be "blamed" for divorce, the courts could make them pay for their indiscretion or failure to uphold their responsibilities as husbands. Parkman (1992) suggests that no-fault divorce has made married women realize that they'd best get paid work, to protect themselves financially in case their husbands decide to divorce them (see also Graglia, 1995). Basically, because states condone marriage as something other than a lifelong commitment, women who may have been stay at home moms a few years ago feel the need to make sure they have a career "just in case."

On the other hand, Garrison (1990) believes that the decline in women's economic status (as a result of divorce) is not related to no-fault divorce legislation. Repeal of no-fault divorce legislation would have little positive effect on divorced women's economic lives, she argues. Garrison is one of several critics of Weitzman who point out that Weitzman's work has not been replicated, and that the data in it is faulty.

Clearly, the reviews are mixed. Thus we do not have answers to the questions of how no-fault divorce affects women. Certainly more women are divorced now than ever before, and many of them have been divorced under no-fault statutes. Researchers have suggested that no-fault statutes—because they make divorce easier—have ultimately increased the number of women and children in poverty.

Property

The unity model suggested by Stetson assumed that all property in a marriage, even children, belonged to the husband. With the passage of a Married Women's Property Act in various states, as well as cases such as *Dege*, this notion changed. A separate-property, or equitable-property, system of

---

B O X **4.2** "Family" Case Citations

General:
Everett v. Everett 215 U.S. 203 (1909)
Zablocki v. Redhail 434 U.S. 374 (1978)

Alimony, Divorce and Property:
Lang v. Rigney 160 U.S. 531 (1896)
DeVillanueva v. Villanueva 239 U.S. 293 (1915)
Armstrong v. Armstrong 350 U.S. 568 (1956)
Vanderbilt v. Vanderbilt 354 U.S. 416 (1957)
Aldrich v. Aldrich 375 U.S. 249 (1963)
Orr v. Orr 440 U.S. 268 (1979)
Mansell v. Mansell 490 U.S. 581 (1989)

Child Custody:
Jarrett v. Jarrett 499 U.S. 927 (1980)
Webb v. Webb 451 U.S. 493 (1981)
Etlin v. Robb 458 U.S. 1112 (1982)
Thompson v. Thompson 484 U.S. 174 (1988)

Child Support:
Roe v. Norton 422 U.S. 391 (1975)
Paulssen v. Herion 475 U.S. 557 (1986)
Rose v. Rose 481 U.S. 619 (1987)
Clark v. Jetter 486 U.S. 456 (1988)
Sullivan v .Stroop 496 U.S. 478 (1990)

ownership came into being. Whichever spouse held title to something (for example, a car or house) owned that something. However, in the 1970s and 1980s, a number of states instituted community-property systems of ownership. Among other things, community-property laws were initially meant to help women in divorce situations. The idea behind community property is that income or assets acquired during a marriage belong to both partners and must, upon marital dissolution, be equally divided between them. Of course the question of equal division is more difficult than it sounds.

In separate-property states, who owns what seems clear. But what about the things two people purchase together that don't have a title? If the two cannot agree on how to divide such possessions, the court will do an "equitable division"; that is, a division that it sees as fair. For example, if one spouse is leaving the relationship with a $75,000 annual salary and the other must take a minimum-wage job at WalMart, the latter will get more property out of the deal. Generally, the court will award more property to the party who has the least earning power, poorest health, and custody of children. Courts tend to divide things more equally if the marriage was long lasting between two people who were nearly equal in wealth before they married, if they both have about equal earning potential, and if there aren't any children involved.

One problem with the division of property is what to do about homemakers. If they contributed to their households through their unpaid work, then how much of the marriage's "stuff" belongs to them? Lindgren and Taub (1993) discuss three ways by which courts have evaluated the contributions of homemakers:

1. Determine the price of their services if those services were provided by paid personnel.
2. Assess the opportunity costs of being a homemaker; for example, wages lost, education lost, and so forth.
3. Assume that both partners are entitled to an equal share of the goods, and make the appropriate adjustments.

During 1980–2000, U.S. courts have changed their views on what is considered dividable property. Educational degrees earned by one spouse while the other spouse supports the family is one example. What are these degrees worth? Today, in making their property-division decisions, many judges consider the fact that one spouse supported the other through a degree program. Judges thus take into account such effort when dividing assets.

Support

Alimony. The word has frightened many divorced men over the years. Alimony, or "spousal support," was awarded more frequently in the past than it is today. However, research cited by Stetson (1997) suggests that since the United States first began recording alimony statistics, in 1890, no more than 19 percent of divorced women have ever been awarded alimony. Weitzman claims that 85 percent of divorced women are not awarded alimony. Traditionally, when alimony was awarded, it usually went to the woman. Today that pattern continues. Weitzman argues that what used to be long-term support for divorced women has become short-term maintenance. Alimony can take two forms: a lump-sum settlement, or a "rehabilitative settlement." A rehabilitative settlement is an amount awarded for a specific period of time, to help a divorced woman (in most cases) get on her feet and support herself. The woman is expected to go to school or get some kind of training during the rehabilitative period. But, Weitzman points out, many women lack the skills necessary to get good jobs, especially if they have been keeping house. Furthermore, women with small children have a compounded problem—child care and the lack of child support.

In the past, alimony was awarded for many reasons. The most common ones were as a form of economic support, as a punishment for the "bad" spouse ("fault"), and as a way for women to maintain the standard of living they achieved by being dependent on their husbands. Today, these three reasons come into play less often. Alimony laws have changed specifically to reflect changing social conditions and ideas. Of course, in states that do weigh issues of fault in alimony awards, women may be the ones who pay if they are considered at fault.

States make decisions about alimony, property, and marriage dissolution using different criteria. Just because a state emphasizes community property doesn't mean it will have fault divorces or award spousal support. Legislatures have debated over what kinds of decisions should be tied together in a marital dissolution. For instance, should spousal support be informed by community property? Should no-fault divorce be tied in with alimony? Should women whose husbands run off with a "trophy wife" be awarded alimony as a form of punishment to their errant man? The U.S. civil-justice system will likely continue grappling with these questions for decades to come.

Lesbian (and Gay-Male) Couples and "Marriage"

As we've seen, legal marriage is applicable only to heterosexual couples. What about couples unable to legally marry, lesbians and gay men? Because this text centers on women and justice issues, we are most interested in lesbians and marriage. However, the whole topic of gay marriage is a hot button in the United States these days. Legislation passed in Vermont in 2000 now allows gay couples to engage in a civil ceremony that "marries" them in the state's eyes—they can file state tax returns together and such.

However, the law is not applicable in other states nor at the federal level, so its national effect is not large. The Vermont Civil Union Law catalyzed national debate about gay marriage, however. And even within Vermont, the issue has generated controversy and political posturing.

Just as with the gay-pride movement in the 1970s, we now hear public voices suggesting that lesbians and gay men should be able to legally marry. Lesbians and gay men have always coupled, but marriage as a legal act has been off limits to them. Some homosexual couples have tried to adopt one another, or done other things to prove to society that their relationship had legal ties. Most efforts such as these have failed. Thus gay couples shifted their attention to notions of domestic partnership in the 1980s. Some applied for marriage certificates; others sued their states. These efforts, too, have failed. For lesbian and gay couples, the closest thing to being married is the Vermont Civil Union Law.

What are the arguments for and against "gay marriage"? In an article in the *Yale Law Journal*, Hohengarten (1994, p. 1495) argues that gay marriage should be allowed under the constitutional right of privacy. As he puts it: "The constitutional right of privacy requires states to sanction and recognize same-sex marriages," because nothing about marriage itself cannot be done by same-sex couples—whether it's loving one another, raising children, running a household, contributing to a community, living a spiritual life, etc. Opponents of gay marriage maintain that it's unnatural; that is, only women and men are "made" to fit together in marriage. Or God condones only Dan and Nan, not Dan and Sam. Of course, God's rules are found in the Bible, a document written by humans. And marriage laws are written by humans. If marriage is a social construction, then who is allowed to marry whom is part of that construction. Regardless of the arguments made, the reality is humans—in any given time and place—are deciding who can and cannot marry. Humans are writing, or socially constructing, the laws, yet they're also reading past some of them and forgetting what they say. If Hohengarten is correct, then reading past the law violates the

---

B O X **4.3**   **Same-Sex Case Citations**

Baker v. Nelson, Minnesota (1971)
Jones v. Hallahan, Kentucky (1973)
Singer v. Hara, Washington (1974)
Thorton v. Timmers, Ohio (1975)
Baehr v. Miike, Hawaii (1999)
Baker v. State, Vermont (2000)

law of privacy. In other words, what people do in their own homes—as long as they are not hurting others—is their own business.

Hohengarten further argues that the case of *Loving v. Virginia* (388 U.S. 1 (1967)) is unmistakenly related to same-sex marriage. *Loving* was about a white and a black person's legal right to marry one another. In this case, the U.S. Supreme Court held that Virginia state marriage laws could not prohibit two such individuals from marrying, particularly as argued under the Equal Protection Clause. It also stated that even though long-held legal or cultural proscriptions may exist against a certain behavior, those proscriptions are not a good enough reason to continue discriminatory practices. The right to marry is thus fundamental and part of the constitutional right to privacy.

Some opponents of gay marriage also ask, "How would the human species continue if women married women and men married men?" Well, lesbians and gay men have coupled for centuries, and the human population has still managed to balloon to alarming numbers. Heterosexual couples outnumber homosexual couples and, at least so far, have ensured future generations. This "death of the species" argument also reveals ignorance. Research suggests that somewhere around 30 percent of lesbians have children from previous heterosexual relationships. And today, lesbians who want to bear and raise children also have artificial insemination available.

Because men earn much more money than women do in the United States, lesbian couples are often not very wealthy. However, if they had some of the benefits of marriage, they might be better off financially. For example, the idea of marital property—property that belongs to both partners legally—provides heterosexual couples a luxury lesbian couples don't have: knowing upon one another's death the property acquired belongs to the surviving partner. There are legal steps which lesbian couples can proactively take to assure this happens, but heterosexual couples are protected by the legal union of marriage.

Even within the gay and lesbian community, there is a lot of debate over the issues of marriage. Some lesbians say they would immediately get married if they could do so; others feel that a commitment ceremony is good enough. Still others see marriage as a patriarchal institution and would avoid it even if it were available to them.

Children and Parenting

Mothering

Maternal instinct. Western society tells us that mothering is instinctual among women. However, if that were the case, most women would "mother" in a similar way. That is what instinct is all about—species members do things in the same way, at largely the same time, to ensure the species' survival. With humans, however, "mothering" varies drastically. Some women are perceived as good, better, or best mothers compared to other mothers. Furthermore, we often judge mothering from a class bias. Mothers who can do certain things for their children—translate "do" into "spend money"—are often perceived as better mothers. Consider mothers who can afford to stay home with their kids versus those mothers who must engage in paid employment. This is an example of walking the line. Some women have no choice but to perform paid labor—yet we have defined some of them as poor mothers. (One young woman lost custody of her child because she had to put the kid in daycare while she attended college classes on an all-expense paid scholarship.)

We have definite ideas about motherhood in the United States. We think of motherhood as "American" as apple pie and hot dogs—an "institution," one might say. We have created an image of who "Mom" is, and an atmosphere surrounding her. The idea of the *motherhood mystique* (McBride, 1973) carries such description even further. The mystique has four parts:

1. Ultimate fulfillment for a woman comes from being a mother.
2. The body of work assigned to mothers fits together in noncontradictory ways; for instance, taking care of a home and family and, these days, often engaging in employed labor.
3. Being a good mother means enjoying all of the work associated with the role.
4. A mother's intense and exclusive devotion is good for her children.

Research and personal stories suggest that each of these assumptions is false. Women can find fulfillment in many ways, not just through motherhood. Likewise, it is not always easy balancing home and family. When women take on paid labor too, they simply get exhausted. And as a mother myself, I didn't always enjoy dirty diapers. Finally, devotion to children can be a good thing, but too much of it can actually harm both mother and children.

The motherhood mystique implies an exalted state—mothers on a pedestal. But of course, the only way off a pedestal is down. Juliet Mitchell (and others; see Adrienne Rich and Shulamith Firestone) points out that motherhood, when "used as a mystique . . . becomes an instrument of oppression" (1966, p. 28). Crittendon (2001) argues that motherhood imposes an enormous cost on most women, a "mommy tax," which can result in financial hardship and social marginalization. Additionally, motherhood is the perfect tool with which to examine quadraplexation. Though motherhood is obviously tied in with reproduction, we can also examine it in light of the other three quadraplexation variables. For example, a part of every mother's life is labor; that is, production. Work can take the form of unpaid nurturing and caring for children at home, or the paid labor required to support those children. Discussions about issues of labor fill a mother's life—is she doing it well enough? Doing enough of it?

Likewise, there are countless virginal images of the Mother Mary, although biological mothers clearly aren't virgins. Sexuality, as part of the quadraplexation process, is another key facet of motherhood. Sexuality reveals itself in a variety of ways. Let's talk about breast feeding. Nursing is the healthiest choice of feeding for babies, especially during the first few weeks of life. However, because U.S. culture has such a breast fetish, nursing becomes sexualized for many women and men. Some women even confess that they can't imagine nursing their children because they consider their breasts sexual objects. Even women who do nurse see the activity as *private* and feel uncomfortable doing it in public. Where does this feeling of shame come from?

Motherhood is filled with walking-the-line situations. Paid labor or not? Not supportive enough or too supportive? Unemotional or too emotional? Nurturing or doting? These questions can wear women down. Though the motherhood mystique suggests that women should love motherhood, in reality many of them dislike a number of aspects of the job (with good reason).

Care of Children

The above discussion highlights the diversity in definitions of the "good mother" and "good" care of children. Suffice it to say, some care is obviously bad—outright child abuse and neglect, for example. However, how do we define less clear cases of child abuse or neglect? Yes, sitting a child on a hot burner or chaining her to a hot-water heater and not feeding her is clearly criminal. But what about failing to feed him fresh fruit, vegetables, or meat at every meal? Is that neglect or abuse? It *is* a class issue. Some women and families simply do not have the money needed to provide enough healthy food for their kids.

Again, quadraplexation tells us that reproduction is a primary function for women. It's women who are responsible for the kids—who call the sitter, who take care of children when they are sick, whose work suffers the most. And these walking-the-line notions of child care plague women's lives. Women are told that they should be raising their own children. Yet they're told to provide for them lavishly as well. Working women are chastised for not spending more time with their children, yet stay-at-home moms are accused of being unintelligent and uninteresting. What should women do? Research finds that women in paid employment actually spend about the same amount of time with their children as nonemployed women do. These statistics contradict the idea that employment reduces a mother's time with her kids. When we also consider our earlier discussion about women feeling that they need to work to protect themselves in case of divorce, these questions get even more complex. Indeed, many women are forced to engage in paid labor because they are single mothers and must feed their kids—regardless of societal attitudes about working versus single moms.

What about nonheterosexual moms? Research suggests that children raised by lesbian couples tend to have stronger self-esteem than children raised in heterosexual households. What might explain this difference? Perhaps such children have to come to terms early about living with "different" families. Thus they learn lessons about strength early on. Or, perhaps being nurtured by two women strengthens a child's sense of self (Swerdlow, Bridenthal, & Vine, 1980). Interestingly, Miller (1982) found that lesbian mothers are more concerned about the long-term development of their children than heterosexual mothers are. This notion contradicts homophobic societal myths that say lesbians don't want or are afraid of children. Indeed, there is no evidence suggesting that lesbians are less capable than nonlesbians as mothers.

Custody of Children

The law has only recently allowed women custody of their children in cases of divorce. Up until the last two hundred years, the common-law system defined children as men's property (just as women were considered men's property). Thus men kept the property from a marriage if it dissolved. Coverture emphasized this right of men, for women had no independent standing or legal right to any property, including their own children.

But with the Industrial Revolution and its economic and social shifts, children became more and more of a liability. As the class system developed, some women were able to stay at home. Children then became expensive. No longer were they needed to work the fields—they were now costly symbols of success. Thus, when children are useful for labor purposes, they belong to men; when they become expensive liabilities, they get handed off to women. Many men have claimed that it's unfair that "women get custody"; they do not realize that this "trend" is relatively recent. Furthermore, gender-blind laws are granting custody to more and more fathers because such laws require that gender is *not* part of the judicial decision-making process concerning parenthood.

Of course, as Weitzman (1985) and others point out, when men do fight for custody, they win 75–80 percent of the time, even without gender-blind laws in place. This points out an interesting reality in U.S. families and courts: Men do not often fight for custody. Why not? They don't want the burden of children? They're afraid they will fail? They don't see themselves as the "real" parent? They think a woman will do a better job? It would be worth asking men to shed some light on these questions.

Not surprisingly, ideological notions of custody have shaped custody laws. Three ideas about custody reign: the *"tender-years" presumption*, the *best-interest-of-the-child test*, and the *primary-caretaker test*. The tender-years presumption says that women should have custody of particularly young children. During their "tender years," children most need a mother's love and nurturing, and presumably nothing can substitute for Mom's touch. This idea is the first one to replace the U.S. coverture rule of male custody. By the mid-1900s, it had spread nationally.

The question of what is in the best interest of the child surfaces in virtually all courtrooms. Judges, case workers, and lawyers repeatedly ask whether living with Mom or Dad is in the child's best interest. In the last two hundred years, the vote has gone to Mom. However, research suggesting that men who fight for custody win runs hand-in-hand with this notion. Men are often more economically able to care for children; hence living with fathers is often in the "best interest" of children. Many working mothers claim they are held to a higher standard in custody hearings (Kellman, 1995), which makes some best-interest arguments hard to swallow. What kind of higher standard? A chaste life, perfectly cleaned house, acceptable friends—in other words, a standard of excellence against which few can measure up.

The primary-caretaker rule asks who has provided most of the child's care. It may not be Mom or Dad—it may be Grandma. In some cases, a grandmother or other relative wins custody. Although the courts generally hold that the best custodial person is a biological parent, it is not always the biological parent who has served as the primary caretaker. Becker (1992) maintains that "maternal deference" should prevail; assuming that a mother is fit, a court should defer to her decision to keep caring for her child.

What about joint custody? This form of caring for children had its heyday in courtrooms across the United States for a number of years. It has one primary drawback—if two parents can't get along well enough to stay married, how can they get along well enough to share care of a child? As with so many things, people initially believed that joint custody would benefit children and parents alike. The parents would get to share the child more or less equally (half the week at Dad's, half the week at Mom's, for example), and the child would get to "have" both parents in her life. But as it turned out, some parents couldn't settle their differences enough to make this arrangement work. So, even in jurisdictions where joint custody was lauded as the best thing to come along in years, courts have used it less and less.

What happens to noncustodial mothers? Quadraplexation variables, as well as general stereotypes, would suggest that noncustodial mothers would feel some backlash from society, friends, and family because they "do not have their kids." This is often true. Noncustodial mothers face all sorts of social censure and guilt because they are not performing the role they should be—taking care of their children as their custodial parent. Herrerias (1995) found that 75 percent of noncustodial mothers voluntarily gave up their children because of emotional problems, financial difficulties, destructive spousal relationships, and legal threats. Most of these mothers would have kept their children if it weren't for these hurdles.

On the other hand, many noncustodial mothers who remain involved with their children find that the quality of their time together improves when they begin living apart (Greif & Pabst, 1988). Indeed, some noncustodial mothers have willingly sought out their status—they want freedom from children, or perhaps want their children to establish better bonds with their fathers. However, social censure and guilt still often accompany this decision—especially if acquaintances and friends start asking, "How could you have made such a decision?"

Remember, for most of human history, especially within the common-law structure, women were *not* given custody. Guilt and societal censure of mothers who aren't raising their kids reflect recent cultural shifts. Fortunately, several support groups have emerged around the country to help noncustodial mothers cope with their decisions and lives.

Support of Children

According to Scott (1985), the feminization of poverty reflects the economic vulnerability of women and their children. This vulnerability comes in part from the fact that many men do not financially support their children. Most women earn less money than men *and* support children. Census data shows that, among custodial parents, about 59 percent received partial or full child support in 1997. About 40 percent received full payments, while the remaining percent received some support. Of course, that leaves one-third of custodial parents who do not receive any support at all. An interesting twist emerged in the 2000 Census Bureau report (based on 1997 data): Custodial mothers who were most likely to receive a child-support award from the court were white, non-Hispanic, and/or divorced and/or had at least some college education (Grall, 2000). Mothers least likely to receive a child-support award were black or Hispanic, had less than a high-school education, and had never married. It seems the "true woman" notion aids women who are seeking support from the courts.

Custodial mothers received more money than custodial fathers in terms of payments. This is understandable, given that fathers tend to make more money than mothers and therefore pay more in child support. Noncustodial fathers were more likely to pay their support than were noncustodial mothers, by a small margin.

How do courts calculate child support? Each state develops guidelines based on parents' incomes and expenses. The guidelines vary quite a bit from state to state, and the differences can be surprising. In some states, judges have substantial freedom to determine awards. In other states, the determination is calculated following a strict mathematical model. Child support is assumed to cover the expenses of shelter, food, clothing, education, day care, and other aspects of raising a child. Some courts count car payments as an expense; others do not. Some noncustodial parents who argue that they "can't afford" a child-support payment because they have to make a mortgage are told that their children come first.

Why do some noncustodial parents fail to pay child support? Some don't have the money. Others refuse to pay unless they're allowed to visit the children. Still others believe that the custodial parent would spend the money frivolously, or not use it for the kids. Justifications abound for both noncustodial mothers and fathers although ideas like "I don't want my ex-wife to use the money to buy a new dress" are ludicrous. Custodial parents may buy something for themselves, such as a dress, without necessarily taking money away from the children. Child support usually goes into one pot—the custodial parent's bank account—rather than being meted out as clothes for the kids, clothes for Mom, electricity bill for the kids, electricity bill for Mom, and so on.

Unfortunately, the courts have not found a way to ensure that noncustodial parents pay the child support they are supposed to pay. The Family Support Act of 1988 (42 U.S.C. Section 666) required states to develop automatic child-support tracking and monitoring systems by 1995. Many states failed to establish adequate systems by that time. States have tried garnishing wages, threatening jail, repossessing cars, putting scofflaws' names and pictures in the local newspaper, and so forth. Some parents move from one state to another to avoid paying support; others drop out of sight for the same reason. Because the system remains faulty, state-based, and largely private, no federal program has emerged to deal with the problem.

For these reasons, Hunter (1983) argues against privatized child support. The civil-justice system would then not be held accountable for the well-being of children. Just as different courts use different means to set child support, they use different ideologies to make decisions; ultimately, they place the well-being of children at risk. What is the alternative if the child-support system fails? These days it is Temporary Assistance for Needy Families (TANF), or what we used to call "welfare." (See Chapter 7 for a more complete discussion.) Bartfield (2000) argues that even though women and children fare much worse than men do after divorce, at least the private child-support system provides some relief. If it weren't in place, women and children would be far worse off.

In some cases, child support is also a means for men to control women, Hunter maintains. Through privatized child support, women are burdened with the obligation of supporting children, while fathers are re-lieved of that duty. The current system forces women to bear the economic repercussions because it offers no better alternative.

Women Criminals

How do these issues of marriage, divorce, and custody play out for criminal women and their families? Let's take a closer look below.

Partner Status

According to a December 1999 Bureau of Justice Statistics Special Report, adult women under correctional care, custody, or control are much more likely to have never been married than women in the general population. In 1998, 42 percent of women on probation were never married, 48 percent of women in local jails were never married, 47 percent of women in state prisons and 34 percent of women in federal prisons were never married (Greenfield & Snell, 1999). As with civilian women, many incarcerated women who *have* been married or partnered have suffered the trauma of divorce, property division, and so forth. It is because of their divorced or nonmarried status that some women engage in crime. (Remember the 2 M's—money and men?)

Children

Women under supervision by justice-system agencies are mothers of an es-timated 1.3 million minor children. Approximately 70 percent of these women have minor children. An estimated 72 percent of women on proba-tion, 70 percent of women in local jails, 65 percent of women in state pris-ons, and 59 percent of women in federal prisons have young children. Women in this population have an average of 2.11 children. About 64 per-cent of women inmates lived with their children before incarceration.

The absence of their kids only worsens the plight of incarcerated women. Indeed, they often have more social and legal problems than male inmates do because of their children. Courts are more willing to take cus-tody away from incarcerated women—and to not return it once the women get out. In some jurisdictions, being an ex-con automatically qualifies a woman for "unfit" status.

What happens to kids whose moms are in prison? About 25 percent live with the other parent, 50 percent live with maternal grandparents, 20 percent live with other relatives, and the rest live with friends, in foster care, or in some other setting. Often only about 50 percent of incarcerated mothers retain legal custody. Even for those who have custody, fewer than one-half of children visit their mothers regularly.

Children of incarcerated women reportedly suffer typical maladies associated with separation—psychological, physical, emotional, and academic problems. Some mothers don't know how to explain where they are to their kids; often both mother and children feel embarrassment, shame, and longing for one another.

Different institutions have established different kinds of visitation programs. Some let children stay on the grounds for several days; others allow only short visits. Because money is tight in most women's programs, many institutions have failed to devise more effective solutions. We discuss the lives of women in prison in more detail in Chapter 9.

The Essence of the Chapter

Though family, marriage, and children have been touted as dimensions of the "private" world, what happens within those relationships has both private and public effects. Child custody and support are affected by employment and other circumstances of both parents, and these circumstances in turn shape family life. The justice system doles out opportunities and burdens for women and men.

The role of quadraplexation plays a clear role in these matters as well: Our ideas about sexuality, reproduction, production, and socialization have direct ties to our families and lives. In the next chapter, we examine the more "public" worlds of education and paid labor and take a closer look at the "private" world of unpaid labor, or housework.

5 Economics: Education and Work

In this chapter we examine women's education and work, both paid and unpaid. These institutions are affected by their social context, as well as by stereotypical notions of what women and men can "do" in life. The fact that we can talk about them in one chapter demonstrates their basic overlap as well as the overlapping of the public and private spheres. Let's start with education.

The Social Context of Education

Lyons (1993) makes several interesting points about women and education. First, it's unclear what educational access for women in the 1990s ultimately means in terms of their ability to influence power and authority structures. Women in the United States are educated at unprecedented rates these days—but what does that mean for their lives? Second, educational access for women, according to Lyons, has not yet resulted in women's intellectual, political, or social emancipation. Many people think of education as the route to bettering one's life, to earning more money, prestige, and so forth. Yet research suggests that the return on education for women is less than it is for men. Finally, even though girls earn better grades than boys do in high school, they score lower on standardized exams such as the SAT and ACT, and receive only 35 percent of scholarships based on these scores. Sad to say, the primary source of scholarship money for women as a group is through the beauty-pageant business. What kind of quadraplexation variable are we talking about here?

History

Historically, men were the educated and women weren't. Historical evidence indicates that men were the only members of society who were taught to read and write. This was true until a couple of hundred years ago. Yes, women were educated in some respects—they learned from family members or friends to read and write, for example. But, by and large, the notion that women needed to read and write was unheard of. "Modern" medicine even suggested that taxing women's brains too much would create problems for society. Why? Because women's brains were supposedly connected to their uterus. Thus, if they used their brains too much, their uterus would suffer. Specifically, they would not be able to have children. In the separate-spheres world of "contemporary" women (read 1700s), the inability to have children was a moral and social shame. This thinking prevailed throughout the world. All patriarchal societies considered it unnecessary to educate women. Men needed to read, women needed to nurture. And nurturing didn't require reading.

In the United States, the nineteenth century witnessed changes in attitudes about education. The evolution of the change was slow, however. The separate-spheres ideology, the medical "advice," the notions we discussed above—all these things posed barriers to change. But still, ideas began to shift. The first college to admit women was Oberlin College, in Ohio. When Oberlin admitted female students in 1833, it did so by making concessions for them. Oberlin established new curricula for women that were intended to help them develop and refine special skills; specifically, cooking, cleaning, and serving. In fact, Oberlin's female students were expected to serve the male students dinner, and to clean and cook. The whole purpose behind this sort of curriculum was to make women better wives and mothers, not better thinkers and world changers. Still, at least they had gotten their foot in the door.

B O X **5.1** **Hobbes on Justice**

Justice of manners, and justice of actions. Again, the injustice of manners is the disposition or aptitude to do injury, and is injustice before it proceed to act and without supposing any individual person injured. But the injustice of an action— that is to say—injury, supposes an individual person injured—namely, him to whom the covenant was made—and therefore many times the injury is received by one man when the damage redounds to another. As when the master commands his servant to give money to a stranger: if it be not done, the injury is done to the master, whom he had before covenanted to obey; but the damage redounds is done to the stranger, to whom he had no obligation and therefore could not injure him. . . .

Thomas Hobbes, *The Leviathan*

Throughout the nineteenth and twentieth centuries, ideas about educating women changed more substantially, as ideas and social conditions shifted. In the mid-1800s, public schooling in the United States became ritualized and routinized because of the work of educational reformers. Through the work of individuals such as Horace Mann, a uniform curriculum, the establishment of "grades" (first grade, second grade, and so on) and the belief in "readin', writin', and 'rithmetic" was put into place in U.S. education. As part of this change, reformers identified women as members of the student population. A hardy and stable democracy needed all its citizens to have a minimal level of reading and mathematical ability. The expectations for female students were still different than for male students, but women were in the classrooms.

On college campuses, administration, faculty, and students alike expected women to study certain kinds of disciplines. They also did *not* expect female graduates to become certain kinds of professionals or to engage in certain occupations, such as lawyering. Medical and educational professionals argued that some areas of study were still too taxing for the female mind and some kinds of work too dangerous, dirty or unseemly for the female person. Throughout the mid-1900s, many people contended that women were going to college primarily to get their "MRS. Degree"; that is, to find husbands. But even those kinds of claims lessened as women made up more and more of the educational population.

To see the kind of situations female students faced, let's consider the policies at Vanderbilt University. Vanderbilt University, in Nashville, Tennessee, opened its doors in 1873 and was, at the time, an all-male institution. In 1887, the faculty unanimously agreed to admit women students "on exactly the same terms as young men" (von Berckefeldt, 2000, p. 154). However, two years later, the faculty board reversed its decision and refused to admit young women as equals. After another few years, Vanderbilt began to admit women "by courtesy" to classes. In 1901, young women won the permanent right to be students on the campus. All this changed once again in the late 1910s, when the university began to suffer from overcrowding. To settle the problem, the administration set limits on the number of women accepted at Vanderbilt. That policy stayed in place until Title IX (see below) was implemented.

In the 1950s and 1960s, educational policy—like much social policy in the United States—shifted, turned, and swung. In terms of students of color, Chief Justice Earl Warren's U.S. Supreme Court handed down the landmark 1954 decision in *Brown v. Board of Education of Topeka* (347 U.S. 590). This decision opened the door of education to all students, regardless of color. *Brown* affected future decisions, such as Title IX. In terms of gender-equity policies, the courts have increasingly paid attention to issues of equal education access and experience since the early 1970s.

Title IX

The biggest change in women's educational opportunities and experiences came with the passage of Title IX. Title IX of the Educational Amendments of 1972 was passed after Congressional hearings that chronicled the long history of sexually discriminatory polices, practices, and attitudes in U.S. schools. Title IX has made it illegal for schools to treat the genders differently in any aspect of the educational process. Thanks to the law, overt discriminatory practices in education have slowed.

Title IX is applicable only to educational institutions that receive federal funds. Such institutions cannot, on the basis of sex, exclude the participation of, deny benefits to, or subject to discrimination any student in attendance. This is true whether the institution is a preschool, elementary school, secondary school, vocational school, private or public undergraduate institution, professional school, or graduate school. Because of the language of Title IX, only vocational schools, professional schools, graduate schools, and public undergraduate institutions are prohibited from discriminating in admissions policies. Title IX has exerted a profound impact on women's educational access and experience. One of the most obvious changes are the raw numbers of women in attendance these days. Slightly more than half of women are undergraduates in this country, one-half are master's-level graduate students, and one-third are professional-level graduate students (Ph.D., J.D., M.D., and so on). Compare these numbers with those of 1971, when women made up just 18 percent of those with four or more years of college (U.S. Department of Education, 2001).

As another example of Title IX's impact, consider the shifts in the academic areas students are studying by gender. In the past, women were expected to study only certain subjects, among them education, literature, and home economics. Today, we see *some* shift in majors by gender, though because of quadraplexation effects, we see some gender strongholds as well. For example, engineering is still largely a male area of study, while social work is still largely female. Some disciplines are witnessing a shift in their student body; psychology, for example. Once a male domain, psychology is becoming ever more feminized. Researchers within the discipline express concern that such feminization will harm the discipline by bringing down both paychecks and respect. This phenomenon has occurred in the past. Clerical work was originally a male occupation but, after the influx of women as a result of World War II *and* with the invention of the typewriter, women became dominant in the profession and the consequent declines of money and respect followed.

Title IX does have its critics. Originally, some individuals feared that it would mean their children would be sharing locker rooms with children of the opposite sex. They worried that men and women would be showering

BOX **5.2**   **Indicators of Progress Toward Equal Educational Opportunity Since Title IX**

College Enrollment and Completion:

- In 1994, 63 percent of female high school graduates aged 16–24 were enrolled in college, up 20 percentage points from 43 percent in 1973.
- In 1994, 27 percent of both men and women had earned a bachelor's degree. In 1971, 18 percent of young women and 26 percent of young men had completed four or more years of college.

Graduate and Professional Degrees:

- In 1994, women received 38 percent of medical degrees. When Title IX was enacted in 1972, only 9 percent of medical degrees went to women.
- In 1994, women earned 38 percent of dental degrees, whereas in 1972 they earned only 1 percent of them.
- In 1994, women accounted for 43 percent of law degrees, up from 7 percent in 1972.
- In 1993–94, 44 percent of all doctoral degrees awarded to U.S. citizens went to women, up from only 25 percent in 1977.

Participation in Athletics:

- Today, more than 100,000 women participate in intercollegiate athletics—a fourfold increase since 1971.
- In 1995, women comprised 37 percent of college student athletes, compared to 15 percent in 1972.
- In 1996, 2.4 million high school girls represented 39 percent of all high school athletes, compared to only 300,000 or 7.5 percent in 1971. This represents an eightfold increase.
- Women won a record 19 Olympic medals in the 1996 Summer Olympic Games.

International Comparisons:

- In the United States, 87 percent of women 25–34 years old had completed high school in 1992, far more than their counterparts in West Germany, the United Kingdom, France, Italy, and Canada.
- In the United States in 1992, 23 percent of women 25–34 years old had completed higher education degrees, which is significantly higher than for women in France and Japan (12 percent each), the United Kingdom and West Germany (11 percent each), or Italy (7 percent).

U.S. Department of Education, 1997

together in schools, that gender-identified restrooms would disappear, that anything distinguishing gender in school would be discarded. These fears were unfounded. Title IX does have exceptions in its language to deal with some of these issues. For example, it is still acceptable to have single-sex sports teams, single-sex housing and locker rooms, and single-sex showers. What is not acceptable is disbursing funds to only one gender. Schools that do this lose much-needed federal funds.

A Closer Look at the Impact of Title IX: Chilly Climate and Single-Sex Classes

Scholars have discussed the term "chilly climate" a great deal since the early 1970s. The expression refers to gender disparities in classrooms and on campuses that affect the learning environment for female *and* male students. For example, differential treatment of students in classrooms by faculty, counselors, financial aid offices, and other academic venues have all resulted in a chilly climate. Often students are unaware of these disparities because they don't know about or they haven't examined the practices of administrators and teachers. Perhaps the best-known work on the chilly climate is that done by the Sadkers (1980). David and Myra Sadker started examining classroom dynamics in the 1980s and found a number of disturbing trends: Teachers often called on boys more frequently than girls, gave them other kinds of attention over girls, and overall nurtured them more than they did girls. Teachers also overlooked and underrecognized girls for their work and participation in the classroom. (See the Sadkers' work for a fuller discussion of the numerous forms a chilly classroom can take.) Campuses showed similar dynamics, on a larger scale. The awarding of scholarship money, access to health information, answers provided by registrars and other personnel—with all these aspects of campus life, female and male students had markedly different experiences.

The American Association of University Women (AAUW) has conducted several large-scale studies on these issues as well. Starting in 1991 with the publication of *Shortchanging Girls, Shortchanging America*, and continuing throughout the 1990s, significant research by the AAUW has supported work such as the Sadkers'. Additionally, the AAUW has documented how such inequities have reduced women's self-esteem, affected their aspirations, and shortchanged them in ways that shape their entire life course.

The chilly climate teaches women, even if nonverbally, that they are less important in a classroom. Consequently, they conclude that they are less important elsewhere, too. As faculty train the next crop of teachers, many now realize the impact of such policies on future generations of students and professionals. Educational methodology now often includes tips on how to get past the chilly classroom and campus, but change has been slow. These efforts come up against powerful gender schemas and stereotypes.

The topic of single-sex schools also came up after Title IX was passed. Segregation in education—albeit by race and ethnicity—was first legally examined in *Plessey v. Ferguson* (163 U.S. 537 (1896)), which said that separate but equal facilities are acceptable. This decision was overturned by *Brown* (1954). *Brown* forced school districts to consider whether separate *can* be equal. The finding in that case was that separate is often not equal. Title IX prompted people to ask whether this is true of gender as well. As we've seen, even in the same classroom, the genders are often treated differently; what about in different classrooms?

Some research has found that, indeed, gender-separate classrooms benefit women because they no longer worry about how they appear or sound in front of men. They also are not dominated by them in conversation. On the other hand, there have been numerous arguments against single-sex schools. One well-known case concerns the admission of young women to the Virginia Military Institute (VMI). This specific case, brought in 1990 by the United States against the state of Virginia and VMI, was on the behalf of a female high school student who wanted to attend the school. She was offered admittance to the female alternative down the road, Virginia Women's Institute for Leadership at Mary Baldwin College. However, that alternative did not provide the same opportunities and experiences as the men's institution did. In this case, the Fourth Circuit Court of Appeals argued that VMI should stay segregated for a variety of reasons; namely, women "don't belong" in paramilitary institutions like VMI, they are a distraction to men, they are intellectually inferior to men, and so forth. The United States Supreme Court did not agree, and the first class of women graduated from VMI in 2001.

In the final analysis, the question is what is best for both genders. Women deserve equity of opportunity and experience; men also benefit from the lessons they can learn from women. Whether we are discussing women's contributions in a classroom or in the lab, it appears that silencing women or separating them from men is questionable at best, and dishonorable at worse.

Sports Programs

Undoubtedly one of the hottest topics related to Title IX policies is sports programs. For many years, people assumed that women and sports did not go together. Sports entailed being active and using one's body, and women were socialized to be passive and immobile. Activity was for men, passivity for women. The idea that sporting might make a woman masculine and muscular only strengthened these convictions. Many people also assumed that women simply were not interested in sports, or that those who *were* interested were lesbians. Recognizing the injustice of such attitudes, Title IX sought to change all this. Whereas people used to believe that athleticism wasn't a woman's way, now they concluded that women were not athletic because they hadn't had opportunities to participate in sports.

Title IX thus introduced the notion of equity in sports. It requires that schools provide equal athletic opportunities to male *and* female athletes. Even now, however, many institutions are not in compliance with this law. Indeed, the number of lawsuits centering on sports equity has increased in the last several years. Clearly, three decades has not been enough to transform attitudes.

Title IX doesn't mean that the government dictates sporting programs to educational institutions; institutions still have much flexibility in the kinds of sporting programs they offer. It *does* mean that educational institutions must pay attention to the opportunities and experiences they are offering to both their male and female athletes if they want to keep receiving federal funding. This often requires some work. Many people unfamiliar with Title IX's effect on sports equity believe that the law has prompted some schools to dissolve certain sports programs for men so that women can have sports programs. That is untrue; the goal of Title IX is to make sure that female athletes, as a group, have the same opportunities and benefits as groups of male athletes.

The preceding point is an important one. Title IX requires schools to have athletic-participation opportunities *proportionate to the student-body population*. In other words, if half the student body is female, half the athletic program must be female (in terms of the number of athletes, not the number of teams). There are few plausible reasons for a school arguing against this, although many institutions try to justify why such a ratio is unrealistic.

BOX 5.3 Some Insights into Sport

MYTH: Male athletes are more skillful than female athletes.

MYTH: Men are stronger and more powerful than women.

MYTH: Some sports are okay for girls and women, but others aren't.

MYTH: Girls cannot be as good at sports as boys.

TRUTH: At 80 percent of all colleges, the football program loses money.

IDEA: The next time you buy a gift for a young girl, buy her sports equipment, a pair of sneakers, or a book about a female sports hero. You can get a book list and a list of suggested gifts from the Women's Sports Foundation if you call 1-800-227-3988 or visit their Web site.

In college level athletics, three criteria determine whether an institution is in compliance with Title IX:

- *Athletic financial assistance:* The school provides the same financial opportunities for female and male student-athletes.
- *Accommodation of athletic interests and abilities:* The school pinpoints the interests and abilities of all athletes on campus, not just male athletes.
- *Other program areas:* The school provides equivalent benefits, opportunities, and treatments for male and female athletes.

Examples of "other program areas" includes equal-quality and -quantity equipment, supplies, locker rooms, and facilities; equitable recruitment practices (an institution cannot spend $50,000 recruiting male athletes and $5,000 recruiting female athletes); equitable scheduling of games and practice times; equitable travel allowances; equitable tutoring opportunities; coaching equity (opportunities, compensation, etc.); equitable medical and training facilities and services; equitable housing and dining facilities; and equitable publicity efforts, to name a few.

Quadraplexation and Education

Quadraplexation variables are ripe for discussion in terms of education. When we consider the reality that even colleges in the 1800s expected women to cook and to serve men, it becomes clear that U.S. educational institutions have a long history of traditional socialization of women. Indeed, schools powerfully teach students what "boys do" and "girls do." Socialization practices run deep and are difficult to change. For example, although the AAUW has pointed out that there are more girls taking math now than in the past, technology has become the new "boys' club" that girls need access to if they want to stay in the game (1998).

Likewise, schools often teach traditional ideology; thus they teach about productive as well as reproductive roles of each gender. For example, women remain the primary K–12 educators. At the K–6 level, some parents and educators argue that young children need women in the schools to feel nurtured. And for female K–6 teachers, the fact that teaching allows them to be at home with their kids at the end of the school day is very appealing. Finally, in all of this lies the undertone of sexuality. In sporting, sexuality is more than an undertone—one of the reasons women weren't welcomed on sporting fields was the fear sports would create lesbians or, at any rate, masculine females. Today, parents and educators debate whether sexuality should be part of the educational process. Sex-education classes in K–12 schools—and the "moral" discussions that surround them—are often concerned with the effects of teaching "sex" to students. Such concerns, I would argue, are particularly focused on the sexual behavior of female students.

This conversation about women and education is not a silent one. In the summer of 1999, a bill was introduced into both the U.S. Senate (S 1264) and House of Representatives (HR 2505) called *Educating America's Girls Act (of 1999)* (also known as the Girls Act). The act identifies issues which must continue to be addressed so that girls needs are met and gender equity in education is reached and addresses educational technology, sexual harassment, athletics, and numerous other topics. Introduction of this bill continues the work of creating equity and justice in education for women and girls.

The Social Context of Work

Women have always worked. Still, newspapers, magazines, and television make it sound as if women have participated in the paid labor force for merely the last 40 years. This is untrue. It's the *social context* of work that has changed, and women's participation in work has changed with it. The problem is that when most people talk about "work," they mean paid labor. But much work is unpaid—and women have routinely done most of it. As economies have changed throughout human history, women's roles—like men's—have also shifted. In earlier days, they may have bartered for the morning milk to feed their families; today, they may bring home paychecks.

The History of Paid and Unpaid Labor

According to Andersen (2000) (citing Tilly and Scott), the best way to grasp the historical transformation of women's paid work in the United States is to follow the development of the capitalist economy. And according to Benston (1969), we must compare "exchange-value" work and "use-value" work. Exchange-value work is done when individuals take their labor into a marketplace and exchange it for money; thus, it's paid labor. Use-value work occurs within the household. It's often unseen by public eyes, and is not exchanged for money in a market. However, it keeps a household functioning day to day. As we examine the transformation of the U.S. economy and its subsequent effect on women's labor, we will see a corresponding transformation in use-value and exchange-value work as well.

Early in the United States, the economy was based on the family. Roughly from the 1600s to the early–mid 1700s, individual families constituted the basic economic units. They produced what they needed and, in essence, survived on their own. People didn't take their labor into a "market" to exchange it for a wage. Most labor was of the use-value kind, whether it occurred out in the fields or in the household.

Starting in the early to mid 1700s and continuing for about two hundred years after that, the impact of the Industrial Revolution kicked in. With industrialization, the household was no longer the center of economic production. People began taking their labor into the market, and began considering use value as less important than before. The separate-spheres ideology, the "true-womanhood" notion, and the idea that women belong in the household and men in the labor market also emerged in this era. These changes in ideology and practice were fueled mostly by the middle class. A symbol of having "made it" in the industrial economy was the ability for a family to have just one wage earner. Thus, for middle- and upper-class women, leisure was a status symbol. For men, having a wife who didn't have to work was also a status symbol. Poor and working-class women, of course, had no choice. They kept performing whatever work they needed to feed their families.

During this era, use-value work was delegated it to what women did in the household. Correspondingly, women's economic role was deemed less and less important. Workers who engaged in use-value jobs for pay (often they were women of color who worked as domestics) were not considered "real" workers because they were still doing domestic work. Their paychecks reflected this attitude toward their labor.

Thus work in this period became marginalized based on gender, race/ethnicity, and class. The same ideology that emerged for the first time two hundred years ago still reigns: women should stay at home with their children, do housework, and not perform paid labor. The irony is that, even though some people make a biological case for these beliefs, these attitudes—as well as exchange-value work—are actually very new in the evolution of humankind.

The family-consumer economy emerged during the twentieth century as an extension of the family-wage economy phase. We are still in this economic phase. The family, as the primary economic consumer (think of the family house, car, vacation, and so forth), needs as many members as possible to satisfy its ever-growing consumptive needs. Women's labor-force participation in this era has gone up and down until recently. Women have participated in paid labor in large numbers during times of war (the image of Rosie the Riveter cropped up everywhere during World War II), but were often "sent home" when the wars ended. However, with changing social conditions, ideas and laws in the 1970s, women's participation in the paid labor force has increased steadily.

Unfortunately, many women who perform paid labor are also performing all the *unpaid* labor required to run their households. That is, they're still doing the majority of cleaning, cooking, laundry, and so forth. The separate-spheres notions developed during the family-wage economy persist.

Quadraplexation and Production

As Mitchell noted back in the 1970s, women's production has always been controlled by others. As a key quadraplexation variable, production is essential to understanding women's lives. Who controls women's labor? In the paid labor market, women's work is controlled by those who control the market: often white men. Because men largely own and control companies, they are deciding rates of pay, benefits, job categories, and the like. Let's understand something here—95 percent of the Fortune 500 companies (the top 500 companies in the country) have men as CEOs. These individuals have enormous decision making power. The decisions made in the paid labor market have greatly influenced women's work, and have resulted in pay gaps, labor-market segregation, and the "glass ceiling," or the limit to how far a woman gets promoted within a company.

In terms of women's unpaid production, one could always argue that women choose to do what they do in their own homes. In essence, then, women control their own labor when doing housework. If it were only that simple. . . . Indeed, women do make decisions about what cleaners to use and how much time to spend on housework. However, society defines the cleanliness of one's house and children, the expected quality of food on the table, and other aspects of the unpaid market.

In other words, even in their own households, women are influenced by how good a job society thinks they are doing. Societies, including women, trivialize and marginalize the work, often because it is "women's work," but scrutinize it nonetheless—a Catch-22, walking-the-line situation. Are women passive creatures, helpless to do anything about such demands? Certainly not, but societal pressure does weigh heavily and many, if not most, women feel the pressure to conform. Such conformity is taught through the socialization process and comes from family, friends, and the media. Furthermore, because women often have primary responsibility for their household, even if they do paid labor, they must figure out how to get all the unpaid labor done. Generally, women in the paid labor force have dirtier houses than those who aren't engaged in paid labor. Of course, upper- and middle-upper-class women can pay someone else to do housework.

Segregation of Production

By its very nature, women's unpaid labor is segregated from men's work. In general, women do housework on their own and remain in their homes while they do it. Certainly there are exceptions to this—some women must go to a public laundromat to do their laundry, some women get together with friends to do certain tasks (wash windows and such). For the most part, however, women do use-value work away from the public world.

BOX **5.4**   *Muller v. State of Oregon*

. . . That woman's physical structure and the performance of maternal functions place her at a disadvantage in the struggle for subsistence is obvious. This is especially true when the burdens of motherhood are upon her. Even when they are not, by abundant testimony of the medical fraternity continuance for a long time on her feet at work, repeating this from day to day, tends to injurious effects upon the body, and, as healthy mothers are essential to vigorous offspring, the physical well-being of woman becomes an object of public interest and care in order to preserve the strength and vigor of the race.

Still again, history discloses the fact that woman has always been dependent upon man. He established his control at the outset by superior physical strength, may, without conflicting with the provisions and this control in various forms, with diminishing intensity, has continued to the present. As minors, thought not to the same extent, she has been looked upon in the courts as needing special care that her rights may be preserved. Education was long denied her, and while now the doors of the schoolroom are opened and her opportunities for acquiring knowledge are great, yet even with that and the consequent increase of capacity for business affairs it is still true that in the struggle for subsistence she is not an equal competitor with her brother. Though limitations upon personal and contractual rights may be removed by legislation, there is that in her disposition and habits of life which will operate against a full assertion of those rights. She will still be where some legislation to protect her seems necessary to secure a real equality of right. Doubtless there are individual exceptions, and there are many respects in which she has an advantage over him; but looking at it from the viewpoint of the effort to maintain an independent position in life, she is not upon an equality. Differentiated by these matters from the other sex, she is properly placed in a class by herself, and legislation designed for her protection may be sustained, even when like legislation is not necessary for men, and could not be sustained. It is impossible to close one's eyes to the fact that she still looks to her brother and depends upon him. Even though all restrictions on political, personal, and contractual rights were taken away, and she stood, so far as statutes are concerned, upon an absolutely equal plane with him, it would still be true that she is so constituted that she will rest upon and look to him for protection; that her physical structure and a proper discharge of her maternal functions—having in view not merely her own health, but the well-being of the race—justify legislation to protect her from the greed as well as the passion of man. The limitations which this statute places upon her contractual powers, upon her right to agree with her employer as to the time she shall labor, are not imposed solely for her benefit, but also largely for the benefit of all. Many words cannot make this plainer. The two sexes differ in structure of body, in the functions to be performed by each, in the amount of physical strength, in the capacity for long continued labor, particularly when done standing, the influence of vigorous health upon the future well-being of the race, the self-reliance which enables one to assert full rights, and in the capacity to maintain the struggle for subsistence. This difference justifies a difference in legislation, and upholds that which is designed to compensate for some of the burdens which rest upon her. . . .

208 U.S. 412 (1908)

Many women working in the paid labor market also are segregated. In fact, women cluster in only 20 of more than 400 defined job categories, and *two out of three* women workers earn minimum wage (AAUW, 1998).

This situation stems from a variety of forces. In the past, diverse people—legislators, judges, husbands, fathers, and women themselves at times—considered certain forms of employment too harsh or tough for women, or too intellectually difficult. Over time, legislation was passed and cases were decided that restricted women's participation in certain work fields. Perhaps the most famous of these cases was *Muller v. Oregon* (208 U.S. 412 (1908)), which discussed, among other things, how women's "physical structure" and "maternal functions" adversely affect her engagement in paid employment (see Box 5.4). In some states, legislation restricted certain jobs to workers who could lift 30 pounds. Most women were too delicate (it was thought) to lift that much, so they were excluded from all jobs falling under that classification. Often touted as "protective" legislation—"We are protecting her from lifting so much,"—restricted women's entry into certain job fields, reducing their opportunities and preserving opportunities for men. The two words, *restriction* and *protection,* are often interchangeable. For some people, they have positive connotations, but in terms of women's experiences, they often have negative implications. They have also contributed to the segregation of women's production.

The Wage Gap

In the United States, women's and men's pay has long been separated by a significant gap. Even in the eighteenth century, legislators discussed what kinds of economies would best help the country. Hamiltonian supporters—those who followed the economic policies of Alexander Hamilton—argued then that paying women less than men would bolster an industrial base for the country. That argument might have been patriotic, but it has not helped women's economic position.

B O X **5.5**   *"Protection"* and *"Restriction"*

If we look up *protection* in a thesaurus, this is what we find: "defend, guard, shelter, shield, screen, preserve" (p. 438).

If we look up *restriction,* this is what we find: "limit, confine, restrain, hinder, impede" (p. 478).

Whether we are calling case decisions such as *Muller* or similar legislation "protective" or "restrictive," it doesn't seem to matter. . . .

The New American Roget's College Thesaurus, 1985

Such attitudes continue to this day. The current wage gap varies depending on what categories are included in the calculations. On average, however, the gap is somewhere around 74 cents. That is, for every dollar a man earns, a woman earns 74 cents. Women earn less than men because of a variety of reasons, including that employers often consider them the secondary workers in a family, or folks who are working only to earn the family's vacation money. Though this *may* have been true in the past, it is not true today in many families. Many women work because their families need that money. Furthermore, in many families, women are the primary or even sole breadwinners.

A joint research effort by the AFL-CIO and the Institute for Women's Policy Research (Hartmann, Allen, & Owens, 1999) found that working families in the United States are losing $200 billion of annual income because of the wage gap. If married women made as much as men, they would be able to raise their families' incomes by 6 percent. There would be even better news for nonmarried women if the pay gap were to disappear: For single working mothers, family income would go up by 17 percent and their poverty rate would be cut in half. Single women would see a rise in their income of 13 percent and a sixfold drop in poverty.

The pay gap has widened and narrowed over time. To understand pay-gap statistics, we need to keep several things in mind. First, the *kind* of workers being discussed is important. Are the statistics encompassing all workers, or just full-time, year-round workers (who usually make more than seasonal workers do)? Considering all workers gives us a better picture of the average worker's salary. Second, do the statistics take into account differences among *groups?* Hispanic women and black women face especially wide pay gaps, primarily because of racial and ethnic discrimination. Third, do the statistics reflect differences in *education?* Generally the more formal education a woman has, the more she makes. In other words, the sources and kinds of any statistics are important to consider.

Until the last few years, the wage gap had begun to narrow. This was good news, but we also need to understand the context of such change. Though some of the gap decrease stemmed from real increasing wages for women, some of it derived from declining real wages for men. Why were men's wages falling? Numerous answers exist, but the most prominent have to do with changes in the labor market and economy and the kinds of jobs being offered these days. The shift from an industrial economy to a largely service economy has resulted in more lower paying jobs. Jobs men typically held, like working in factories, are starting to disappear. Women, too, feel these labor-force changes and once again are experiencing a widening gap. Census Bureau data (1999) shows an increase in the gap over the last few years. The peak decrease in the gap came in 1996, when the ratio of men's to women's pay was .74. However, in 1998, the ratio had fallen to .73, and in 1999, to .72. These are tiny regressions, but the gap will likely widen further as the economy continues to change and fluctuate.

Pay Equity and Comparable Worth

The wage gap has attracted attention long before now. The Fair Labor Standards Act of 1938 prohibited discrimination in compensation for equal work on the basis of sex. The Equal Pay Act of 1963 made the same statement, and the Civil Rights Act of 1964 prohibited discrimination in compensation because of sex, race, color, religion, and national origin.

However, these acts fell short of their promise because of a basic, flawed assumption: that men and women do "equal work." A better way to handle pay-equity issues is through *comparable-worth* notions. Women and men do not work the same kinds of jobs, so emphasizing equal pay is like using oranges in an apple pie. Comparable worth is about paying women a comparable wage to that of men. It recognizes that women and men generally do not do the same or equal work but, rather, comparable and equally *valuable* work. How is comparable worth determined? By comparing the skills, training, degree of danger or responsibility, and so forth of different jobs. For example, a female nurse has a lot of responsibility and holds people's lives in her hands, and so does a male firefighter.

The *Fair Pay Act of 1999* (S. 702/ H.R. 1271), introduced by Sen. Tom Harkin (Iowa) and Congressperson Eleanor Holmes Norton (District of Columbia), represents a federal-level attempt to define comparable worth. The act is still in committee, so there currently is no federal-level comparable-worth/pay-equity policy for nationwide application. Some individual organizations, communities, and states have developed their own guidelines and rules.

Critics of comparable-worth policies fear they will sabotage free-market forces, create a socialist economy, and so forth. But these arguments ignore the real issue: Where is the justice in paying women less than men? Perhaps women should not come in to work on Fridays (or leave early Thursday afternoon), given that they earn roughly 70 percent of what men earn.

More about Paid Labor

Valian (1998) points out that gender schemas influence how we think about ourselves and our work. She argues that men tend to see career success as a result of their own skills and abilities while women tend to see career success as a result of luck or hard work. This mind set fits in with the things women are taught *about women* and, Valian argues, actually inhibits women from advancing professionally. Men and women may start in the same place professionally but, because the male schema is to put work first, men reach the top of their professions more quickly. Women put their work in second or third place and therefore discount their professional and personal accomplishments. As a psychologist, Valian examines gender inequities from a different vantage point than I do as a sociologist; nonetheless, her work provides some insight into women's attitudes and approach to paid labor.

Sociologists tend to see the issues discussed in this chapter as created by a macrosocial structure. Though women "rate" their work in relationship to other things in their lives, structural and organizational practices also keep them from succeeding as much as men do. The pay gap, comparable worth, segregation—all these things are structures that humans create. Other examples include the glass ceiling, "sticky walls," and "sticky floors." The glass ceiling keeps women from ascending the promotional ladder. Though more women are in boardrooms now than in the past, the glass ceiling still keeps many of them out of the CEO chair. Sticky floors and sticky walls refer to women's inability to move horizontally in their career choices—it is as if they eventually cannot move in any direction. From a psychological point of view, women may be "doing this to themselves," (i.e., choosing careers which allow only so much mobility so they can, in addition to working, attend to family matters). From a sociological point of view, such phenomena are a large part of gender inequity. Let's look more closely at the glass-ceiling phenomenon.

An essay published by Dataline (1991) suggests that the glass ceiling is a more complex obstacle than we might think and that understanding its complexity may help us to dismantle it more quickly. The article suggests there are three levels of the glass ceiling: the *apprenticeship*, the *pipeline*, and *Alice in Wonderland*. Each level may or may not exist in an organization and, even if all levels do exist, one may be stronger than the other two.

The *apprenticeship* occurs at the entry level in many fields. In medicine, it is the residency and intern period; in law enforcement it is the rookie year. Many fields have an apprenticeship period during which the new apprentice learns the rules of the game. At this level, management weeds out people who don't "make the grade." Can she or he handle the job? Often a kind of hazing takes place during this period—sometimes in the form of sexual harassment. If you can't handle the ribbing, then get out, the message goes. Such an environment creates a glass ceiling in and of itself; one can't move up if one "washes out" at this level.

The *pipeline* is analogous to middle-tier employment—after the apprenticeship period but not at the top level of management. Within the pipeline, the glass ceiling manifests itself in three ways:

1. The pay gap
2. The process of credential building (a process by which only certain people have opportunities to acquire credibility)
3. Use of recruiting services and strategies that unconsciously or explicitly discriminate against some groups. Such services and strategies limit who moves up to the next level of the organization.

Alice in Wonderland, the third and highest level in the glass ceiling, is not achieved by many women. Often the standards used to judge people at this level are much higher than for previous levels. However, for many women, managers make these evaluations using different criteria than used for the men (is she "tough" enough to do the job?). Such changes can feel schizophrenic in nature—how does one keep up when the rules are so different? Many women cannot. Add to that the very visible role women play at this level—they often become the token female achiever for a company—and the scrutiny and pressure to succeed may be unbearable.

If these levels of the glass ceiling do exist, then the phenomenon is multifaceted. It includes the impact of entry-level, midlevel, and upper-level decisions and policies. Upper and middle management construct such decisions and policies within organizations, and all individuals must deal with them. Of course, many organizations have difficulty engaging in self-examination; they would do well to ask how quadraplexation variables may be affecting the work environment of employees at each of these levels.

Quadraplexation and "Work"

We can use each of the four quadraplexation variables as "lenses" through which to view work; indeed, they are interwoven into this complex institution. Production obviously falls in the discussion. Let's also think about reproduction. Babies, children, families, housework—all are part of the reproduction variable, and they constitute "work." Socializing children becomes part of this familial work process as well. Children must learn the do's and don't's of society. Teaching such lessons, while rewarding, can also be taxing—particularly if parents are struggling to balance both paid and unpaid labor.

Women's sexuality also comes into the "work" picture and may become part of a walking-the-line situation. Should a female professional look like a mom; i.e., nonsexual? Like a working woman; that is, businesslike but nonsexual? Like a man? Should she "use" her sexuality to promote herself on the job? At home? Can we define her as a sexual being at work? Does her sexuality affect her work? Women's appearance, far more than men's, becomes central to their work evaluations. Many women in criminal-justice professions also face complex questions about their sexuality: Is she "man" enough to do this job?

Title VII

The history of women's paid work in the United States has been one of both blatant and subtle discrimination and injustice. Because of changing societal attitudes in the 1950s and early 1960s, Congress enacted Title VII as part of the 1964 Civil Rights Act. As we saw earlier, addressing equal-protection challenges is up to each state. Title VII is a federal action. It has been amended three times: the 1972 Equal Employment Opportunity Commission, the 1978 Pregnancy Discrimination Act, and the 1991 Civil Rights Act. It protects people by making certain actions by employers illegal. But it cannot "doubly" protect people—black women, for instance, cannot claim to be hurt twice (for being black, and for being women) by one situation. Title VII is the most comprehensive equal-employment-opportunity statute ever passed. It was not the first; the Equal Pay Act came earlier but has had less impact. Title VII centers on creating equal employment opportunities for all people. It also tries to counteract the impact of stereotypes on people's labor opportunities.

Title VII is applicable in both the public and private sectors to employers, labor unions, employment agencies, and training programs that have more than 15 employees. It examines possible discriminatory employment situations or conditions that have occurred "because of sex." However, it only vaguely defines that term (see Box 5.6); it leaves the definition to the courts. This ambiguity has raised discussion since 1964. The legislation asks the following question: "Is the employment practice of discriminating against *(women, people of color, Jews, etc.)* a sufficient or necessary condition for the work to get done?"

1. A *sufficient condition,* or action by the employer, is discriminatory if all women (or other group members) are affected by it. In other words, is there something about the job that would make the employment practice of discriminating against women acceptable? The courts have largely said "no" to this question.
2. A *necessary condition,* or action by the employer, is discriminatory if the action would not have happened if a person were the opposite gender. In other words, is the employment practice of discriminating against women necessary to get the job done? This second question is the one more widely asked by courts.

How do the courts define discrimination? They use the following three interpretations:

BOX 5.6   Title VII of the Civil Rights Act of 1964

a) It shall be an unlawful employment practice for an employer (1) to fail or refuse to hire or to discharge any individual, or otherwise to discriminate against any individual with respect to his compensation, terms, conditions, or privileges of employment, because of such individual's race, color, religion, sex, or national origin; or (2) to limit, segregate, or classify his employees or applicants for employment in any way which would deprive or tend to deprive any individual of employment opportunities or otherwise adversely affect his status as an employee, because of such individual's race, color, religion, sex, or national origin.

b) It shall be an unlawful employment practice for an employment agency to fail or refuse to refer for employment, or otherwise to discriminate against, any individual because of his race, color, religion, sex, or national origin, or to classify or refer for employment any individual on the basis of his race, color, religion, sex, or national origin.

c) It shall be an unlawful employment practice for a labor organization (1) to exclude or to expel from its membership, or otherwise to discriminate against, any individual because of his race, color, religion, sex, or national origin; (2) to limit, segregate, or classify its membership or applicants for membership, or to classify or fail or refuse to refer for employment any individual, in any way which would deprive or tend to deprive any individual of employment opportunities, or would limit such employment opportunities or otherwise adversely affect his status as an employee or as an applicant for employment, because of such individual's race, color, religion, sex, or national origin; or (3) to cause or attempt to cause an employer to discriminate against an individual in violation of this section.

d) It shall be an unlawful employment practice for any employer, labor organization, or joint labor-management committee controlling apprenticeship or other training or retraining, including on-the-job training programs to discriminate against any individual because of his race, color, religion, sex, or national origin in admission to, or employment in, any program established to provide apprenticeship or other training.

- *Disparate treatment* is discriminatory when an employer treats people less favorably—for example, not promoting them—because of their sex, race, color, origin, or religion. Disparate treatment is similar to the common, everyday notion of biased or discriminatory treatment. The employer's motivation is problematic; not promoting an employee because they are a woman or are of color is disparate treatment.
- *Disparate impact* is discrimination that involves employment practices that look gender or race neutral but in reality are not. Practices such as imposing weight limitations, height limitations, educational criteria,

veteran status, and so forth are intended to produce a group of employees with certain characteristics. Not hiring someone because they cannot possibly make it into the hiring group is disparate impact. Such discrimination practices often result in class-action law suits.

- *Overt or facial discrimination* occurs when employers overtly establish one policy for one group and another policy for a different group; for example, one policy for women and one for men. There is only one legal way to engage in such a practice: to establish a *bona fide occupational qualification* (BFOQ). Can the employer prove that there is some reason that only men can hold this job? Only women? Such an argument holds in only rare cases these days, but they have held in the past. The first case to test this definition was *Dothard v. Rawlinson* (433 U.S. 321, 347 (1977)). A woman who applied to be a correctional officer was denied the job because she was not tall enough. At the very least, this is a form of disparate impact. However, the state of Alabama argued that such a job required a male correctional officer and, therefore, maleness was a BFOQ. Since then, cases dealing with safety issues for pregnant women, or with privacy issues such as bodily searches, have been discussed in the courts.

When an employer violates Title VII, several things may happen. At the federal level, individuals can file suit with the Civil Service Commission; for all other circumstances, one must file with the Equal Employment Opportunity Commission (EEOC). The EEOC was created within the Title VII legislation, and is a five-member bipartisan board appointed by the president.

Individuals filing Title VII violations must be timely; depending on the case and circumstance, they generally have only three to ten months to file a case. Success in securing remedies under Title VII comes by strictly following the rules. Many Title VII cases, as with many civil cases, are settled out of court. Some critics argue that settling only hides cases that should be tried in the public; others counter that it more quickly resolves the issues at hand so both parties can get back to their lives. Also, many states have their own fair-employment-practice laws. Thus litigants may follow state rather than federal guidelines.

If an employer is found guilty of Title VII violations, the court may mete out several kinds of sanctions. Sanctions are intended to serve one or more functions, such as compensating someone for a wrongdoing (a cap is in place for monetary settlements), penalizing the wrongdoer, and/or preventing the wrong from occurring in the first place, or occurring again. Ideally, a correlation exists between the type of sanction imposed and the harm incurred. For example, if an employer refused to hire someone for a Title VII reason, the court may force the employer to hire that person or to provide her or him with compensatory damages. We would do well to

---

B O X **5.7**   Select Title VII and Title IX Case Citations

Title VII:
Alexander v. Gardner-Denver Co., 415 U.S. 36 (1974)
Steelworkers v. Weber, 443 U.S. 193 (1979)
Hishon v. King & Spalding, 467 U.S. 69 (1984)
Meritor Savings Bank, FSB v. Vinson et al., 477 U.S. 57 (1986)
Flight Attendants v. Zipes, 491 U.S. 754 (1989)
Auto Workers v. Johnson Controls, Inc., 499 U.S. 187 (1991)

Title IX:
Cannon v. University of Chicago, 441 U.S. 677 (1979)
Iron Arrow Honor Society v. Heckler, 464 U.S. 67 (1983)
Grove City College v. Bell, 465 U.S. 555 (1984)
Franklin v. Gwinnett County Public Schools, 503 U.S. 60 (1992)

---

realize Title VII has benefitted many groups of people as much, if not more, than it has benefitted women.

Sexual Harassment and Affirmative Action

I have put these topics together in one section because they both affect women's labor and education. Both also have links to quadraplexation, as well as people, conditions, and ideas. If we fail to understand that variables such as production and sexuality are a large part of sexual harassment, or that affirmative action is affected by the ideas of people and social conditions at any given time, then we fail to truly understand the context of these occurrences. Let's start with sexual harassment.

Sexual Harassment

Let's understand what sexual harassment is and is not. First of all, sexual harassment is about uninvited, unwanted, and unwelcome sexual advances—whether touching, commenting, or joking. Moreover, it doesn't happen just between a superior and inferior. Anyone can sexually harass anyone else. A student can harass a faculty member, an employee an employer, a boss an employee. The main point is that a person uses it to control another person.

Sexual harassment is a form of terrorism. Perpetrators engage in it to control their victim. We are unsure of the true extent of sexual harassment, either in the workplace or in schools. The issue came to a head with the Anita Hill/Clarence Thomas hearings and, later, the Tailhook scandal. Anita Hill charged that Clarence Thomas, a U.S. Supreme Court nominee in 1991 under then-President George Bush, had sexually harassed her when she was in his employment. The hearings proved quite graphic and touched off a public controversy concerning the topic. The Tailhook debacle took place among U.S. Navy personnel at a convention. Several women said that officers approached them inappropriately or forced them into sexual behaviors.

Sexual harassment has only recently been defined although it has been around for many years. Historically, the courts saw sexual harassment as a private matter. They didn't want to become involved in it and didn't want to hold employers or educators responsible. Its formal definition was proposed by Eleanor Norton Holmes, then chair of the EEOC, in 1980. The earliest employment sexual-harassment cases focused on harm suffered through job loss, job security, income loss, and loss of career advancement. These cases were often called *quid pro quo* cases (I'll rub your back if you'll rub mine). Later, stress on the job—created by harassment—was also added to the definition. Stress on the job could come from remarks made by others, posters and other physical-environmental factors, and so forth. These cases are commonly referred to as *hostile environment* cases. Sexual harassment was the first legal concept that defined a situation mainly affecting women. That is not to say men are not sexually harassed at work; they are. However, we don't know how much sexual harassment actually goes on, and I do believe that women are its primary targets. Moreover, this form of terrorism is apparently the worst at the apprenticeship level. Perpetrators use it as an excuse—if you can't take it, then get out.

Sexual harassment has significant consequences. Women will quit their jobs if the harassment becomes unbearable. Often co-workers, friends, or family tell them to simply look the other way, get over it, or just "deal with it." But none of these responses is easy. Because many employers don't take harassment seriously, just "dealing with it" can have devastating consequences. If a woman quits her job because of it, where does her next meal come from?

Sexual harassment on the campus is part of the chilly climate we discussed earlier. When a faculty member suggests sex in return for a good grade, or help on a project for a promised assistantship, that's sexual harassment. When an individual feels uncomfortable on campus or in an office or classroom because of unwanted advances or comments, or an uncomfortable physical environment, that's also sexual harassment.

Affirmative Action

Affirmative action is about opening up the labor force and educational institutions to groups who have historically been denied entrance to them.

Affirmative action moves women out of "women's work" (and people of color out of race-coded jobs), and affords students access to all fields. It is about achieving a balanced representation of workers in all areas, and a balanced representation of students on campuses. Because most people find jobs through word of mouth, or consider certain schools through word of mouth, a segregated labor force and school population arise. Why? Word of mouth perpetuates the status quo; I talk to the people I know, you talk to the people you know. Trouble is, we both talk to people like us. Affirmative action pushes employers and school administrators to cast a wider net when looking for workers or students. As with many topics we've been discussing, affirmative action has a long history, although the concept is relatively new.

President Lyndon B. Johnson formally created affirmative action with Executive Order 11246 in 1965. The impetus for the order came from Johnson's stated belief that passive forms of nondiscrimination, such as simply saying, "do not discriminate," may not go far enough to redress the situation. He envisioned affirmative action as a way to decrease discrimination. When Richard M. Nixon was president, he expanded the order by establishing goals and time lines. These gave companies a clearer sense of what they would need to do to comply with the order.

Jimmy Carter's administration put all the federal-enforcing efforts for affirmative action together under the auspices of the U.S. Department of Labor. Before then, all companies enforced affirmative action in their own way. This move created the Office of Federal Contract Compliance Programs (OFCCP) in 1978, which still exists.

Except for the passage of the Americans with Disabilities Act, the administrations of Ronald Reagan and George Bush put affirmative action in reverse. For example, the attempt to repeal Executive Order 11246, that required all government contractors and subcontractors to take an affirmative step towards hiring minorities and women, was put forth during the Reagan administration. While such a step was thwarted then, it set the tone for arguments against this critical policy. During these administrations, politicians and others started using buzz words like *reverse discrimination, quotas, preferential treatment,* and *hiring less qualified people* to describe affirmative action. Yet these phrases have nothing to do with affirmative action. Let's explore why.

Reverse discrimination: The assumption here is that affirmative action shortchanges—and thus discriminates against—white men. I have yet to see this happen. Who still runs the Fortune 500? Where are all the black and Hispanic faces on college campuses *across the country* (not just in Detroit and San Antonio)? Furthermore, any individual who thinks he has been discriminated against can file suit, funded by the federal government. Reverse discrimination cries generally come from individuals who are angry because they're losing their historically unfair advantages.

Quotas: These are ordered by judges when an employer or institution has engaged in such heinously discriminatory behavior that a quota is the only way to punish a them. If the company fails to enforce the quota, they can be fined.

Goals: These are established by many companies as flexible percentages meant to achieve a diverse workforce and student body. A goal is not a quota. It is not court ordered; it does not come from the heinous discriminatory acts of past.

Preferential treatment: To some folks, encouraging specific groups of people to apply for a job or school is "preferential treatment." Such encouragement is part of the historical practice of affirmative action. U.S. citizens have done this for a long time—encouraged Lutherans to go to Lutheran colleges, the sons of Navy men to go to Annapolis, and so on. The difference? Critics didn't call that preferential treatment then; they call it that now just because it is being applied specifically to women and people of color.

Hiring those less qualified: Affirmative action is about increasing the flow of information and the applications for jobs and schools from many different sources of *qualified* people. It isn't about getting a job simply because you are a certain gender or race. All sorts of people have been hired and promoted for all sorts of reasons—both before and after affirmative action.

The sameness/difference debate that we saw in Chapter 1 lies at the core of our discussion about affirmative action. Should we consciously work to find "different" people to fill jobs—that is, bring race and gender to the forefront of people's minds? Or should we treat everyone the same? What do you think?

Women Criminals, Education, and Work Training

If civilian women face such difficult realities, what about incarcerated women? Research has suggested that criminal women face similar difficulties, although within different circumstances. Many people mistakenly believe that prisons provide a free college education for prisoners. The fact is, very few prisons offer prisoners opportunities to study for a college degree. Most male prisoners, if they get any kind of education in jail or prison, finish a Graduate Equivalency Degree (GED). Some institutions also offer an associate's degree, a two-year degree commonly offered by community or technical colleges. These realities are a shame, for research has demonstrated that the more education a prisoner receives, the more his or her chance of recidivism, or repeating of crime, falls. Contrary to the public's perceptions, educating prisoners is much cheaper in the long run than not educating them.

Women's prisons do not offer as extensive educational experiences as men's prisons. Yes, most women's institutions do offer some kind of post–high school training. However, like other resources in women's prisons, these offerings are few and often gender specific. Prison administrators justify such circumstances in many ways—for example, women aren't the breadwinners, or they don't need to be trained for specific employment. Such notions are inaccurate. The vast majority of women in prison are mothers who, upon release, will need to support their families. Not educating or training women in prison simply releases them into the same social milieux that caused their problems in the first place—with little way of creating a different life for themselves or their children. True, incarcerated women tend to be more educated than incarcerated men (meaning that more women have a high school diploma), but while nearly all institutions have basic educational courses, only some offer a full college degree.

Some women's prisons have vocational and job-training programs, but most of them center on cosmetology, sewing, clerical skills, and the like. And as we've seen, these sorts of jobs have notoriously low pay and few benefits. They're also tedious and back breaking. In other words, prisons "train" female inmates for a life of lesser economic self-sufficiency. Institutions that do offer nontraditional vocational training programs, such as "construction technology" or electrical certification, say that many women inmates do not like them. This isn't surprising: Imprisoned women, like civilian women, have absorbed traditional attitudes that tell them it is better to be a hairstylist than a carpenter. Likewise, prison staff often resist supporting such programs. A further problem exists, however: Some jobs—such as hairstyling—require practitioners to be licensed by the state. But in many states, ex-cons cannot hold such a license. Another case of walking the line. And of course, as is typical in institutions, many of the skills the inmates learn are used to maintain the institution itself; for instance, cooking, cleaning, and groundswork.

Numerous programs in women's institutions thus have been designed to make inmates conform to white, middle-class, WASP notions of women. The corrections system hasn't yet realized that such notions will not help these women. Specifically, many middle-class women do not need a good career to survive in the world; they can become stay-at-home wives and mothers. And if they do choose a career, it's not likely in cosmetology or clerical service.

The Essence of the Chapter

Understanding the impact of walking the line, quadraplexation, and people, conditions, and ideas gives us fresh perspective on women, work, and education. Further understanding the legal, political, and social changes that have come about particularly in the last 40 years adds to that inquiry. Gender schemas have shaped our ideas about women and men—whether we are talking about incarcerated or nonincarcerated women—and legal changes catalyzed by changing attitudes and conditions have been reflected in the justice system to some extent. The next chapter discusses women as participants in the justice system.

6 Women Participants in the Justice System

"Women are often denied equal justice, equal treatment and equal opportunities."

—Feinman

In this chapter, we briefly examine the history and experiences of three groups of female justice professionals—lawyers, correctional officers, and police. Though many additional justice occupations exist—paralegals, wardens, judges, stenographers, and so on—the complete list could encompass an entire book by itself. I've selected these three occupations purely by choice. We will also consider different definitions of discrimination, as well as the role of quadraplexation.

Defining Discrimination and How It Works

The U.S. Commission on Civil Rights (Rothenburg, 1995) identifies three forms of discrimination: individual, organizational, and structural. *Individual discrimination*, by which persons act in discriminatory ways, is the most commonly understood form. Individual discrimination may be conscious or unconscious, intentional or unintentional. It includes a manager's not hiring someone because he or she does not like the applicant's race or some other characteristic. It might also include hiring someone because of the applicant's appearance rather than his or her competence. When people who are concerned about their property values going down take steps to discourage unwanted groups from moving in, that is also individual discrimination. Name calling, jokes, unwanted or threatening physical contact—these are all forms of individual discrimination.

Organizational discrimination is practiced by individuals but reinforced by organizational procedure, policies, and practices. When organizations establish rules that limit certain groups' access, that is organizational discrimination. Height and weight requirements, religious or cultural requirements, standardized testing—all of these practices are forms of organizational discrimination. Their ultimate effect is to shut the organization's door to certain people.

Structural discrimination is the overarching effect of all discrimination that gets embedded in the very fabric of a society. If individuals responsible for hiring make discriminatory decisions, and the company they work for requires the use of a standardized test as part of the interviewing process, we have an embedded structural process. Meaning? The individual discrimination is furthered by the policies of the organization. The organization, because of its employment policies, shuts out future opportunities for group X. Members of group X cannot find gainful employment and thus have to live in the poorer parts of town. Their children attend second-class public schools. When they get old enough to look for employment, they cannot get a job back at the same organization. A vicious cycle results and creates a systematic process of discrimination.

Congressional actions such as Title VII and Title IX have attempted to stop this sort of cycle. Advocates of these actions recognize that lack of access to quality educational institutions can reduce individuals' opportunities to succeed and that discriminatory employment practices have hindered the advancement of certain groups.

Women in the criminal-justice system, especially female employees of the system, have faced much individual, organizational, and structural discrimination in the last two hundred years. Because the criminal-justice professions have been deemed primarily "men's work," and because such

---

BOX **6.1** Wolgast on Justice

We imagine that justice is an ideal or standard from which injustice departs. That we have such a standard seems necessary, for how else will we recognize a case of injustice when we come upon it? We need justice the way we need a pattern or standard that something can fail to fit. Though the idea is natural, I argue that it's mistaken. And from this mistake others flow, such as the antinomies that have no rational solution in the face of morality's demand for one. My approach here involves looking not at the concept by itself but more broadly at its grammar, at the ways and contexts in which justice is invoked. . . .

Elizabeth Wolgast, *The Grammar of Justice*

work is considered tough, dirty, primitive, and dangerous, those already entrenched in it have not welcomed women. The kinds of discriminatory practices we just discussed have reinforced the message. Title VII and Title IX have dramatically opened up the justice professions to women, although work remains.

Belknap (1996) notes that regardless of which area we examine, female workers in the criminal-justice system face a number of hurdles: the perception of women as tokens or as recipients of "preferential" treatment; lack of access to the "old-boy" network; a higher set of expectations; sex stereotyping; male resistance; and the imposition of chivalry. True-womanhood ideas and separate-spheres ideology, as well as quadraplexation effects, sex-role stereotyping, and chivalry, have seriously effected the roles women have played in this arena. Indeed, women were initially "allowed" into the justice professions only after its existing practitioners decided that certain aspects of the work would benefit from a "woman's touch"; for example, women or children on the streets, and women and children in penal institutions. In some instances, women were allowed to enter these "men's worlds" because they believed women could teach "wayward" members of that gender how to be "true" women. Society regarded this early involvement by women as a form of protection and rehabilitation. However, such reformers were often not like the women they helped. They were largely middle-class women of privilege, many of them with some formal education. Becker (1963) called them "moral entrepreneurs."

In the Courts

Women and people of color have historically been excluded from practicing law. Women, in particular, were seen as too delicate to participate in such a dirty and uncivilized profession. If you look back at the *Muller v. Oregon* decision discussed in Chapter 5, you get a sense of how the justice system viewed women. Such attitudes were common in 1908 and reflected beliefs that had prevailed since the early Industrial Revolution.

The first woman to practice law in the United States was Maggie Brent (1601–1671). However, Ms. Brent was not a bar-admitted lawyer. The first woman admitted to the bar (Iowa) was Arabella Mansfield, in 1869. We know little about the practice of law by women between Brent's and Manfield's time. We do know that women could not attend law schools or gain admission to state bars. The underlying rationale for these restrictions was simply that women were women. Practitioners and others argued that the law was synonymous with male characteristics and traits, such as aggression and indecence. Those with power and influence highlighted the differences between women and men—the private and public worlds, the notions of true womanhood—to keep the profession segregated.

Women who did go into law commonly came from families of lawyers and judges. Just as today, their reasons for going into law varied. Some perceived the law as the family business; others wanted to learn how to handle their own business, economic, and legal affairs. Still others went into the law to help those less fortunate then themselves—poor and destitute women, prostitutes, immigrant women, and such.

Legal Training

The legal profession in the United States was formalized in the last half of the 1800s. At that time, all lawyers had to have college degrees and go through formal law-school training. Pheobe Couzens was the first woman to be admitted to law school in 1868 at Washington University (St. Louis). The first woman to graduate from law school was Ada Kepley, in 1869, from Union College of Law in Chicago (now the University of Chicago). But such early examples give the wrong impression; many more women were turned away from law schools. Some women established their own law schools in response. However, the established schools looked down on them. At graduation, matriculating students received diplomas, not law degrees.

Over the decades, schools slowly began admitting women. Harvard Law, for example, was one of the last schools to admit women—and held out until 1950 to do so. The most prestigious schools admitted women only after putting them through a thorough interrogation about their personal lives and plans. Women who "passed" the interrogation were accepted. Given the social timbre at the time, this kind of interviewing was legal and accepted. As a final hurdle, these law schools reminded female students that they were taking the place of men who could be sitting in classes.

In the 1970s, Title IX opened the way for women in law schools. Between 1966 and 1975, the number of female law students increased tenfold. Currently, about 47 percent (ABA, 2000) of all law students are women. That said, the enrollment of women in the *top* law schools in the country is below average, while the lower-tiered schools have more women than the average. It's easy to say, "Well, at least they're in the door." However, *where* one attends law school influences other opportunities such as clerk positions, internships, and employment offers. Progress is not solely a numbers game; opportunities and attitudes must also change.

The number of female law-school faculty is also increasing, albeit slowly. Currently, about 31 percent of faculty are women. However, of those, only 6.4 percent are tenured (ABA, 2000). Many of the women cited in this text are law-school faculty. Further increases in their numbers should help women's prospects. Nowadays, most textbooks, case law books, class discussions, and male faculty ignore the presence of women in the law and women as judges, lawyers, academics, and litigants. Many law-school professors teach only one point of view—the male view. Because our legal system is grounded in precedent, the legacy of the male viewpoint and legal decision making finds its way into law school classrooms. Dusky (1996) criticizes legal training in this country. She remarks, "Like country clubs all over America, our system of legal education favors affluent white men" and "the law and the institutions that do its works are designed to serve the elite and maintain the status quo" (p. 10). She goes on to say, "Intellectual movements, large-scale political events, debates on social issues, theoretical musings, and ideology . . . apparently have no significance on the teaching of law at most schools . . . the walls of most law schools and the skulls of most law professors are impenetrable" (p. 11).

One of the hottest debates raging now in law schools centers on teaching method. Historically, law in this country has been taught using the Socratic method, by which professors toss out a hypothetical legal situation and students are expected to apply to it legal principles. Though Socrates was a great thinker in many ways, his method of raising hypothetical questions has an unfriendly, harsh, and intimidating quality. Such an abrasive teaching form is most understood and accepted by male students, critics argue, because it characterizes the culture of men.

The Practice

Whereas Mansfield was the first bar-admitted lawyer, Myra Bradwell became famous for *not* gaining admittance to the bar (Illinois). Bradwell had studied the law under her husband and passed the Illinois state bar in 1869. When she applied for her license, however, she was turned down. She appealed her case to the U.S. Supreme Court, which eventually overturned the earlier decision (*Bradwell v. Illinois* 83 U.S. 130 (1873)). There were four reasons she initially was not granted the license:

1. Because of coverture, as a married women she could not enter into contracts. (Single women were denied entry because the courts/bars believed that women should not be encouraged to remain single or to compete with men.)
2. The common-law tradition did not provide for women to be lawyers.
3. If women were permitted to practice law, they might also seek to hold public office.
4. Admitting women to the bar (licensure) would mean they would be exposed to the obscenities that sometimes emerged in the courtroom.

Ideas about true womanhood, separate spheres, and quadraplexation all clearly influenced this set of explanations. Indeed, the above four reasons are examples of individual, organizational, and structural discrimination. And the discrimination still occurs. We've already mentioned the scarcity of women in the most prestigious law firms. But women face other problems in the law as well: not making partner (only 14.5 percent of women are partners) (ABA, 2000); difficulty in achieving promotion and tenure in academe (6.4 percent of women faculty are tenured); less client contact; less courtroom experience; lower pay (men average $69,680 per year; women, $50,648—a ratio of .73) (ABA, 2000); specialty segregation (meaning women often specialize in family law and the like while men are found in areas such as tax law and corporate law); sexual harassment and hostility from colleagues, judges, and clients; lack of respect; lack of admittance to the "old-boy" network (44 women hold general-counsel positions at Fortune 500 companies) (ABA, 2000); and the "mommy track" (tracking women into less interesting or significant cases, for example, because of fears they will put their family first). Because law is still not considered a woman's domain, many women in the legal profession continue to fight the idea they do not belong or are less knowledgeable, tough, or competent than men.

Such discriminatory practices occur because of sex, not lack of ability. To counter such realities, many women are hanging out their own shingles or leaving the law after practicing for a period of time. A good place for women to turn is the government; interestingly, 42 percent of legal-aid attorneys and public defenders are women (ABA, 2000). When you consider that women make up just 29 percent of all attorneys, the proportion of women in government law is quite large. The government pays less than the private sphere, but it also offers more stable employment without the pressure to make partner and conform to the corporate or business lifestyle.

Because the law is still seen as a man's profession, practitioners feel they must be aggressive, tough, unemotional, ambitious, and upwardly mobile to "make it." If women behave aggressively in court, judges, clients, and opposing counsel may call them bitchy, hysterical, or histrionic. If they appear cool and unemotional, the same folks criticize them for being arrogant and unsupportive. Such choices are perfect examples of walking the line.

To combat such practices and attitudes, advocates for women have established task forces on women in the law at the state and national levels. These task forces have found that the law itself is gender biased. Though it appears neutral on the surface, much of it is patriarchal. We need to re-examine the teaching of the law, the practice of the law, and the law itself to assess women's role and effect within them. In 1987, the American Bar Association (ABA) took a step in this direction by creating the Commission on Women in the Profession. The Commission found that although women's participation in the ABA has increased (women make up 26 percent of ABA members), in the last few years their numbers have declined steadily. The reasons? Perhaps this effect stems from the numbers of women who are leaving the law; perhaps it comes from something else.

Whatever the explanation, we should monitor it to ensure that women's voices are still heard within the legal profession.

In the Prisons

What do we mean by corrections? For our purposes, corrections officers work with *convicted* offenders who are in prison. That can be very different from working in a jail, where the population tends to be about 50 percent awaiting trial and 50 percent convicted but of misdemeanors. Furthermore, prisons are often inflexible, rigid neomilitary institutions. Many women feel uncomfortable working in such a situation.

Women first entered the correctional field as reformers of "wayward" women prisoners. Many of them came from the middle and upper classes. In Chapter 9, we talk more about the "Lady Visitors" and then "Matrons" of early prison systems. Men "allowed" such women into the system because they worked with female inmates (so men didn't have to). Moreover, these women reformers and prisoners largely kept to themselves, thereby relieving male administrators from the responsibility.

Early corrections reformers operated within a system that largely ignored women. For example, women's prisons received scant funding and even fewer resources for diverse programming. Some reformers contributed their personal resources to help inmates. Once such work became an established profession and the Reform Era passed, women's prisons still lacked money and decent facilities. But even the Lady Visitors stopped coming, because their attentions were turned elsewhere. Prison "Matrons" now worked with female inmates.

Remember, we are still talking specifically about women working in women's prisons. The idea of women working in men's prisons has surfaced only in the last 30 years. Though there are some female correctional officers in men's prisons now, the "true-woman" ideals and sexist and stereotypic notions of what women can and cannot do still affect their employment in the field.

This continued segregation creates some serious problems. For example, in many jurisdictions, female correctional officers receive inadequate training. Even though most states offer some kind of training or have a training academy, that training generally focuses on male offenders. Because women tend to work in women's institutions, such training has limited applicability for their situations.

Furthermore, most states have only one women's prison. Thus employees at such prisons often come from the surrounding communities. Feinman (1994), citing the Center for Women Policy Studies, has found that women in corrections are interested in their work and see it as leading to current and future career opportunities. However, other research suggests that female officers do not often see corrections as a career goal. According to this research, these women tend to have lower job satisfaction and less positive attitudes on the job. Many of them chose this line of work because of the money or the prison's location. Remember, male prisons abound; in virtually any state, male officers could find work at a male prison within a reasonable distance from home. For most women's prisons, it is *the* job in the community. So, whoever needs employment goes there. Many college-educated women who start in corrections leave after a period of time. They tire of the locked-in culture and the low status of the profession and often turn instead to law, probation, or parole.

Sexual harassment and other problems for women workers abound, especially in a male prison. As with police, many male prison workers don't believe that women are tough enough to handle the work. They thus see women as security risks; they feel forced to choose between protecting women officers and grappling with the inmates. This can lead to differential treatment by co-workers and superiors alike. It may also prompt administrators to assign women less challenging or dangerous tasks.

Do female officers prefer to work with men or women? That depends on the officer. Some would rather work with women because they are generally less violent. Others disdain working with women because they see them as more emotional and in need of a more nurturing kind of care. That nurturing kind of care requires energy and time—two resources that officers may not have. Some officers prefer to work with male inmates and male officers. Several studies have also found that male offenders respond to female correctional officers (CO's) in a positive manner; specifically, they often make an effort to improve their appearance, language, and behavior around them.

In her 1986 study of women in corrections, Zimmer (1986) found that female CO's tend to adopt one of three work styles:

- The *institutional role style*. These officers adhere closely to the institutional rules and work hard to maintain an institutional, highly professional manner. They try to enforce rules in a fair and consistent manner, but their preoccupation with obedience to the rules can lead them to be rigid and inflexible.
- The *modified role style*. Such officers do not believe that they can perform their work as well as their male colleagues can. They therefore sympathize with male officers who oppose their presence. These women tend to fear the inmates and to avoid direct contact with them. They rely heavily on their male co-workers on the job.
- The *inventive role style*. These female officers closely ally themselves with the inmates. They find support in their relationships with the inmates and express little fear of them. They much prefer working in

---

B O X 6.2   Case Citations

Dothard v. Rawlinson 433 U.S. 321,347 (1977)
Price Waterhouse v. Hopkins 490 U.S. 228 (1989)

---

direct contact with the inmates rather than doing chores behind the scenes. Though Zimmer has argued that these roles are unique to women, she could not empirically back up that argument.

Stohr et al. (1996) report that the behavior of female and male correctional officers is more similar than different, but that workplace perceptions of the genders are more different than similar. Why would workplace perceptions be different? I would argue that they differ largely because of quadraplexation. Think about it: Women officers engage in production (their work) and deal with sexuality in the way they present themselves in general. Some face reproduction issues, too; meaning that they may have to deal with pregnancy while on the job, or with the burdens of working motherhood. Socialization tells them they need to be "good" workers *and* "good" mothers; the job tells them—what? Be tough, stand your ground, yet remember "you are a woman." Wright and Saylor (1991) note that female officers have the same level of job satisfaction as men but experience a higher stress level. Doubtless the balancing act they're managing plays a role.

Most women in the corrections field have "women's" jobs—social worker, teacher, clerk, and counselor. Few of them work as prison guards. Though their numbers are greater in women's prisons as we've seen, there are not many such institutions. And though some women work in men's prisons, even in men's maximum security prisons, those numbers are small. With the passage of Title VII, some states hired women into men's prisons right away; others took a more gradual approach. Some states still do not allow women in their maximum-security units (U.S. Department of Justice, 1991).

In Law Enforcement

In 1998, women constituted 25.2 percent of all police employees, 62.5 percent of civilian employees employed by police departments, and 10.5

percent of all sworn officers (Sourcebook, 2000). Such numbers represent the history of women in law enforcement. Let's approach this discussion in two parts: 1910–1971 and 1971 on.

Formal police departments first arose in the United States in the 1800s, and women became involved in them in the latter part of the century. How and why did women become involved in policing? As with correctional officers, the primary reason was the need for a "woman's presence" in dealing with perpetrators and survivors of crime. These early participants were not police officers. Rather, they were "matrons," "safety workers," or "operatives." These labels made distinctions between the female workers and the "real" officers, the men.

Major battles ensued over the use of women in police departments. As in the legal arena and prisons, male police-department personnel felt that police stations were the wrong place for "real" women. As Feinman (1996) pointed out, men argued that women would be "contaminated and demoralized by contact with such depraved creatures," in particular the association with the worst kind of fallen woman, the prostitute. Still, women persisted in having a presence in law enforcement. In 1910, Alice Wells became the first policewoman in the United States, in the city of Los Angeles.

Female police officers face many pressures. Martin (1989) cites a lack of *anticipatory socialization* as one example. In other words, because women learn different lessons from society than men do, they have less experience with aggression and other male characteristics and behaviors. Female officers often need to learn new facial expressions and voice intonations to suggest an authoritative stance. Specifically, female officers train themselves to smile less frequently than women in the general population do.

Women often face hostility from male workers who fear that female partners can't hold up their end of the work. The most commonly heard complaint is that women do not have the physical strength to do the job of policing. Of course, much of police work these days requires more brains and technological expertise than brawn. Indeed, much police work consists of filling out paperwork.

Women also face opposition from outside the force. Civilians on the street do not always feel comfortable with female officers, although this circumstance varies by situation. Furthermore, male officers' wives and girlfriends may feel threatened knowing that the men are working closely with women on the job. Such opposition, along with additional forms of discriminatory behavior (sexual harassment, pay differences, differing expectations, and so on) makes it difficult for women to get ahead on the force. Promotional opportunities and attractive assignments seem difficult for female officers to secure. The fact that many women work in law enforcement but that women make up only 10.5 percent of sworn officers speaks volumes about their prospects.

Quadraplexation and the Three Justice Professions

While each of the three justice professions we've explored in this chapter has its own history, responsibilities, training, and so on, we can look at all three of them through the lens of quadraplexation. Indeed, this analysis actually brings to the forefront the similarities among the three. Also, in the discussion that follows I will refrain from using the terms "woman lawyer," "woman correctional officer," or "woman police officer"; I want to talk more generally about women on the job.

Let's talk first about *socialization* and *reproduction*. Women in all three professions feel pressure from the responsibilities of motherhood. They most likely do not want their children to "get in the way" of their jobs, but they find it difficult to get to the phone or leave work if there's an emergency with the babysitter. Working in a closed-in, "tight" environment in a prison, for example, many administrators perceive such personal issues as annoyances. The attorney working toward partner in a private law firm is expected to put in billable hours; this is what defines competence and contributes to the firm's and her own reputation. The police officer worried about her kids at home can be perceived by colleagues as not having her "mind on the job"—a dangerous attribute, especially in some situations.

What about *production,* or the paid labor itself? In all three professions, women earn less than men and cluster in the "women's" areas or specialties; for instance, lawyers in family or juvenile law, CO's in women's prisons, police officers working with rape survivors or delinquents. Such specialty segregation still runs rampant in each profession, and erodes both pay and prestige. Moreover, women in all three professions face numerous forms of verbal, nonverbal, and physical sexual harassment, a lack of respect for their abilities and knowledge, and a long struggle up a steep slope. While the numbers of women in each profession have increased, numbers alone don't indicate acceptance and honor. These numbers have risen largely because of legal reforms; in particular, Title VII, Title IX, and affirmative action. But such legal reforms do not guarantee *attitude* reform. The *production* part of women's lives also includes their unpaid labor, such as all-important voluntary involvement in professional associations and unpaid labor at home.

Finally, the role of *sexuality* in these professions is key. For many people, the idea of women as sexual beings clashes with the image of women chasing a criminal down the street, wrestling a convict to the floor, or putting an alleged drug dealer behind bars. Believe it or not, some judges even advise female lawyers to put on skirts to argue their cases.

Without a doubt, legal policies such as Title IX and Title VII have profoundly improved the picture. Without such legislation, we would not see anything close to the influx of women into the three justice professions that occurred during the twentieth century. Furthermore, our thinking about what happens "on the job" would also not be where it is today. For example, the defining of sexual harassment in 1980 influenced what workers can say and do on the job, especially in male-dominated workplaces. This is not to suggest that sexual harassment does not still occur in any of these occupations; it certainly does. But at least now the targets of such behavior have a way to fight back.

The Essence of the Chapter

We hear "lip service" these days about women taking care of themselves and their children. Yet, historically, women have been denied entrance to certain professions. If discrimination grounded in gender schemas and quadraplexation continues, how will women survive? It has only been through the legal "loosening" of such gender-scripted realities that women's economic lives have improved—a little. The next chapter looks at the effect of poverty on women and children and asks, Is the law helping here?

7 Women and Poverty

What did Virginia Wolfe say about why women were poorer than men? "They were having children."

The trouble with being poor is that it takes up all your time.
Willem de Koonig

Poverty is an economic condition people live in, not a personal characteristic. Numerous writers and social critics have commented on the reality that *poverty is something we create in society*. Poverty exists because we allow it to exist, and because we (the "we" here is the generic society "we") must feel it has some import. Others claim that poverty exists because it supports the wealthy classes in some way—it provides jobs, it distinguishes the "haves" from the "have nots," and so on. Poverty, as a created institution, strongly affects women's lives, especially because women's economic status is different from that of men's. Indeed, poverty is part of quadraplexation. Economics affects every aspect of a woman's life—production, reproduction, sexuality, and, yes, even socialization. In the United States, it is costly to be a woman. Later in this chapter, we will look at the "Cost of Being Female" Index developed by Headlee and Elfin (1996) to investigate this. We will also examine the effect of court cases and legal policy on women's economic lives. But let's start with the notion of the feminization of poverty.

Poverty

Consider the ideologies and fetishes of U.S. society—the Protestant work ethic, the image of "pulling yourself up by your bootstraps," economic success, money. Clearly, having money and wealth is important. Many people believe that *not* having money and wealth stems from an

119

individual's shortcomings—he or she didn't work hard enough. When the U.S. government first started collecting poverty data, it believed that poverty could be eradicated from U.S. society through government-sponsored programs.

In 1959, the government established something it called the *poverty threshold* (also referred to as the poverty rate). It deemed that the average family spent one-third of its budget on food—the so-called breadbasket measure. The government used that figure to calculate how much it would cost to feed families of various sizes. It then multiplied that figure by three. Voila! Households that earned under that amount were defined as poor. The thresholds were used mainly for statistical purposes such as figuring out how many people are poor in the U.S. As you can image, these calculations pose some problems.

The federal government also set up *poverty guidelines*. These are numerical configurations used to determine who is eligible for financial assistance through various programs. The figures change every year and are calculated based on how big a family is and where its members live. The guidelines determine who is eligible for food stamps, Head Start, food-assistance programs, school lunches, and so forth. The poor are often a forgotten population. It is especially useful during a political campaign (at least for some candidates!). Such silence about the poor may suggest they are fewer in number; this is not the case. The number of poor people in the United States has stayed roughly the same over the last decade.

Who Are the Poor?

Who tends to be poor in the United States? The answer depends on the definition of *poor*. If we look to government reports to answer this question "officially," persons of color, especially blacks and Hispanic/Chicana/Latino

---

BOX 7.1   Von Hayak on Justice

It is of course not to be denied that in the existing market order not only the results but also the initial chances of different individuals are often very different; they are affected by circumstances of their physical and social environment which are beyond their control but in many particular respects might be altered by some governmental action. The demand for quality of opportunity or equal starting conditions appeals to many and has been supported by many who, in general, favour the free market order. . . .

Friedrich von Hayak, *The Mirage of Social Justice*

TABLE 7.1   Median Household Income, 1999

Race	Median Income
Overall	$40,816
White, non-Hispanic	$44,366
Black	$27,910
Hispanic	$30,735
Asian/Pacific Islands	$51,205
American Indian/Native Alaskan	$30,784*

*Represents a three-year average, 1997–1999.

Source: U.S. Census Bureau.

peoples, are poorer than the rest of the population. At least a quarter of the black and Latino/a population have been poor since the poverty threshold was defined. Almost 20 percent of children under the age of 18 are also poor. Poverty is greatest in metropolitan areas (central cities), less in non-metro areas (such as rural communities), and least in suburban communities.

The poverty rate has also changed over time. In the late 1950s, when it was first measured, it was around 22 percent. It reached its lowest ebb in 1973, at 11.1 percent. The rate rose steadily through the 1980s and started to come back down in the mid-1990s. In 1999, the last year with available data, the rate sank to 11.8 percent, the lowest rate since 1979. This number represented 32.3 million people, and a historic low for major racial and ethnic groups in the United States. The median household income for 1999 was $40,816 (see Table 7.1).

Of all family groups, single women with children under six; especially black or Latina families, suffer from the worst poverty. In 1999, 50.3 percent of female-headed households with children under six were impoverished. Of all families headed by women, the poverty rate is 27.8 percent; the rate for married couples is 4.8 percent. Apparently, having a man in the house dramatically boosts a woman's economic position. Race also helps. Female-headed households in which the householder is white (not Hispanic) had a poverty rate of 22.5 percent in 1999, while black female-headed households, Hispanic origin households, and Asian/Pacific Island female-headed households had rates of 39.3 percent, 38.8 percent and 23.1 percent, respectively.

The Feminization of Poverty

The term "feminization of poverty" was coined in the 1970s when feminists started paying closer attention to women's lives. Originally, the phrase was meant to point out that "the poor" were primarily women and their children; two-thirds of all poor people fit these criteria. Why did it take economists, politicians, and scholars so long to spot this reality? As we saw above, the U.S. Census Bureau didn't even start computing poverty rates until 1959, and the primary group of interest then were the elderly. This first group had the attention of policy makers, including President Lyndon B. Johnson, who made the war on poverty a primary component of his presidency. But with the advent of the women's movement, people began to realize that many women, too, were in economically dire straits. Why?

Why Are Women Poor in the United States?

To find out why women make up a disproportionate number of the poor in the United States, let's look again at quadraplexation. In terms of production, women's *balkinization* in the paid labor force contributes to their secondary economic status. When women cluster into specific occupations—"women's work"—their paychecks shrink. The *wage gap* also harms women economically. (See Chapter 5 for fuller discussions.)

The capitalist market which seeks to maximize profit, also keeps women poor. Many scholars have identified that women are the secondary labor market and thus disposable. Employers use this rationale to "justify" paying women less, thereby increasing profit margins. Managers often use the phrase "for the good of the company" to unite workers. Yes, anything that benefits a whole company benefits both male and female workers there. But because women, as a sector of the labor market, have less power, their ability to combat the evils of capitalism is less.

Sexual harassment—both a production and a sexuality factor—also plays a role in women's economic lives. Women have quit their jobs to get away from harassers. Some of them find worse jobs the next time around—or no job at all. Some women feel that the only way to get paid more or be promoted is to give in to harassers' demands.

Scott (1985) argues that the feminization of poverty comes from women's segregation in the paid labor force and from all of the unpaid labor women do. In other words, women's poverty comes in part from their role in production. According to Scott, because women also run the PTA, keep the Little Leagues going, watch other women's children for free, and so forth, they run out of time to earn more money, go to school, or acquire additional training which might possibly influence paychecks. We do this to help one another, but often it may hurt us also. Scott also maintains that the feminization of poverty should be redefined. Originally the expression referred primarily to statistics—two-thirds of all those in poverty were women and their children. Scott urges a more contemporary definition: the feminization of poverty is the "economic vulnerability of women who are the sole support of their children."

As we saw in Chapter 4, the lack of child support also contributes to women's poverty. The absence of decent child-care options in the United States compound the situation. Child-care workers themselves, many of whom are women, do not make a lot of money. Still, having to pay out of pocket for child care can cost as much as a paycheck. It is another walking-the-line situation—work to pay the bills, but then hand over your earnings to pay the sitter. These circumstances stem in part from the assumption that women should be the primary caretakers of children, that women are responsible for births out of wedlock, that women should look to men to support them comfortably, and so on. Child care (which is both a reproduction and production issue) is obviously a hot topic. As Collins (2000) noted, only one in 10 potentially eligible low-income families actually gets the child-care assistance it needs, and no state is currently serving all eligible families.

The expectations that society places on women in terms of their sexuality also keep women poor. Men and women alike expect women to look a certain way, to dress a certain way, to smell a certain way, and so forth. Meeting these expectations costs money. Society expects men, too, to look and smell a certain way, but it judges women a lot more based on their appearance. In a capitalist market structure, women pay a pretty penny to look pretty!

Why Are Women Poor Globally?

As the World Watch Institute (Jacobson, 1992) points out, gender bias and discrimination have led to an increase in the poverty of women worldwide. Discrimination against women—which includes inadequate birth-control opportunities—has boosted birthrates in many Third World countries. In many such regions, multiple births catalyze a downward economic spiral for women. "Women are the primary breadwinners in subsistence economies . . . research shows they work longer hours and devote a larger share of their earnings to supporting their families" (p. 5).

Jacobson also points out that gender bias in subsistence economies ranges from wage discrimination to exclusion from development programs, to legal barriers to owning land, to violence against women. All these forms of discrimination exacerbate poverty by preventing hundreds of millions of women from obtaining the credit, education, training, health services, child care, and legal status they need to improve their prospects. As a result, not only do families remain poor, but the economies of many Third World nations lag far behind their economic potential. Jacobson notes that "investing in women is the most direct way to lift families out of poverty" (p. 5). We discussed a similar insight in Chapter 5, when we looked at the joint report by the AFL-CIO and the Institute for Women's Policy Research (IWPR): Get rid of the pay gap, and poverty drops off. All families, whether single headed or married, are then better off.

The Role of Government

What many people call the U.S. social welfare system dates back to the 1930s and President Franklin D. Roosevelt's New Deal. During the 1930s (the decade of the Great Depression), FDR felt personally responsible for the well-being of the U.S. population. Before the Depression, when people fell on hard times, they often turned to their families for help. However, the Depression proved so cataclysmic that many families could no longer turn to one another for aid. The Social Security Act (SSA) of 1935 created an unprecedented government program—it sought to protect a group of citizens against some of the maladies of contemporary social life. The SSA set up an old-age pension. It also established a fund for temporarily unemployed individuals; for those who were needy, aged, and blind; and for widows with children, women with children whose husbands had abandoned them, and women whose husbands could no longer work. Later, this program was named Aid to Families with Dependent Children, or AFDC.

Such programs sought to help people by providing income supplements. In the 1960s, Lyndon B. Johson took the "War on Poverty" one step further by starting the Food Stamp program, Medicare and Medicaid, and the School Breakfast Plan. These programs, however, had a different intent—to help people become self-sufficient. At the time, people considered them a necessary governmental obligation.

But problems surfaced—Vietnam, an oil embargo, increasing numbers of poor—and by the end of the 1970s, politicians and the public began expressing dissatisfaction with these "welfare" programs. The ideological tide had turned. This sentiment gained strength through that decade and, by the time the 1980s rolled around, it had achieved tidal-wave proportions. Beginning in the 1980s and through the 1990s, the push has been to "get people off welfare" or to restrict programs. Critics have sung loudly and longly: "Welfare doesn't work; welfare is bad."

The real problem with the welfare system was the rules. The system was created in such a way that it did *not* help people become self-sufficient.

B O X **7.2**   **Case Citations**

Wyman v. Rothstein, 398 U.S. 275 (1970)
Shapiro v. Doe, 396 U.S. 488 (1970)
Goldberg v. Kelly, 397 U.S. 254 (1970)
Jefferson v. Hackney, 406 U.S. 535 (1972)
Van Lare v. Hurley, 421 U.S. 338 (1975)
Bowen v. Roy, 476 U.S. 693 (1986)

Because of bureaucratic red tape and rules too numerous to list, the system overburdened itself and those who used it. The rules become so complex that the system bogged down and sometimes stalled. Some scholars argue that it isn't the intent behind the social welfare system that is bad; rather, it's the administration of that system. The system itself created a form of dependency through its arcane rules and expectations. For every small step its users took forward, system managers, such as social workers, told them to take a giant step backward. Here are a couple of examples:

- If a woman took a job to supplement the subsidy she received on welfare (to earn money for rent or food, for example), her welfare subsidy was cut. Often she took a job *because* the subsidy was below poverty level.
- A man in the household put the family's welfare subsidy in peril— even if he was only a boyfriend and not a parent.

In both kinds of cases, women had to make a choice—paid labor or not? A relationship or not? The welfare system perpetuated the process of walking the line by controlling poor women's lives with its onerous rules. Worse, it kept them poor.

The Personal Responsibility and Work Opportunity Reconciliation Act of 1996

In 1996, Congress passed the Personal Responsibility and Work Opportunity Reconciliation Act (PRWORA). The new law replaced Aid to Families with Dependent Children (AFDC) with the Temporary Assistance to Needy Families (TANF) program and transformed the United States' welfare system. TANF funds are tied to a new five-year limit on federal welfare benefits, tougher work requirements, stricter child-support provisions, and increased pressure on states to reduce overall welfare caseloads. Many states adopted even shorter lifetime limits on welfare receipt or stopped providing benefits for a period of time before letting recipients reapply.

The new federal welfare rules also include discussions about aid in family-violence situations, to non-native born persons, and for eligibility for school lunches. The TANF program gives states primary responsibility for social welfare programs, and states have responded to this challenge in a number of different ways. TANF limits funding for certain benefits, but states do not have to follow those suggestions. If they do want to support additional programs, they must spend their own money.

What kinds of problems do these changes pose, especially in terms of women and economics? Well, let's look at some aspects of education. Under TANF, government-paid vocational education is limited to one year. Most training programs in community and technical colleges require two years. What, then, should students do if they receive support for only half their training? Also, to TANF, postsecondary education does not count as an acceptable work-requirement activity, even though higher education has a direct link to better employment and higher earnings (and lower recidivist rates!). Here again, what happens to the welfare mother looking to help herself and her children by obtaining a college degree? News reports since 1996 have presented both positive and negative stories about the impact of these changes in social welfare rules.

Violence against Women

The intersection of poverty and violence against women tie directly to economics. Individual women and their children must figure out how to secure a life after violence shatters it. Regardless of whether a woman is rich or poor, domestic battery, rape, or stalking can all devastate her economic status—to say nothing of her psychological and physical health. Though violence against women may seem a private concern on the surface, it's a problem that the country as a whole must face. Women in dire economic straits owing to violence need housing, jobs, child care, and security to get their lives back on track.

As we will see in Chapter 8, many batterers control their partners by limiting their access to cash, checking accounts, and their own paychecks. Batterers also prescribe their victims' educational opportunities, work lives, job-training opportunities, and so forth. Some batterers have purposefully damaged their partners' credit rating, thereby preventing them from securing housing and other economic resources. As domestic-violence and sexual-assault workers and researchers have noted, survivors often teeter on an economic seesaw. Violence can leave them economically vulnerable through loss of employment, medical and legal fees, and loss of housing and property.

The recent welfare "reforms" have continued the cycle of violence in some ways, as well as subjected women to more walking-the-line "choices." Because of limited opportunities and programs, and strict regulations, many women in violent situations find themselves in a more precarious position than ever. How can they get out if the government won't help them get back on their feet? Cutting back on food stamps programs, (federal) job training, child care, and the like makes it nearly impossible, especially for poor and working-class women, to support themselves and their children should they find their way out of violence. Poor women in violent situations need to know that some sort of economic security is out there for them. They must have access to housing, jobs, child care, physical and mental medical care, and safety. Governments need to take such things into account when designing programs.

What Can We Do?

According to the National Advisory Council on Violence Against Women, all of us—individuals and organizations alike—can do a number of things to help women in violent situations. Ideas follow. (All the programs of the National Advisory Council on Violence Against Women can be found at http://www.ojp.usdoj.gov/vawo/agendaforthenation/welcome.html.)

1. Eliminate the economic crisis facing many victims of domestic violence, sexual assault, and stalking by designing and implementing programs to provide stability to victims and their families immediately following victimization.
2. Donate security and communications services or underwrite the costs of security-enhancing products and services for women requesting such assistance through community-based programs or the courts.
3. Provide incentives, including technical assistance, for private law firms and individual attorneys to offer free, low-cost, or sliding-scale representation for women survivors of sexual harassment, sexual assault, and domestic violence.
4. Design and implement welfare policies and practices that enhance both safety and self-sufficiency for all welfare clients, including victims of domestic violence, sexual assault, and stalking.
5. Prohibit, in law and administrative policy, any discrimination against women survivors of domestic and sexual violence in any area of insurance, including health care, life, disability, auto, renters, homeowners, and property insurance.
6. Review and modify national, state, and local housing policy, and expand funding as necessary to increase all women's access to safe and affordable housing.
7. Expand the capacity of domestic violence and sexual-assault programs to help women achieve greater economic independence.
8. Expand programs that address "sticky-floor" and "glass-ceiling" phenomena, with the goal of increasing all women's overall economic security, resources, and options.

Criminal Women and Poverty

Studies in social class indicate that one's social class significantly impacts one's life chances. People with access to greater economic resources are physically and mentally healthier, better educated, and happier overall. In terms of crime, middle- and upper-class members are less likely to be victimized, arrested, or convicted of a crime.

Reiman (1998) argues that "justice is a two-way street but criminal justice is a one way street" (p. 157). He suggests that, when the justice system focuses on the criminal behavior of individuals, it "literally acquits the existing social order of any charge of injustice!" (p. 157). What does that have to do with women's criminality and poverty? The argument lies in the same vein as the "poverty is socially constructed" argument, except that it is about the criminal-justice system. We socially construct a criminal-justice system and, at the same time, live in a society that prefers to place all responsibility for crime on individuals themselves. Society prefers not to look at the existing social system and examine which of its features push people to engage in crime. As with so many other things, we have an individualistic orientation to crime. "They did it, they should pay for it." If we stopped to examine the lives of women, where (socially constructed) poverty affects women more than men, we might better understand the lives of "criminal" women. But we generally do not do that because of the invisibility of women. As Reiman further notes, "It is not merely the guilty which end up behind bars, but the guilty poor" (p. 136).

Most information on "criminal" women comes from arrest and incarceration data. Moreover, many of these women are poor, are of color, and have used some form of social assistance. Many of them are mothers, are single, are survivors of violence, and have had interrupted work lives. (We will talk about these women more in Chapter 9.) Their lives often hang by a precarious thread. If we consider the kinds of crimes women engage in—property crimes such as welfare fraud, petty theft, and so on—we realize that many women engage in crime because they are desperate.

> Women prisoners have a host of medical, psychological, and financial problems and needs. Substance abuse, compounded by poverty, unemployment, physical and mental illness, physical and sexual abuse, and homelessness, often propel women through the revolving door of the criminal justice system (Owen & Bloom, 1995).

If we consider the combined impart of a woman's education, occupation, and income, we can surmise her social-class position. This is the standard "objective" measure of social class used by sociologists. For many women in prison, their objective social class position falls toward the lower end of the social class ladder. Hence, some women who find themselves incarcerated are there because they haven't been able to pay the fines associated with their crime.

Furthermore, many of the crimes women tend to engage in, such as prostitution, are intended to generate money. Debate has swirled around the topic of prostitution—whether women like it, whether it represents a form of violence against women, whether it is consensual. I don't want to argue these points in this section; the fact is, women engage in prostitution for money. Researchers have found that prostitution, along with events such as beauty pageants, can bring in significant money for women. However, most prostitutes walk dangerous streets earning just $10 or $20 a trick.

This point about money is important. It means that women do money crimes; men do money crimes *and* violent crimes. Women generally aren't shooting people's heads off or mugging them. They engage in different crimes for different reasons. Though some women in prison have killed their abusers, they generally take such actions only after years of abuse. Prosecutors, judges, and defense attorneys have debated the definition of Battered Women's Syndrome, and whether victims "like it," and so forth. However, the bottom line is that a battered woman's fear and anxiety may intensify owing to an economic stranglehold and the feeling that she has no other way out.

The presence of children adds to the picture. Think about Scott's definition of the feminization of poverty—women's economic vulnerability especially when they are the sole support of their kids. Some women find themselves homeless because, given the frail economic thread they're hanging by, they can no longer feed their children and pay rent. To what lengths would you go if you found yourself in this position?

The Cost of Being Female

In their book *The Cost of Being Female*, Sue Headlee and Margery Elfin (1996) propose an index to hypothetically measure such costs and then apply the index to a variety of different situations. The index measures "the costs of discrimination against women in Amercian society" (p. xxi). Headlee and Elfin suggest that the cost of being female (COBF) is larger today than pre–World War II. They also argue that class and race, as well as country of residence, strongly influence COBF. They then assess the COBF in the following areas:

1. the workplace
2. politics
3. social life
4. education

5. health
6. different countries and generations

Their conclusions? The COBF is

> costly and unjust. Gender discrimination prevents half of our
> population from moving up as far as their talents will bring them
> and deprives the nation of the best use of its human capital. . . . If
> we paid women better, we would have less poverty among
> female heads of household and fewer women on welfare. . . . Fi-
> nally, as a matter of simple justice, fairness and human decency,
> we should eliminate discrimination against women (p. 214).

Well said.

The Essence of the Chapter

The cost of being female in society is like so many other things—socially
created. When we realize that human beings created the programs in place
in the United States and around the world that *do not* help women, we can
begin to see that human beings can therefore change these programs. We
have recognized this in the past. Examining women's poverty and their
work, educational, and family status becomes a circular discussion then—if
we want to arrive at justice for women, we must deal with the circle of life
we place them in. A related topic is the connection between violence
against women and women's control over their own bodies—a link that we
examine in the next chapter.

8 Women, Their Bodies, and Violence

One cost of being female is the cost of violence. Except for pregnancy, we will largely discuss issues of violence against women in this chapter. The chapter focuses on women's bodies, but, unfortunately, such a discussion almost always leads to an exploration of violence. Let's start our discussion with pregnancy and its effects on women's bodies and lives. After that, we will examine general violence against women and then specifically look at rape, domestic battery, pornography, and advertising.

Pregnancy

As far as we know, women have always had the ability to become pregnant. Over the vast majority of human history, laws affecting pregnancy have been minimal. However, women have been subjected to *social* rules concerning pregnancy for some time. Social judgments about who should be pregnant have upset many women's lives and plans. Women who are deemed too young, too poor, too "of color," too uneducated, or too something else have often come under society's scrutiny. Add to this the contemporary discussion of contraception, and we have a hotbed of issues relating to women's bodies.

Contraception

We use contemporary terminology to discuss contraception—reproductive choice—but we need to realize that we have been having these discussions for a long time. In the United States, the "scientific" world got involved in public discussions of reproduction and contraception as early as the 1800s. Particularly in this country, but also in other parts of the world, population control has been debated for centuries. As the United States became an ever more popular port of settlement, more and more immigrants arrived. With the influx of immigrants (the largest of which came in 1907), came a discussion focused around keeping the "native" (that is, white anglo) population "pure." These discussions certainly had racist and xenophobic elements, but they were discussions nonetheless. Talk of population control often centered on immigrants in the nineteenth century for fear that foreign-born peoples would overpopulate the United States. However, such debates also targeted poor women and women of color already living in this country.

The eugenics movement represented the low point of such thinking. The word *eugenics* (from the Greek "eugenes," or "wellborn") was coined in 1883 by Francis Galton, an Englishman and cousin of Charles Darwin. Phrases such as Herbert Spencer's "survival of the fittest" also cropped up in conversations during these years when eugenics societies proliferated throughout the world. Under the name of eugenics, proponents sought to both plenish, or populate, the world and yet limit human numbers based on desired genetic characteristcis. In the United States, the eugenics movement reached its peak in 1920 and strongly affected immigration laws and racist beliefs.

For example, the Immigration Restriction Act of 1924 favored immigrants from northern and western Europe while restricting the entry of persons from southern and eastern areas of Europe. Government officials and scholars, among others, deemed these latter types "biologically inferior." Numerous states also required citizens of various backgrounds, including both native born and foreign born, to be sterilized. Certain Nazi practices were eugenic. Some people would argue that these practices still happen today when parents test for the genetic composition of their unborn babies. Eugenics, then, also constituted a contraceptive method—a way to keep certain woman from becoming pregnant.

Numerous authors often cite *Griswold v. Connecticut* (381 U.S. 479 (1965)) as the first contemporary case relating to contraception and reproductive choice. Nevertheless, as early as 1937, the American Medical Association had already recognized birth control as an essential part of medical practice and education. The *Griswold* decision allowed married couples to make their own choices about contraceptives; case attorneys argued this U.S. Supreme Court case as an issue of privacy. *Eisenstadt v. Baird* (405 U.S. 438 (1972)) gave the same right to unmarried persons.

What about abortion? Debates about this procedure have reached feverish pitches in the United States. Yet the reality is that abortion before "quickening" was legal and acceptable in this country long before 1800. By the 1840s, however, it had become a medicalized and commercialized practice in urban centers. Between the 1840s and 1860s, several states enacted the first anti-abortion laws. Note that this change regarding abortion happened during the rise of the professionalism of medicine. The newly organized and more prestigious medical profession wanted control over a domain they claimed as theirs. Also at this time, the medical profession began slandering and deriding midwifery—the primary way by which women had delivered babies.

Once in place, anti-abortion forces proved strong. It was not until the U.S. Supreme Court decision in *Roe v. Wade* (410 U.S. 113 (1973)) that the tide turned. *Roe* was decided on the grounds that women had a constitutional right to privacy, including deciding what to do with their own bodies. The U.S. Senate heard the "Human Life Statute" nine years after Roe as an attempt to overturn the decision; however, the Senate subsequently voted down the statute. For the last 20 years, women's ability to decide what to do with a pregnancy has faced innumerable challenges. One of the biggest blows came with the *Webster v. Reproductive Health Services* decision (492 U.S. 490 (1989)), which let states restrict women's access to abortion by imposing guidelines on services offered to women through publicly funded institutions (such as refusing to allow public employees to perform abortions in public hospitals).

But reproductive choice extends beyond abortion. Technologies such as Norplant, in-vitro fertilization, donor insemination, and contract parenthood/surrogacy all influence women's choices. As a culture, we have attached moral arguments to each of these choices. From the viewpoint of quadraplexation, choice has everything to do with reproduction. But if we delve further, we realize that the other quadraplexation variables also come into play. Reproductive choice relates to women's labor—both paid work and unpaid home work. Choice also affects—and is affected by—the socialization variable; specifically, what women are taught about being "good mothers." Finally, I would argue that much of the discussion of reproductive choice goes straight into the face of sexuality. As we ground the discussion in morality, we consciously or unconsciously grapple with sexuality. After all, how else do most women become pregnant in the first place? Finally, reproductive choices often force women to walk the line.

Perhaps the most recent issue concerns women's behavior during pregnancy. Should a woman work while pregnant? Have sex? Have a cigarette or a drink? This counts as a walking-the-line issue also, because many mothers-to-be are in a no-win situation. Their behavior is coming under closer and closer scrutiny by all sorts of people—family, friends, clergy, and justice professionals, to name a few. Numerous legal cases have examined a woman's behavior during pregnancy and have found her unfit, negligent, or engaging in gross misconduct.

Violence Against Women

We can examine violence against women from many different angles— kinds of violence, definitions, causes, and so forth. Belknap (1996) makes several statements about women and violence, including that women fear crime more than men do. This fear produces a victimization mind set and often sets women up to think of themselves as victims—indeed, mothers often socialize their daughters to be victims. But, as Belknap also points out, "It is not necessary for all men to victimize all women in order for all women to be afraid of male violence" (p. 130).

Defining Violence

Hamner and Maynard (1987) argue that defining violence against women can be difficult. Violence can take several forms, depending on who is defining it and where the definition is coming from. For example, Hamner and Maynard see legal definitions as the narrowest of all definitions of violence. Even though they carry a certain degree of authority and formality, they tend to omit many behaviors and attitudes that women regard as violent. That reality gives common-law definitions of many behaviors—domestic abuse, sexual assault, sexual harassment, and so forth—much power. Even though some lawmakers pass laws as gender-neutral, the ability to define what is and is not violent has enormous impact on people's lives, especially women. Feminist opinion generally agrees that the power to define violence works to the advantage of men and to the disadvantage of women.

Professional and expert definitions of violence tend to be broader than legal definitions, regardless of how the legal definitions are constructed. These broader definitions derive from professionals and experts in fields of study such as family violence, child abuse, pornography, and so forth. These individuals' interpretations of violence can pose problems as well. For one thing, there are many different expert opinions. However, the public often accepts these ideas as authoritative, even if experts' statements about violence don't accurately describe survivors' actual experiences.

Women's definitions of violence tend to be the broadest, because they come from actual experiences. From these experiences, and the verbal sharing of them among women, the definitions of violence often include behaviors that women perceive as threatening, violent, or harassing—often behaviors that neither legal nor expert definitions include. Women, then, often find themselves in disagreement with the other two kinds of definitions and may find themselves tottering between two worlds—their own experiences and descriptions or conclusions coming to them from other sources.

How do we explain violence against women? Psychological explanations that suggest that perpetrators are sick, demented individuals have proven the most popular. Social-structural explanations, by contrast, suggest that violence is a response to societal situations such as stress, blocked goals, bad economic situations, bad housing, poverty, and lack of employment or job choice. These explanations require society to examine itself; thus they don't have as strong a voice. Feminist explanations often focus on the ways in which society denigrates women's lives. Liberal feminists urge

---

B O X **8.1**   Rawls on Justice

Justice is to be understood in its customary sense as representing but one of the many virtues of social institutions, for these may be antiquated, inefficient, degrading, or any number of other things, without being unjust. Justice is not to be confused with an all-inclusive vision of a good society; it is only one part of any such conception. It is important, for example, to distinguish that sense of equality which is an aspect of the concept of justice from that sense of equality which belongs to a more comprehensive social ideal. There may well be inequalities which one concedes are just, or at least not unjust, but which, nevertheless, one wishes on other grounds, to do away with. . . .

John Rawls, *A Theory of Justice*

---

the passing of laws and the teaching of lessons that spread the word about violence against women. The legal system must also work to punish those who commit violence. Radical feminists see violence as part and parcel of a patriarchal society—only by changing patriarchy, they argue, will we eliminate violence.

Sexual Terrorism

Regardless of how we define violence, many authors argue that violence affects *all* women's lives. Sheffield (1987) calls the overwhelming reality of violence in women's lives *sexual terrorism*. In her view, men use sexual terrorism as a system to frighten and control women. That system manifests itself in both the actual and the threatened use of violence to keep women under men's control. In this system, all women—regardless of age, color, ethnicity, social class, and so forth—learn that they are potential victims of violence. Women's subordination in society, then, rests on the power of men to intimidate and punish women sexually. Sheffield argues that sexual terrorism sustains the power of patriarchy because it ensures women's compliance to male wishes, desires, and ideas. It operates on a variety of levels:

1. The "good girl/bad girl" dichotomy tells women that they will be punished if they are bad (if they wear skirts that men consider too short, for example).
2. Mass-media images—music, film, television, advertising, photography, literature—all contain violent lessons about womanhood.
3. The sexual-terrorism system legitimizes and provides social support for those who have contempt for women—for example, battering men who claim that they have a right to subdue their "nagging" wives.

Terrorism runs smoothly because, in part, it has the following components:

1. An *ideology* that defines women as inferior
2. A set of *propaganda* that disseminates information supporting that ideology
3. The use of *indiscriminate and amoral violence* to keep women in a state of fear

The Continuum of Violence

Take a sheet of paper and draw a horizontal line across it. At each end of the line, put a short vertical line. You've now constructed a continuum of sorts. Let's place on this continuum all of the forms of violence against women we can think of. Verbal and physical abuse, rape, torture, prostitution, incest, unnecessary surgeries, forced heterosexuality or pregnancy or motherhood, cosmetic surgery, advertising, pornography, female infanticide, lesbicide, witch hunts, slavery, sexual abuse, battery, slashing, stalking, genital mutilation, suttee, femicide. . . . The length and content of this list probably surprises you. It includes a multitudinous (and incomplete) list of behaviors directed at women solely because they are women. Some scholars argue that each item requires things from women—compliance, adherence to traditional ideas of womanhood (true womanhood, for example), a belief in a woman's nature, acceptance of male superiority. This list is similar to Stout's *Continuum of Male Controls and Violence Against Women* (Stout, 1991, p. 307). Stout suggests putting femicide at one (closed) end of the continuum because femicide is the ultimate—and final—act of violence against women. The continuum is open on the other end to demonstrate the ongoing and continual violence still directed at women. Stout's list includes language, research differences, differential treatment in many social settings, sexist advertising, and so on.

Domestic Battery

Just naming this section is difficult. What do we call the beating of a woman by her significant or ex-significant other? Many people use the term *family violence,* but numerous scholars have argued that that expression masks the true nature of what happens in violent households. Others use the terms *domestic violence, domestic battery, women battery,* and so forth. I have chosen to use the term *battery* because it implies the violent nature of this situation, and domestic because we are talking about what's going on in the domestic world—the world of women, according to the separate-spheres argument.

Men have beaten women since the beginning of time. Nevertheless, people in the United States didn't talk about this publicly until the 1970s. I prefer to think of battered women as survivors rather than victims and use that terminology throughout this discussion. Of course, *survivor* applies only to those women who continue to live despite being beaten. Four battered women are murdered by an intimate in this country every day. Some people call the marriage license a license to hit, but apparently it is also a license to kill.

The subject of domestic battery raises so many questions. Why don't battered women leave? What is going on? Who tends to batter? And why? People on the street (like you and me), police officers, judges, and battered women themselves all ask these questions. For a long time, legislators, judges, and police personnel have considered domestic battery a private, family issue. This assumption made courts reluctant to deal with it. Cops, too, often found battery cases annoying and complex. Of course, these attitudes affected the lives of battered women. In her book on the history of domestic violence on the U.S. east coast, Gordon (1994) argues that how we defined domestic violence/battery has varied significantly over time. For a long time, Americans didn't publicly discuss it. However, as societal ideas changed, and as we began to slowly broach the topic, definitions changed also. For example, in the 1950s, the era that saw the development of psychology and psychiatry, people often cloaked discussions of battery in language such as "hysterical woman claims husband hit her." Some men who beat their wives suggested that they did so because of their "frigidity." Who are battered women? Who are batterers? Probably the best place to start is with a discussion of the battered household.

Battering Households

My definition of violence in households is probably different from your definition. How people think about family violence is so varied. Indeed, some people think it is okay for husbands to hit their wives, or for parents to spank their children. Other people consider these actions absolutely incorrect. Because I see this as an unsettled discussion, I prefer to examine household characteristics that lend themselves to violence. All violent households do not necessarily have all these characteristics, and these variables may vary in intensity. However, I would argue that if a household displays all of these characteristics to some degree, then a violent family environment likely exists.

Control and power are two defining characteristics of a violent household. The batterer wants to rule the other members of the household; that is how he keeps his position in the "pecking order." To achieve that control and power, batterers use a variety of mechanisms. They impose rigid rules on the households, so they can know who fits where in the hierarchy at all times. They also believe that they are always right and that they know best.

Violent households also tend to be *isolated*, geographically and socially. Batterers maintain their power and control by defining whom family members can and cannot see, talk to, visit, spend time with, work with, and so forth. This isolation also depends on the *silence* of the family members—batterers thus tell their victims/survivors not to talk about what goes on behind their closed doors. Often this silence and isolation is coupled with a sense of *denial*, a feeling among victims/survivors that "it's not as bad as it seems" or that "it's bound to get better" eventually.

Fear and terror cement the whole set-up into place. Let's face it: Many of us live in households where people get angry sometimes, or people try to tell each other what to do and how to do it. What separates these households from those where battery occurs are the fear and terror borne by battered families—fear of what might happen if a family member doesn't follow the rules, if she talks to people she isn't supposed to, if she makes the bed a different way, if she tells someone what is going on.

One of the most frequently cited analyses of violent households is the work of Walker (1980). Her discussion makes even more sense when we couch it in the above environmental variables. In a house of fear, terror, control, power, denial, isolation, and silence, violence can become an inescapable cycle. Walker identifies three stages: (1) contrition (the honeymoon), (2) tension building (the "eggshell" stage), and (3) battery. During the honeymoon stage, the batterer might bring flowers and say "I'm sorry, this will never happen again." But, honeymoons rarely last. Ultimately, tension begins to build again. At some point, a trigger in the batterer's mind sets off an abusive episode. The abuse can last for some minutes or several days. The cycle from one abusive episode to the next also shortens over time. From anecdotal sources, some battered women say *they* prefer to trigger the violence because then *they have some control*. This does *not* mean that they are causing the violence. It means that they know, given the cycle, that violence will occur again at some point and that triggering it at least lets them know exactly when it's coming.

How does the cycle continue? Think about the above variables. A batterer batters to show he is powerful, then says "I'm sorry." But, the cause of his behavior doesn't disappear simply because he battered. Thus his frustration builds back up and he does it again. All the while, that sense of building reverberates through the household. To keep this cycle going, the batterer instructs the household members not to talk about what's happening, not to talk to so-and-so, period, and so forth. And here's another important point: A batterer's abusive behavior doesn't have to always be physical—the mere raising of an eyebrow can get household members to follow the rules. Why? Because they associate the raised eyebrow with past episodes of violence. Once the batterer establishes the cycle of violence, he doesn't have to use physical abuse all the time. (For example, how many parents spank their children and then, to control their children's behavior at some future point, they say something like, "Do you want another spanking?") Elizabeth Pleck (as quoted in Jones, 1994, p. 164) says, "The single most consistent barrier to reform against domestic violence" has been the "family ideal" image. In other words, the ideal says families are loving and nurturing entities and parents always look out for their children and love them completely. Furthermore, all family members are protected from harm and taken care of. Of course, try explaining this ideal to members in a violent household. . . .

Battered Women

Who are the women living in abusive relationships? The American Medical Association has urged physicians to screen all women whom they see in ER, surgical, primary care, prenatal, pediatric, and mental-health settings for exposure to domestic violence. Why? Because battering can happen to any and all women. For much of the last three decades, researchers have tried to characterize the typical battered woman with lists of variables describing her and her behavior. However, contemporary researchers maintain that battered women are diverse. They come from all social classes, colors, ethnicities, religions, and so forth. Some battered women are passive; some fight back (what Pagelow calls "mutual combat"). Many battered women *do* leave battering relationships, but they often return for any variety of reasons (economics, fear, emotional needs, threats, and so on).

I think it is of utmost importance to understand that women respond to violence in their lives at an individual level—that is, their responses stem from their own best attempts to handle the situation. We cannot always understand others' motivations. Some folks talk about how alcohol and drugs worsen family violence. Yet some battered women prefer their partner drunk or drugged because he "nods out." For as many kinds of battered women, there are that many kinds of responses to the abuse.

Why do battered women stay? They do so for many reasons: religion, guilt, economics, love for the abuser, low self-esteem, lack of alternatives and support systems, a history of abuse in their family of origin, isolation, a belief that they're crazy, fear. The fear is especially well grounded; many women are killed by their abusers after they leave or file for divorce. But "Why doesn't she leave?" is the wrong question to ask. It doesn't call for an answer; it makes a judgment. "It mystifies. It transforms an immense social problem into a personal transaction and at the same time pins responsibility squarely on the victim. It obliterates both the terrible magnitude of violence against women and the great achievements of the movement against it" (Jones, 1994, pp. 131–132). Jones argues that battered women are battered "because they will not give in" (p. 94). So, sometimes they fight back, sometimes they lie low—whatever they choose, they're still fighting back, meaning they're doing their best to survive. Battered women are ingenious, resourceful, and brave. They do get out.

Common Law and Domestic Battery

As Jones points out, English common law thought of assault as something that happened only between two men. Thus, historically, assault has not been applied to the relationships between men and women. English common law also set up an adversarial courtroom system that has, ultimately, strongly influenced how the U.S. justice system handles cases of domestic battery. Battered women may want their husbands arrested but not jailed. Or jailed forever, or neither. But the system defines this relationship as adversarial—which means that no matter how the battered woman calls it, she must play it by the court's rules. She may not want him arrested, but the jurisdiction has a mandatory arrest policy. She, and the cops, become the batterer's adversaries. Because an adversarial situation pits two parties against one another, courtrooms automatically pit battered women against their batterers—publicly. As a result, she may be placed in a situation of greater harm. Thus battered women are "damned if they do" (resist the battering through legal means) and "damned if they don't" (walking the line *again!*). If a battered mother runs away with her kids, she's kidnapping. If she leaves her kids behind, she's abandoning them.

Batterers

According to Gordon (1994, p. 97), a batterer's "sense of entitlement" is so strong that "it was experienced as a need." Batterers use battering because it works. They don't turn to violence as a last resort; it's their weapon of choice. How does a seemingly nice guy turn into an abusive menace? Batterer typologies cite many characteristics: possessiveness, emphasis on tradition; sense of male privilege; desire for control; poor feeling differentiation (meaning they don't know if they are sad, angry, depressed); low self-esteem; vulnerable self-concept; feelings of helplessness, powerlessness, and inadequacy; jealous; dependency; rigid ideas; dual personality; bad temper; poor impulse control; tendency to blame others; trust issues; use of drugs or alcohol; misogynistic ideas; stress; lack of control; and poor communication abilities. Many researchers suggest that this list of "explanations" is nothing more than a list of excuses masquerading as reasons for unacceptable behavior.

Many scholars do agree that numerous batterers possess a "dual personality." They seem nice to the outside world, but are abusive in private. Often we hear people say things like, "I can't believe he beats her—he's so nice." Bingo. That is exactly how the dual personality plays out. Even in well-publicized cases of battery (O.J. and Nicole Simpson, for example), people say such things. Besides the dual personality, batterers often have two kinds of self-presentation. Some batterers may present both. One presentation is the "charming and yet confused or mystified" kind—a passive, go-along-with-the-situation response to accusations of battery. Such batterers often say things such as, "I'll do anything to clear up this little misunderstanding," or "I don't know . . . why I'm here, what happened . . , what's going on. . . ." The other presentation is the "self-defense and denial" kind; often these batterers become intimidating and angry and claim, "She's crazy."

The Domestic Abuse Intervention Project (DAIP) in Duluth, Minnesota—a leading organization in batterer programming—requires batterers to examine themselves and their behavior through the lens of a set of variables. For example, they must ask themselves questions such as "What did I intend to happen when I used that behavior?" and "How do I blame my victim for my behavior?" and "What can I do differently in the future?" The DAIP recognizes that different domestic-battery case workers attribute battering to different causes; each has his or her own theoretical explanation. But workers do agree on this: Batterers must take responsibility for their actions. Thus, they must start learning to understand, their own behavior.

Some batterers successfully talk their way out of an alleged battering situation, even if the incident has attracted the attention of police. This may happen in a variety of ways. Some batterers are better "talkers" than others and "weasel out of" the law. Others present improbable situations (such as being physically challenged) and therefore don't seem able to batter. If batterers admit to the abuse, they often justify it by saying things like "She's dumb," "She's a nag," or "She's nothing without me in her life." Listening to these accusations, one might well ask why a batterer would want to stay with such an undesirable woman. Of course, these statements are excuses for his own behavior, not accurate descriptions of the victim's behavior.

How do we help batterers stop battering? Programs such as the one at DAIP have had significant success. Other programs emphasizing family therapy for the batterer and his survivor(s) try to get the family unit back on track in a nonviolent manner. Anger-management and stress-reduction classes have also proved worthwhile.

Why Batter?

Some researchers attribute battering to individual characteristics, such as a lack of self-control or mental illness. The societal perspective looks at the bigger picture and suggests societal-level stresses and strain—unemployment, anomie, lack of education, and so forth. Feminist explanations blame patriarchy and male dominance for teaching men that they are the leaders and women are the followers.

Pence (in Jones, 1994, pp. 99–100) has described the cultural context that encourages battering:

1. A set of hierarchal structures that seem natural and that dictate that some people are in charge and others subordinate
2. The cultural objectification of women in pornography, videos, TV shows, beauty contests, and so forth
3. A combination of (a) psychological conditioning that trains women to take care of and understand men, (b) economic arrangements that plunge women into poverty when they're alone, and (c) legal license that permits men to coerce women by threats and violence

Attempts to "explain" domestic violence have led to the development of theories such as the "battered women's syndrome." First hailed as an insightful explanation, this theory has become less convincing to contemporary scholars. The syndrome portrays women as passive creatures under the control of abusive men. However, we know that not all battered women are passive creatures; they all react in different ways to their situations. The syndrome, then, doesn't accurately describe women who fight back *or* women who don't fight back. "Why didn't you fight him off?" "If you are so weak, how could you fight him off?"

As we've seen, the courts have been reluctant to impose criminal sanctions on batterers for many decades, because they've seen domestic battery as a private, family issue. However, the courts have been quick to impose themselves on women who defend themselves against the abuse. This imposition ultimately becomes yet another "walking-the-line" example. Studies demonstrate that, on average, abusive men who kill serve two to six years in prison, while abused women who kill serve 15 years. She kills to save her life, he kills to control—and serves less time.

Rape and Sexual Assault

Rape is pervasive. It cuts across all lines within U.S. society, including age, race, and class. National statistics show that the ages of rape victims range from six months to 93 years. At its core, rape is an act of violence and has little or nothing to do with sex. Rapists use sex as a weapon of control and power. The number of women affected directly by rape is astonishing. According to the National Coalition Against Domestic Violence, a rape is committed every six minutes in the United States; one out of every seven married women is raped by her husband; one-third of all women will be sexually assaulted in their lifetime; and 70–75 percent of all rapes are committed by someone whom the victim knows. Statistics released by the National Center for Victims of Crime (1992) estimate rape survivors are almost nine times more likely to attempt suicide than those who haven't survived rape.

Rape Culture

Martha McCaughey, at a guest lecture she gave at Emory University, defined a rape culture as one in which:

1. Rape and other forms of violence against women are common.
2. Rape and other forms of violence against women are tolerated (prevalence is high, while prosecution and arrest rates are low).
3. Victim blaming and racist myths of rape and other forms of violence against women are commonplace.
4. Images of rape and other forms of violence against women abound.
5. Images of sex and violence are intertwined.
6. Women do not enjoy full, legal economic, and social equality with men.

Not all scholars agree on whether a rape culture exists. Some suggest that the notion lets us wallow in the victimization of women; others suggest that it gives men too much power in a patriarchal world. We need more information to decide whether a rape culture exists in the United States.

The Criminal Law, Reporting, and Conviction Rates

The FBI Uniform Crime Report indicates that one in every 10 rapes gets reported. According to the National Coalition on Sexual Assault, only one in 60 gets reported. This figure is based on the number of women seen at sexual-assault centers across the United States. Let's clarify the difference between the words *sexual assault* and *rape*.

When the common law first defined rape as a crime, it did not consider the woman the victim. Rather, men in her family—her father, brothers, uncles, or husband—were the ones seen as truly harmed. They felt the burden of having a soiled and impure women in their midst. In some states in the U.S., the law required the woman to marry the rapist—and expected her to be happy about it. At least someone would marry a defiled woman. Over time, people have defined rape and its consequences differently.

The FBI defines rape as the violation of a woman by a man who is not her partner. Gender is thus an inherent part of this definition. Sexual assault, on the other hand, is a much broader crime. It refers to the sexual violation of one human being by another human being. The violation is sexual in nature but does not necessarily use a sexual organ. A pop bottle or a mouth may be the tool of violation. This broader definition affects the statistics and reporting of this crime. Reporting appears to depend on several factors, including survivor characteristics, alleged offenders' characteristics, characteristics of the situation, and so on. Because sexual assault statutes—which exist in all states now—are broader than rape definitions, sexual-assault centers report more occurrences. These counts more accurately reflect the kinds and amounts of violence occurring; the FBI's reliance on the term "rape" leads to undercounting and inaccurate reporting of reality.

With all of these statistics, another astonishing fact comes to light: The conviction rate nationally is just 5–10 percent, as reported by the FBI Uniform Crime Report. When we include rape by acquaintance, the conviction rate falls to a minuscule 1.75 percent. Sexual assault has the lowest conviction rates of all violent crime.

Types of Rape and Rapists

Numerous typologies these days describe different "types" of rape, as well as different types of rapists. One can examine stranger rape versus acquaintance rape, marital rape, date rape, campus rape, gang rape, stalk rape, and on and on. Researchers often attach the extent of rape to some type of rape; for example, the FBI estimates acquaintance rapes as approximately 75 percent of all rapes. These numerous perspectives make discussion of rape both easier and more difficult—easier because they give us a clearer sense of the diverse situations of rape, more difficult because they cloud the definition of rape and its underlying point. Rape is about power and control, about degradation and harm.

Many women have partners who force them into sex. Numerous wives do not think of this behavior as rape, nor do many husbands. But sex accompanied by fear, or threats, with or without physical force, is rape. Some wives submit to sex to prevent or defuse beatings but don't see the situation as rape. There are only 19 jurisdictions in the United States where rape in marriage is against the law. The conservative estimate says that one in seven married women is subjected to marital rape (Russell, 1990).

In his book *Men Who Rape* (1990), Nicholas Groth identifies three groups of rapists—power rapists, anger rapists, and sadistic rapists. He also defines statistics and rape differences. The power rapist commits up to 70–75 percent of all sexual assaults, and usually plans these attacks. We can equate power rapists with acquaintance or date rapists. These rapes are the least likely to get reported, as the victim usually knows the perpetrator. Groth identifies this category of rapist as having low self-esteem and feeling out of control. He feels he has a right to control his victim to gain a feeling of power in himself.

Anger rapists, as described by Groth, commit an estimated 25–30 percent of all rapes. These crimes include "stranger rapes" and often manifest excessive violence. Anger rapists tend not to plan the attacks. They identify people as either "good" or "bad"; unfortunately, their victims fall into the "bad" category, as defined by the rapists.

The remaining 2 percent of rapes committed come under the sadistic category, according to Groth. Usually a mentally ill person commits these rapes, often using excessive violence. Sadistic rapes frequently result in the death of the victim.

Groth's model is one among many typologies. Scholars often argue that such typologies pose problems. For example, some researchers believe that they almost constitute forms of profiling and, thus, become essentialist. Essentialism, as pointed out in Chapter 1, is when all members of a group are lumped under one label; it becomes a form of stereotyping. We can talk about types of rape and rapists, but the bottom line is that rapists can be anybody, and rape survivors can be anybody. However, victims often know their attackers. As a form of sexual terrorism, rape has all the characteristics associated with other forms of sexual terrorism, such as domestic battery and sexual harassment.

The Victim and the Myth

A perpetrator's view of a victim may derive from the many myths about rape and sexual assault that run rampant in U.S. society. These myths include the following:

- Women provoke men to rape by the way in which they dress.
- Women deserve to be raped.
- Women say "no" but mean "yes."
- Women who are raped asked for it.

Unfortunately, rape perpetrators are not the only people who believe these myths. The following examples suggest just how widespread this ignorance is:

- The presiding judge in a rape case called the five-year-old victim an "unusually promiscuous young lady."
- A juror in a Fort Lauderdale rape trial stated that the victim "asked for it" because of her clothing.
- A Pennsylvania judge declared a rape suspect not guilty despite a police witness to the attack. The judge said to the defendant in open court, "This was an unattractive girl, and you are a good-looking fellow. You did something stupid."

Beneke on *Men on Rape*

Beneke (1982) suggests that the threat of rape drastically affects women's lives because it:

1. Alters the meaning and feel of the night
2. Alters the meaning and feel of nature
3. Makes women more dependent on men
4. Makes solitude less possible for women
5. Inhibits women's expressiveness
6. Inhibits the freedom of the eye
7. Requires women to earn more money. (If you don't feel safe walking home after work or riding the bus, you need a car.)

If you're a woman, think about your individual behavior in terms of the above items. You probably understand what Beneke is saying.

The Impact of Rape on Women of Color

When famed blues singer Billie Holliday was raped at age 10, she was taken, still bleeding from the attack, to the local police station. "Instead of treating me like somebody who called for help," she said, "they treated me like I had killed somebody . . . they threw me into a cell and gave me filthy looks and snickers." After a few days, she was taken to court. Her rapist was sentenced to five years—and she was sentenced to a Catholic institution (Griffin, 1986).

Because of the stereotypes of our racist society, the cries of "rape" by a black woman often lack legitimacy. During the same week as the "Central Park Jogger" case (in which a group of black men was brutally raped a white, middle-class woman), 28 other rapes or attempted rapes occurred in New York City. Nearly all the victims were black or Hispanic women, and the media ignored nearly all of them. "The image of black women in our society is that they are chronically promiscuous, loose and whores" (Davis, 1983). These attitudes lead to less reporting of rape and further harm, both physical and psychological, to black women. According to Sheffield (1987), the "good girl/bad girl dichotomy has particularly troublesome consequences for black women within our society." Sherffield notes that "rape laws were initially enacted to maintain property rights of white men (property being the wives of these men) and as a means of social control of black women and men. While the rape of a white woman by a black man was a capital offense, the rape of a black woman was not a crime."

Davis (1989) states that "the most insidious myth about rape is that it is most likely to be committed by a black man" (Davis, 1989). The reality is that 97 percent of all rapes are intraracial, not interracial. This myth of the black rapist, as perpetuated by a history of racism within law enforcement, becomes evident when we look at the following facts: Between 1930 and 1967, of 455 executions on rape convictions, 405 of the convicts were black (Davis, 1983). Moreover, there is a disproportionate number of black men in prison on rape convictions (as well as many other crimes). Given these facts, it's no wonder that women of color are afraid that law-enforcement officers will harass their male family members and friends. Thus, these women have yet another reason not to report sexual assault.

Other Facets of Rape

As we've seen, rape has many facets. Until recently, criminal justice personnel and scholars rarely discussed the question of whether a rape victim consented to the attack. Today's "No means no" refers to the issue of consent. These days, sexual assault statutes recognize that a rape survivor does not even have to be conscious to say "no" to an attacker; legislators assume that rapists know their behavior is inappropriate. Therefore, a woman shouldn't have to say no for the crime to be defined as rape.

The feeling of being doubly violated constitutes another facet of rape. Our criminal-justice system still struggles with rape in the courtroom. Often a trial boils down to one person's word against another person's word. Trial transcripts reveal prosecutors asking questions of rape survivors, such as what kind of clothes they were wearing, whether or not they struggled against their rapists, and why they were where they were. They don't ask men such questions.

What Can We Do?

Ideas about how communities and society as a whole can address rape and sexual assault. But so far, the criminal and civil justice systems have placed the responsibility of avoiding rape squarely on women. This responsibility must shift to fall on the men living within our society.

The silence must be broken—men must talk about rape, and men must educate men about rape. "It is men who rape and men who collectively have the power to end rape" (Beneke, 1982). Largely men have taught men to ignore a woman's saying "no" and to assume she means "yes." Men must learn that no means *no*; that consent to sex requires understanding and respect between equal partners. Men must learn that rape affects their lives also—that their lovers, mothers, grandmothers, sisters, and children may suffer sexual assault.

Our educational systems must change, including greater opportunity for sexual-assault awareness programs within our schools, These programs would give young people a chance to hear the truth about rape. In time, perhaps attitudes will change.

We also must rethink our understanding of "gender." Women have been socially engendered as powerless and dependent on the men who assault them. "Sexual terrorism is maintained by a system of sex-role socialization that encourages men to be terrorists in the name of masculinity and women to be victims in the name of femininity" (Sheffield, 1987).

Attitudes about women must shift. Rape is the ultimate expression of sexism. Women have been objectified within the media which we see everyday. Pornography has made women sexual objects; has made rape something she enjoys; has allowed women to be reduced to body parts (mutilated) for men's sexual gratification.

We must no longer accept violence toward women. Advertisements, movies, and television shows inundate us with images of rape and violence. Many of these images promote violence against women—and we need go no farther than the neighborhood convenience store to purchase them.

Finally, we must stop blaming rape survivors. We must fight to disprove the myths surrounding sexual assault. Women do not ask for rape—any woman has a right to dress as she chooses, to go where she chooses—these choices in no way give men the right to rape. Women are no more responsible for rape than a banker is responsible for the behavior of a bank robber. Women may be guilty of bad judgment ("If only I hadn't gotten drunk; if only I hadn't gone home with him"). However, bad judgment is not a "rapeable" offense. We must educate ourselves regarding sexual assault in order to educate others about sexual assault.

Pornography and Media

Television and Other Media

What is a "soap opera"? This question probably conjures up images of those daytime shows about sex, titillation, murder, and mayhem. The plots in these shows move forward slowly to keep watchers enthralled over time—the shows even have magazines and Web sites devoted to their content and characters. To media scholars, soap operas (and radio shows before them!) are mainly vehicles for advertisers. Indeed, some critics suggest that television itself is nothing more than a way for capitalism to sell its wares. Perhaps a cynical statement, but an interesting one.

So, what are advertisers selling? Products, services, solutions, the good life . . . often sex and sexuality. Many advertisements target women as consumers because women spend more money than men do on products advertised on TV. And many advertisements use women to sell the products. Indeed, advertising gives us specific messages about women and men, about families and moms and dads, about women's relationships with men, about all sorts of issues associated with gender. The media—no matter what—are actually in the big business of socialization. Andersen (2000) argues that the socialization business entails the symbolic annihilation of women because it trivializes, condemns, or narrowly defines women. At the same time, it depicts men in high-status roles by which they dominate women. The media also portray people of color, people of different physical and mental abilities, and people of low social classes as different than "the norm." They are sillier, unintelligent, funnier, or more feral than the "average" middle-class, abled, white person. Though media sources are working to give the impression that our society has achieved equality for all, the media themselves haven't made this achievement in the images they portray.

Think of what the media emphasize—for example, superficial changes like "the first woman to ever fly a fighter jet." Yes, it is great to pat women on the back, but by continually emphasizing firsts, the media give us the sense that women have made it, or that they're even "taking over." But women *haven't* made it.

Television is arguably the central cultural arm of U.S. culture. A few souls still claim that they don't watch TV, but they are rare. For most citizens, television provides a direct link to expected U.S. norms. It thus is an agent of the established order, of capitalism, of advertisers.

But television certainly doesn't stress equality. A few shows over the last two decades have worked at it—*Cagney and Lacey, Murphy Brown, Judging Amy*. These shows represent women and men in complicated, nonstereotypical roles. But if you think this is standard TV fare, switch the channel. Even shows such as *Roseanne* reemphasized that working-class women are fat and funny. In reality, most TV shows portray men in more occupations, more often in charge, and more aggressive in their behavior. Men are the prime actors. Likewise, 80 percent of TV shows portray violence. Here's what we *don't* see a lot of on TV: capable elderly, realistic and educated blacks (although we now have black TV, so this *may* change), respectable native Indians or Hispanics/Latinas/Chicanos, temporarily or permanently challenged individuals, and lesbians and gay men.

Newspapers, too, perpetuate differentiation by sex. The next time you read the obituaries, note the differences in what they say about men versus women. Richardson (1988) points out that obituaries are gendered as is where a story is placed. Certain stories appear in the "women's section" (Most people think of these as the "living," "lifestyle," or "home" sections); others go in "sports."

Magazines, too, tend to be gender specific. Men's magazines focus on finance, sporting, and sex. Women's magazines center on cooking, housekeeping, fashion, and makeup—and ways to get and keep men. We like to think things have changed because we have *Ms.* and *Working Women*, but these magazines present both an updated style and traditionalism. They don't describe *social solutions* to the problems in women's lives. Instead, they offer personal, individualized solutions. There is a big difference between those two approaches. By offering individual solutions to pay gaps, sexual harassment, day care, and rape, magazines tell women that they need to take care of these things themselves. Yes, that is true. But, if magazines also offered social solutions, then two things could happen. First, women as a group, and women as individuals, would benefit from any resulting changes. Furthermore, the tendency to blame the victim would decrease, because society would not hold individual women responsible for those changes they shouldn't *have* to make.

The sexism shown in popular culture has changed in that it has become less blatant and more subtle. But, it has not necessarily declined. Media images of women and men continue to enforce gender, race, and class stereotypes, albeit more quietly now. Even in the "news"—that supposedly objective example of the media—the low percent of women reporters, anchors, print journalists, editors in chief, and publishers is astounding, even in news coverage of women's issues.

Why?

Andersen (2000) suggests four explanations for these media representations. The *reflection hypothesis* says the media simply reflect the values of population. Therefore, if the population and culture are sexist and prefer to see women and men in traditional roles, then that's what they get. The *role-learning theory* proposes that images encourage "proper" role learning and must therefore represent what the culture wants its members to learn. *Organizational theories of gender inequality* suggest that the media portray women and people of color in certain ways because these individuals hold subordinate positions in organizations. These realities in turn influence the way the media portray them. Finally, *ideas about capitalism and the media* postulate that producers simply foster images that support sales of sponsors' products. Such an explanation does beg us to ask what a scantily clad woman has to do with fishing gear, but. . . .

Advertising

Several decades ago, Goffman (1979) identified "genderisms" in advertising. In his view, these indicated the relative importance and status of the people portrayed in the advertising. Genderisms are:

1. Relative size
2. Feminine touch
3. Function ranking (man directs, woman is directed)
4. The family (men with boys, women with girls)
5. Ritualization of subordination (women in lower body positions, subordinate positions)

6. Licensed withdrawal (women less oriented to the situation, such as not completely in touch with what is going on)

The next time you watch television, see whether you can spot these genderisms. When you flip through a magazine (pay attention to what kind it is, too), look for genderisms in the ads. What do you find?

You may be wondering what this discussion has to do with inequality and justice. Think about the name of this chapter: "Women, Their Bodies, and Violence." The portrayals of women in advertising certainly involve their bodies. Advertisers use sex to sell, and passivity and secondary status to influence. These images emphasize the true-womanhood and separate-spheres ideals and reward those who adhere to them. Furthermore, women's bodies often become the central theme of a show or an ad. These realities have consequences for women's lives psychologically, behaviorally, and economically. They may even have violent consequences as well. For example, let's consider the line between advertising and pornography.

Pornography

As with many topics in this book, a discussion of pornography could be a book by itself. But let's start with this mental exercise: Imagine people making love. The images that arise in your mind may be diverse, but they likely include mutual pleasure, touching, warmth, an empathy for each other and each other's bodies, shared sensuality, a sense that the lovers are there because they want to be. Now imagine sex that features force, violence, or unequal power. The images may be blatant, such as whips and chains; they may be subtle, such as unequal nudity or powerful and submissive positions. Whether subtle or blatant, these scenes likely have a feeling of tension, a sense of drama coming from the fact that one person is dominating another.

How do we define pornography? This is actually difficult to do. Indeed, the debate over this question has proved long and heated. Let's look to the Latin origin of the word for clues. We find *porne,* meaning a prostitute, female captive, or slave, and *graphein,* meaning to write. Note the specific gender connotations in this literal translation: the writing, or depiction, of female slaves. This definition lends itself to a contemporary definition of pornography as the portrayal of women in degrading, humiliating, violent, exploitative, and offensive sexual manners. According to this definition, porn harms women.

Some writers contrast pornography to "erotica," coming from the Greek *eros*—meaning erotic, free-will love of a consensual, reciprocating, and mutual manner. In its literal translation, erotica makes no gender distinction, and equality and consensuality are paramount. Erotica, then, is considered tasteful and artistic, not violent or degrading. And although it is sexually explicit and arousing, it is about equals. Pornography, by contrast, shows women as unequal and inferior.

But this is only one way to define pornography. There are other ways, which add to the difficulty of our task. Why is porn so difficult to define? The reason is that people object to it or support it for all sorts of reasons. Some oppose pornography based on Christian theology and argue that it corrupts minds. Others argue on a more secular ground that pornography is immoral because it influences men's behavior in bad ways. Yet others argue that it's bad because it portrays violence against women. Still others suggest that we must accept pornography as part of the societal landscape, to protect the First Amendment right to free speech. Some groups who rarely see eye-to-eye, such as right-wing women and feminists, may find a common ground over pornography. Yet other groups, such as feminists "in general," may not see eye-to-eye because their definitions of what pornography is and how we should handle it are widely different.

Antipornography feminists theorize that pornography causes rape and other forms of violence against women. Like battering and rape, pornography is about the power imbalance between women and men, and men's ability to dominate and subjugate women. These arguments are based on three beliefs:

1. Pornography both reflects and promotes male dominance in society.
2. Pornography sexually objectifies women.
3. Pornography depicts physical assaults against women, and these depictions serve as behavior models.

Some people argue that pornography is the documentation of actual crimes against women. Certainly this argument raises significant justice questions.

Themes in Pornography

Pornography presents numerous themes. They include notions such as "pain is glamorous," "women are passive," "women participate in their own victimization," and "women are dependent." Pornography also promotes the idea that it is appropriate for men to define women's behavior and sexuality (where have we heard that before?), and that men are entitled to unconditional access to women's bodies. But porn continues other themes—"visual" themes, if you will—that include the following:

- women being bound and gagged or portrayal as animals
- ambiguous facial expressions
- punishment
- men in powerful positions/women in vulnerable positions

- women completely or partially nude while men are fully clothed
- submission of women
- phallic symbols
- high heels
- women portrayed as meat

Numerous studies conducted since the mid-1960s have examined the connection between pornography and its possible harmful consequences. The Presidential Commission on Obscenity and Pornography (1971) found that pornography *does not* cause harm to women or society and urged the decriminalization of it. This report met with much criticism from those who opposed pornography. Two decades later, the Attorney General's Commission on Pornography (1986) concluded that a causal link *does* exist between certain kinds of pornography and sexually violent and abusive crimes. This report drew criticism from members of the other camp, particularly those who saw the report as too conservative and believed that it distorted the statistics.

During the 1980s, numerous studies examined the link among pornography, violence, and sex. Among the most discussed was Malamuth's findings, which linked pornography to sexual violence, and the work of Baron and Strauss, who found that rape increases in direct proportion to the circulation of men's sex magazines. Malamuth and Donnerstein's book (1984) found that after repeated exposure to pornography, viewers became desensitized to women's pain and degradation and callous toward rape and other violent acts.

Linking Pornography and Advertising

Perhaps this seems far-fetched—pornography and advertising together? There is actually a thin line between the two, and we must discuss it. Why do advertisers use women to sell sports cars? So they can have a job? Well, yes, but do they have other reasons as well? We've already discussed the idea that advertisers use sex to sell things. But in sports-car ads, how is the woman portrayed? What is she wearing? High heels? Jewelry that looks like a choker and banded wrists? Is she sitting in the car while a man is standing up and leaning over her? Recall the characteristics of pornography. We should not forget that pornography is one form of the mass media. Thus, the characteristics that we find in pornography show up in other media forms as well. Advertising, yes, but also TV, movies, videos, and so forth. Does this mean that "the media" are active participants in violence against women and their bodies? What do you think? Remember, the media are in the big business of socialization. Commercials persuade people to buy products and spend multibillions of dollars; they also sell gender stereotypes that perpetuate ideas about who women and men are. Advertisers meticulously plan the images they create, because mistakes cost money, including the use of the stereotypes to appeal to people's sense of the familiar. But what else are the media selling, or creating, or teaching, besides the familiar?

The line between pornography and advertising and, for that matter, any other form of media is thin. On television, in cartoons, videos, movies, and song, women are bound and gagged, treated as meat, shown in submissive positions in high heels, and so forth. If you take a moment to look for these details, you will be surprised by the number and nature of the pornographic images and violence against women portrayed in the U.S. media. In terms of justice in women's lives, these daily reminders of women as secondary creatures have devastating consequences.

Women Criminals, Their Bodies, Prostitution, and Violence

Given that prostitution is a criminal offense, that people disagree as to whether it should be defined as a crime, and that it has something to do with women's bodies, it seems appropriate to discuss the topic in this chapter. Prostitution is not just about women's bodies; it's also about violence and quadraplexation. Additionally, though many prostitutes spend at least short periods of time in jail, other women defined as criminals who spend time in jail and prison are beginning to discuss the violence they encounter in those institutions. Let's start with prostitution.

Prostitution: Its History and Effects

Where does the word *prostitution* come from? Some scholars suggest that it derives from the Latin *prostituere*—meaning "to cause to stand in front of." This source implies that the prostitute publicly shows and offers her body for sale. Modern commercial sex—or "sex work"—has roots in ancient Greece, where licensed brothels appeared about 500 b.c. In a more contemporary analysis of the United States, Luchetti and Olwell (1982) say that prostitution began "in earnest" in this country during the gold rush of the 1840s and 1850s. Most prostitutes in the western United States at this time were Asian (often brought to the United States by kidnappers as indentured servants), Indian, and Euro-white. Prostitutes in the south at this time tended to be black and mixed-race women. Prostitution wasn't defined by any geographical region. Historically, it has been defined as the most deviant form of behavior for women. (There's that sexuality variable!)

According to Luchetti and Olwell, prostitution fell into three status classes in the latter 1800s. The most profitable, upper-class women worked in the *class houses*. Young women worked for the madams of the houses and received substantial wages, in addition to room and board. Retention in the class houses depended on two things: physical appearance and the ability to attract and keep customers. (Talk about quadraplexation!) Failure to maintain these two standards led to discharge, and thus unemployment. If they were lucky, women discharged from class houses, and women who couldn't make it to class houses in the first place, might find residence in a *second-class house*. These jobs paid less and required more work. If a women couldn't maintain her quota in the house or if customers or the madam of the house didn't perceive her as acceptable, she went to a *corrupted boarding house* or *crib*. A cramped room with a cot and a chair, cribs were every prostitute's worst nightmare. She turned tricks on the street and brought them back to her crib, making 50 cents to a dollar for every trick. She was the one most likely to get a sexually transmitted disease, be physically attacked, or even be murdered.

Women turned to prostitution for several reasons during this era. For many, someone they trusted introduced it as a way to pay off a debt. For other women, submission to sex was directly linked to her survival; this was particularly true of black women in the South. Regardless of the reason, a prostitute was a "fallen woman." She certainly did not fit into the mold of the "true woman," as she was neither pure nor pious. Chances are, she wasn't considered domestic or submissive either.

Attitudes toward prostitution in the 1800s reflected the Madonna/ whore, Mary/Eve dichotomy. Though some writers (for example, Kingsley Davis, 1937) suggest that prostitution served to protect the family, most social commentators saw it as an evil of society. This notion showed up in the works of theorists in the latter 1800s (such as Lombroso) as well as the prostitution movements even earlier in the century. In 1832, John McDowall established the New York Magdalen Society, which distributed literature condemning prostitution. McDowell used literary sensationalism to recruit reformers to "save" prostitutes. This work, as well as the work of other reformers at the time, brought upper-class women into social-reform work. These progressives strived to save the souls of prostitutes by reforming them into "true" women.

By the 1840s, reform organizations began to recognize that women's poverty and men's exploitation of women (through pimping) were the primary causes of prostitution. Reformers argued that only economic equality would help women become self-sufficient enough that they would not have to resort to prostitution. The same argument stands today. So, members of the nineteenth-century women's movement, working largely as moral entrepreneurs, did help some women "escape" prostitution. These reformers also saw their job as protecting prostitutes from sexually transmitted diseases.

These attitudes carried into the 1900s as well. Many theorists in the past 30 years have continued to discuss the prostitute as a "whore." For example, Flexner (1969) argues that society suffers four social costs because of prostitution:

1. Personal demoralization
2. Economic waste
3. Spread of sexually transmitted diseases
4. Social disorder and crime

James's (1977) research elucidated several aspects of the U.S. economic system that make prostitution an alluring and viable alternative to women. First, prostitution offers many unskilled, semiskilled, and low-skilled women an occupation by which they can make more money than in almost any other field. Prostitution also provides adventure and allows for some degree of independence. Given the focus on women's sexuality and role in a patriarchal society, prostitution can also give women a way to act out the traditional role of woman. Finally, prostitution gives some underprivileged women the opportunity to have some privileges. Critics of James that this model ignores the harshness and violence of the average prostitute's life and lets the economic benefits of prostitution overshadow the stark realities of the work.

Some recent research finds prostitutes discussing themselves as contemporary businesswomen. Some prostitutes have created special-interest groups such as COYOTE (Cast Off Your Tired Ethics) (in San Francisco) and DOLPHIN (Dump Obsolete Laws—Prove Hypocrisy Isn't Necessary) (in Honolulu). Such organizations have strived to legitimize the decisions that prostitutes have made for themselves. These groups point out that prostitution can count among the highest paying fields available to women. Many women turn to prostitution because they can fare far better at it than they can by working a "straight" job. Yearly incomes can range from $8,000 (massage parlor) to $100,000 and more ("call girls").

Are Prostitutes Victims or Criminals?

For years, scholars and criminal justice professionals labeled prostitution a "victimless" crime. Most criminologists now call it a public-order crime—a crime which disrupts the public order. Not all scholars would agree with this definition; indeed, many feminist scholars contend that prostitution is a crime against women rather than a crime of women. Why? Well, let's consider some issues: The average age of recruitment into prostitution is 14; the average age of prostitutes is 23; and many women are "out of the life" by their late 20s. These last two facts are related to women's appearance (the quadraplexation variable of sexuality). More than 50 percent of prostitutes are runaways; about 75 percent are survivors of incest. Most come from homes where they grew up with violence and abuse. Ninety-eight percent have to answer to pimps who sexually, verbally, and physically assault them. Many are destitute, homeless, sick, and drug addicted. Feminist scholars believe that, far from James's explanations, many women enter prostitution to escape poverty and domestic violence. Though prostitutes come from all social classes, poor women and women of color are most at risk of getting pulled into the profession. Moreover, "managers" often move them from city to city on a circuit.

Much discussion has focused on the criminalization of prostitution. Should prostitution be considered a crime? Does the criminalization of prostitution only worsen women's lives? Would women be better off if prostitution were decriminalized? The San Francisco Task Force on Prostitution found that prostitution actually takes several different forms—street walking, the pornographic media industry, live theater, bordellos, and such. However, even though street prostitution comprises only 10–20 percent of all prostitution in San Francisco, it gets the most attention from politicians, police, social workers, and the media. The Task Force recommends the decriminalization of prostitution. It further suggests that city leaders take the funds they're currently using to fight prostitution and instead dedicate the money to helping those with greater needs in the community, such as the homeless. And even though both women and men participate in prostitution (men as customers and pimps), women are arrested most frequently and labeled the most deviant. Thus, while there are minimally two participants in the transaction, women bear the brunt.

Even prostitutes in parts of Nevada, where the trade is legal, do not have it easy. Although news reports often depict the brothels as clean and wholesome, many are unsafe, dirty, and unhealthy. Prostituted women are trapped in positions of virtual slavery; they are routinely raped and assaulted, but the house is paid to keep quiet.

Prostitution and the Media Image

The glorification of prostitution by the media is outrageous. Images such as Julia Roberts's *Pretty Woman* depict a life not known by the average street walker. First of all, most prostitutes do not live lives of luxury and joy. Secondly, many people consider them the scum of society; individuals who deserve their fate. They often face disrespect and pity. That's a hard line when most prostitutes turn to the trade simply to survive.

Legal and Law-Enforcement Issues

Most common law defines prostitution as "offering or agreeing to engage in, or engaging in, a sex act with another person in return for a fee." The

California Penal Code defines it as anyone "who solicits or who engages in any act of prostitution (including) lewd acts between persons for money or other consideration." Prostitution is not illegal unless state statute prohibits it. Arizona and Nevada are the only two states that leave the choice to each county rather than prohibit prostitution on a statewide level. By deciding to become a prostitute, a woman does not forfeit any constitutional or legal rights. For example, a prostitute who has been raped can bring charges (Rush, 2000).

Still, the law often shows a bias, subjecting prostitutes to more legal backlash than it does their customers. The media images of police busting up prostitution rings tend to be a lot of hype. Communities will sometimes go on community clean-up campaigns, and you'll see cops loading women into vans on the news. However, in most communities, police largely leave prostitutes alone as long as they don't cross the unwritten boundaries.

Cops tend to think of dealing with prostitutes as a boring or annoying aspect of their job. Often local law-enforcement agencies and the town's prostitutes set up a "deal," a "red-light district" where prostitutes can ply their trade. When prostitutes are arrested, the police generally release them the next morning. Most prostitutes have been arrested 30 or 40 times. Of course, the longer their record, the less likely or able they will be to return to conventional society.

International Trade

Prostitution has yet additional facets when we look at it on a global level. Numerous written and video documentaries of the horrible lives of young women trafficked forcibly from one country to another have been made. Some are kidnapped—but others are promised a better life in another country. Taken from their familiar surroundings, they become like cattle in the international sex trade. Their managers (or captors) force them to live in squalid conditions, feed them poorly, refuse them adequate medical attention, and force them to turn numerous tricks in a day for virtually no money on return. Law enforcement has had a hard time controlling this trade. Sometimes informants tip off brothels before police officers can arrive. For foreign-born women arriving in the United States, where they know little of American culture, it can be virtually impossible to escape this brutal life.

Violence and Criminal Women

Research finds that violence in the form of rape, assault, and prostitution has shaped the lives of criminal women for ages. Many women criminals have worked as prostitutes. Many women have also suffered sexual and physical abuse, whether as children or as adults. They are survivors trying to recover and move on with their lives. Estimates suggest that many young women who run away from home do so to escape abuse in their household of origin. As runaways, they become status offenders—and begin accumulating a record. Life on the streets is hard; many turn to prostitution to survive. Drugs, interpersonal violence, struggle, and hardship follow. If such a woman bears children, she now has to support them as well as herself.

The Bureau of Justice Statistics (1999) reports that, of women incarcerated in state prisons, about 60 percent describe past physical and sexual abuse, over one-third cite abuse by an intimate partner, and just under one-quarter report claim abuse by a family member. Some of these violence survivors end up in prison and jail because of the violence—battered children who batter as adults, battered women who fight back, women who assault, and so forth.

Quadraplexation and Women's Bodies and Violence

Perhaps nowhere is it more fitting to talk about quadraplexation than when we discuss women's bodies and violence. All of the issues covered in this chapter focus on women's sexuality. Even discussions of pregnancy have often centered on morality and whether a woman is moral and good enough to have children. Pornography, advertising, rape, battery—all have links to sexuality. Different people—employers, partners, capitalists, and others—use these forms of violence against women as weapons, to "sell" sex or entice men. Whether it's women trying to earn money, as in prostitution, or women staying with batterers out of economic necessity, production also plays a role. How can we not talk about economics and labor when we are also talking about women selling their bodies on film or in person? Furthermore, as a society we socialize women into a set of specific gender roles. Thus we shouldn't be surprised that some women see many of these activities as legitimate and acceptable.

The Essence of the Chapter

I often find that the topics discussed in this chapter weigh most heavily on me, because they are so poignantly personal. They can affect someone's life even if she is just sitting and listening to a discussion about them. Unlike most discussions of paid labor, education, and even poverty, discussions about women's bodies and violence often bring tears and fright. Do women have the right to control their own destiny? Their own bodies? Their own minds? Of course they do. Why society often fails to realize that these questions involve matters of life and limb is beyond me. The scholarly answer is that the patriarchal legal system—the "law as male"—fails to truly understand women's plight. There's yet another area where this lack of understanding plays a major role: what society does with women in prison. They, too, lose the right to control their own destiny, bodies, minds, and lives.

9 The Housing of Women Criminals

"In here, God knows, life is not a rose garden . . . nothing lovely flourishes here. Little that is good is nourished here. What grows here is hypocrisy, obscenity, illness, illegality, ignorance, confusion, waste, hopelessness. Life in prison is a garden of dross, cultivated by those who never check to see what their crop is."

Jean Harris

We have spent time up to this point talking about "women" and their history, rights, and so forth. But in that discussion, we made an implicit assumption. By "women," we really meant "civilian" women; that is, women who are not under the thumb of the justice system, as arrested individuals, individuals awaiting trial, or incarcerated persons. Though "civilian"women may not have perfect lives, they do live in a different world than do women under the control of the justice system. You probably noticed this while reading the section at the end of most chapters that mentioned women criminals. Generally, those discussions centered on incarcerated women. This chapter focuses on women's prisons, and the lives of the women within those walls. Throughout time, many people have thought of women criminals as the lowest of the low on the scale of humanity. Because criminality is norm-violating behavior, some individiuals see women who engage in such behavior as decidedly not "true women."

A History

The public often criticizes prisons for being too easy on women, but in reality, prison life is harsh. Some critics would say it is harsher for women than for men. Women's prisons suffer from underfunding and understaffing, much as men's prisons do. But, men's prisons were built for men. That is, the U.S. prison system was not built with women in mind—something that has important implications for how the prison system handles, treats, and assesses women. A brief history of prisons demonstrates why this is the case.

The Notion of Punishment and Prison

This book isn't about the history of corrections, so we'll keep our discussion here brief. But I hope this section will give you enough of a sense for how the U.S. prison system arrived at its current point. The idea of an "organized" correctional system is relatively new—it evolved only over the last couple of hundred years.

Before that system emerged, Western communities generally thought that people should be publicly chastised for their criminal and delinquent behavior. Thus townspeople witnessed floggings, shackling, and hangings in the city square. For the Puritan communities of the American colonies, the idea that the Devil had found his way into a person's soul justified public punishment. Community leaders often felt that people would resist Satan if they saw what came of succumbing to his temptations. These public displays of punishment were meant to deter people from engaging in behavior. Of course, not all punishments resulted in people's hanging or

---

BOX **9.1**   **Solomon on Justice**

Vengeance is the original meaning of the word *justice*. The word "justice" in the Old Testament and in Homer too virtually always refers to revenge. Throughout most of history the concept of justice has been far more concerned with the punishment of crimes and the balancing of wrongs than it has been with the fair distribution of goods and services. "Getting even" is and has always been one of the most basic metaphors of our moral vocabulary, and the frightening emotion of righteous, wrathful anger is an essential part of our emotional basis for our sense of justice, just as much as benign compassion and sympathy. Our resentment of injustice is a necessary precondition of our passion for justice, and the urge to retribution its essential consequence. "Don't get mad, get even"—whether or not prudent advice—is conceptually confused. Getting even is just an effective way of being angry, and getting angry, as Aristotle argued long ago, already includes the desire for vengeance. . . .

Robert C. Solomon, *A Passion for Justice*

beheading; some communities segregated some people from others for a period of time. The structures that held people (we now call them prisons, penitentiaries, or jails) were often not built specifically for that purpose. Rather, they were unused or abandoned buildings.

The earliest visions of a structure built to house people included the Jeremy Bentham's Panopticon and prisons described by John Howard in his book *The State of Prisons* (1777). One of the earliest classical criminologists, Bentham argued that communities should build a specific sort of building to contain wrongdoers and social undesirables. He envisioned a building three storeys high, with an open courtyard in the center and each floor visible from the courtyard. In the middle of the courtyard stood a tower with walls covered by fabric. Individuals within the tower could watch those in the outer building. Bentham felt that this "panoptic" (all-seeing) arrangement could prove useful in a variety of settings—factories, hospitals, mental institutions, children's institutions, and criminal adults' institutions. Today, most people associate the Panopticon with the housing of criminal adults.

Bentham was really describing what became the modern prison, an institution intended to deter crime among the general population. As a classical thinker, Bentham saw deterrence as the key force behind corrections—people would avoid crime if society just figured out how to deter them. Along with other classical thinkers such as Cesar Beccaria, Bentham argued that punishment of offenders should be swift, certain, and severe enough so that offenders "felt the pain" of their wrongdoing. The Panopticon itself would surely turn people away from criminal behavior. Who would want to live in an environment where someone watched them every minute of the day?

In his investigation of European prison conditions, Howard wrote that prisons should allow offenders their own cells, cleanliness and sewage, and provide sufficient food. Also, men, women, and children should all be separated from one another. This notion of segregation by prisoners' age and gender endures even today. Indeed, from the time of Howard on, women's prisons evolved as segregated institutions.

Women's Prisons

As you might have guessed from the above discussion, criminal women and men (and children) used to be housed together in one building (often an abandoned structure originally built for another purpose). When reformers such as Howard argued for segregation by age and gender, prisons began moving women out of the "big room" and into other parts of the building—often the attic, as it could hold the relatively few women prisoners. These rooms lacked light, heat, and running water.

Once installed in the attic, the women were all but forgotten. They had little contact with jailers or others, and scant opportunities to get fresh air or exercise. Prison administrators assigned them menial tasks, such as mending male prisoners' clothes. When fights broke out among the women, they had to resolve them on their own. This ignoring of women prisoners has persisted over the last two hundred years.

In the 1800s, prisons relocated women to a separate building somewhere on the grounds of the institution. Correctional philosophers touted this change as a way to keep order among the women, who then couldn't compete for the men's attention. But, once again, women found themselves in abandoned, isolated parts of the property. Jailers often ignored them or exploited them, by having them mend, sew, or garden. They were probably sexually exploited as well. The first prison in the United States devoted entirely to women was Mount Pleasant Female Prison in New York, opened in 1835. It remained the only prison for women until the 1870s.

By the mid-1800s, another reform movement gained momentum. This one originated with middle-class women who needed a productive way to spend their time. They became known as correctional reformers. They set their sights on "fallen women" who, with guidance from proper women (themselves, of course), could get back on the "right" track. Among the best known of the reformers was Elizabeth Fry, a Quaker who worked tirelessly to correct "wayward" women. Her work garnered international acclaim, and was cutting edge at the time. She, and those like her, had the time and money to work with women inmates one on one, to establish centers and programs, and to advise wardens on how to work with the women. They became know as "Lady Visitors," and they worked diligently to instill notions of true womanhood in imprisoned women. Although most female prisoners would never be able to attain such virtues, the movement took on a life of its own. Some scholars in the field would claim that it continues to affect our ideas about women in prison to this day.

This reform movement urged the complete physical separation of women prisoners from men—off to a place where women could do the work of righting themselves. Thus the women's prison was born. In 1874, the state of Indiana opened the Indiana Reformatory Institution, the first *completely separate and independent* prison for women in the United States.

Alongside this change came the advent of female personnel—Matrons—in women's prisons. Prison system administrators expected Matrons to serve as role models for inmates, to develop close relationships with them, and to teach them to be "good and true women." However, many Matrons came from similar social and educational backgrounds as the prisoners. They hailed from the working classes (that's why they had jobs in the prisons) and had little formal education. Many of them were widows. The ramifications of this reality is that although system administrators wanted the virtues of middle class womanhood taught to the inmates, they were hiring individuals who themselves didn't know what that meant.

In the 1870s, as states built additional prisons for women, these structures varied in style. Generally, though, they fell into two categories—the cottage style or the dormitory style of prison. Both styles were referred to as reformatories. The cottage style featured numerous small buildings dotting the prison grounds. Administrators and correctional philosophers intended these cottages to serve as symbols of domesticity and true womanhood— little "homes" where women could learn to be "better" mothers and so forth. These prisons provided considerable educational facilities as well. With the dormitory style, women lived in dorm-like environments but still had opportunity to learn the art of homemaking. Not all women were considered reform material. Some women were considered criminal "to the core" and thus were lost souls. Yet the reformers had faith that many women were indeed "savable."

By the early 1900s, however, the idea behind reform for women faded. War, alcohol, the Great Depression—all of these developments and more turned attention away from such institutions. Administrators tightened the rules in women's prisons, revoked opportunities, and cut budgets. Reformatories became custodial institutions—more like today's prisons than reform centers. This decline of the women's-prison movement continued until the 1960s, when once again discussion about women's issues rose to the surface of U.S. society.

Contemporary Life in Women's Prisons

Perhaps because of the reformatory age, many view women's prisons today as "cushy" compared to men's prisons. But as the rest of this chapter reveals, being a woman in a U.S. prison is anything but "cushy."

The Daily Grind

The number of women in U.S. federal and state correctional institutions has reached an all-time high—78,000 on any given day. Another 60,000 women are in county and city jails. These numbers total about 6 percent of the U.S. prison population. Most of these women have children. Many of them are women of color. Racial or ethnic discrimination makes their prison experience even more difficult. Owing to language and cultural barriers between prisoners and their keepers, conflicts erupt over food, cultural practices, and the like. Moreover, correctional programming—educational, vocational, psychological, and so forth—rarely addresses the needs and problems of incarcerated women. The reasons that may have affected why she ended up in prison in the first place—inadequate education or income, mental health or relationships issues, and so forth—are rarely dealt with satisfactorily within the institution. These issues are discussed later in the chapter. When women finish serving their time, many of them are even less equipped than male ex-cons to earn a living and support a family.

Regardless of how we might feel about "criminals," prison is harsh. Inmates can't go to the fridge for a snack, take a shower whenever they want, get an aspirin for a headache out of the medicine cabinet. Officers constantly monitor conversations. Going to KMart is out of the question, and figuring out what to have for dinner doesn't cross one's mind. Generally, inmates rise for breakfast at 5:30 or 6:00 A.M., and stand ready for their first "count" by 6:30 or 7:00. Their day continues in this ritualized, controlled cycle until bedtime and last count.

In his survey of 304 women in a southern prison, Stevens (1998) found that the goals of women inmates change over time. For example, whereas independence counted as most women's second highest goal before incarceration, it was their highest goal after incarceration (41 percent and 56 percent, respectively)—not a surprising finding. Financial security, something many incarcerated women have never known, was important to only 18 percent of respondents before incarceration but became a primary concern after incarceration for 41 percent of respondents. Doubtless, financial independence has a direct link to general independence. In other words, women certainly learn lessons while in prison, though not necessarily the ones we might expect.

Number of Women's Prisons

Most states have just one women's prison. One. Even with the enormous acceleration of prison building in this country over the last 20 years, most prisons are built for men. This reflects the invisibility of the female inmate. Lack of facilities means all sorts of other "lacks"—in education, medical support, access, and so forth. Read on to find out more. . . .

Location of Women's Prisons

Besides being scarce, most women's prisons—are located in rural, isolated places. That may not seem like a big deal to most of us, but it is to an incarcerated woman. Let's say you're the woman. The state you live in has only one institution, and it is located in the rural, southern part of the state. But you're from the northern part of the state. What are your chances of seeing your kids? Moreover, what kinds of programs might that prison offer? What kinds of opportunities might you have to do community-based rehabilitation work?

Grading and Policies

The term "grading" in relation to prisons refers to what most people think of as maximum, medium, or minimum security. Most U.S. women's prisons are graded as minimum security. Some are medium security; newer ones may have a maximum-security wing. This grading system poses a problem: In states that have just one institution for women, all female prisoners— regardless of their crime—go to the same place. There, they are subjected to rules made to cover the behavior of all women prisoners.

As a result, most women's prisons have an extraordinary number of rules, both trivial and serious, to govern all inmates' behavior. Although female inmates are less likely to be violent than male inmates, they are more likely to be sanctioned for rule violations. McClellan (1994) found that women were "written up" for "drying their underwear, talking while waiting in lines, displaying family photographs, and failing to eat all the food on their plates." Men are not typically sanctioned for such things. Contraband and bad behavior in a women's prison can include lighting another woman's cigarette, borrowing someone's comb, and having an extra bra. Indeed, the policies in women's prisons often treat inmates as if they were children (Belknap, 1996). Furthermore, prison personnel use inmates' rule-violating behavior as a way to control their access to family visitation, which already constitutes a problem for many incarcerated women (see below). Thus, it appears that women prisoners break rules more often than men, *But,* it is often the number of rules they must conform to that generates this impression.

Mothers and Motherhood

The majority of women in prison (75–80 percent) have children. Of these roughly eighty thousand women, 70 percent have children under the age of 18 (which amounts to about 200,000 youngsters). By contrast, 50 percent of men in prison are fathers. These parenthood differences sharply delineate female and male prisoners. Visitors, employees, and the inmates themselves can *feel* the presence of kids in women's institutions, but not in men's institutions. The feeling may be physical or emotional, but the children are there in spirit. This difference has everything to do with reproduction and socialization. Most of us identify women as the primary caretakers of children—and women in prison feel this responsibility. As Byrne-Pollack (1990, p. 129) notes, the "loss of children is cause for acute worry and depression" among incarcerated women. These inmates carry much guilt for missing a lot of their children's lives. They also know or find out quickly that all states have laws permitting the termination of prisoners' parental rights (Amnesty International, 1999a).

Studies have also found that many women in prison tend to hold traditional ideas about women's roles; this too would suggest that they feel deeply concerned about their children. Because of their status, women offenders face unique social and legal problems regarding their children.

What happens to kids whose moms are in prison? About 25 percent of them live with their other parent, about 50 percent live with maternal grandparents, another 20 percent live with other relatives, and the rest live with friends, in foster care, or in some other setting. Only about 50 percent of mothers in prison retain legal custody of their children. Those who lose custody feel a profound hollowness. In a survey of 150 female inmates in Ohio, Hungerford (1996) found that 75 percent of them were generally satisfied with the living situation of their children while they were in prison. Most (86 percent) of the children were living within an extended kin network, and only 10 percent were in the formal custody of the state. Often family members of the incarcerated women stepped forward and offered to take their children.

However, such generosity does not always come out of love and respect for the imprisoned mother. Hungerford found that many caregivers were angry and upset with the mother for ending up in prison. Many caregivers must change their lifestyle significantly to care for the child or children, and often face new financial pressures in fulfilling their promise. The resulting resentment and hostility prompts some caregivers to withhold child visitation. Fewer than one-half of imprisoned mothers with custody see their children regularly. The visits are often sad occasions, held in large, public rooms, and constantly monitored. Though some institutions have created bright, public rooms with toys for children, most meeting spaces are stark.

Children of incarcerated women suffer from maladies often associated with separation from their mother—psychological, physical, emotional, and academic problems. Such problems count among the hidden costs of incarceration (Dressel, Porterfield, & Barnhill, 1998). They include, but are not limited to, bed wetting, poor school performance, depression, early pregnancy, poverty, and substance abuse. Many mothers feel anxious, depressed, or ashamed in explaining to their children why they can't be with them. States have typically done little to remedy this problem. That is too bad, for maintaining strong family ties during incarceration decreases recidivist rates and motivates women to succeed in prison (Amnesty International, 1999a). Women rarely get help with this situation from the men in their lives. Husbands, boyfriends, and brothers often drop women quickly after the women end up in prison; visiting day at a women's prison is a virtually all-female affair (Church, 1990). Contrast this to visiting day at men's prisons, when wives and girlfriends line up. I would argue that this is another example of patriarchy at work.

The news for women prisoners is not all bad. Institutions have established different kinds of visitation programs so that mothers and children can spend time together. Shakopee Institute for Women in Minnesota has a separate building in which women and their children can be together in a somewhat homelike setting for up to several days. This kind of program helps maintain the bond between child and mother and alleviate the problems that separation creates. Other programs that strengthen family ties include the Elizabeth Fry Center in San Francisco and the Massachusetts Houston House.

Physical and Mental Health

Health care in women's prisons often relies heavily on part-time staff doctors and mental-health professionals. The most common problems in a women's prison are gynecological, but prisons rarely have a gynecologist on staff. Women must convince a guard that they are sick enough to see a doctor, and then must wait days or weeks for an appointment. No more than half of U.S. prisons offer gender-specific health care such as mammograms and Pap smears (Amnesty International, 1999a). Sadly, HIV/AIDS is a growing problem among women in prison; there are reportedly more than two thousand HIV-positive women in prison who don't receive effective health care or treatment.

Inadequate care poses especially serious problems for pregnant women who don't receive adequate prenatal attention. Furthermore, many jails and prisons transport women out of the prison to a hospital for birthing. Prison officials shackle the women to the transport vehicle and then to the hospital bed, right up until and during labor.

Prisons often skimp on mental-health care as well. If women complain about "nerves" (anxiety and depression), physicians or physician's assistants give them drugs such as Valium. Prisons find it much easier to hand out medication than to treat the real causes of anxiety and depression. Indeed, many women in prisons are drugged specifically to keep them quiet, which seriously hampers their mental and physical functioning. Some prisons put women in isolation cells as a form of treatment for mental health issues, but don't provide accompanying therapy. Numerous women in prison are interested in forms of therapy—individual as well as group counseling. Parenting classes and other forms of psychological training—such as Alcoholics Anonymous or Narcotics Anonymous—would benefit the recovery and reformation of women inmates. A 1998 study by the National Institute of Corrections found that only 27 departments of corrections reported offering substance-abuse programs for women. Only 19 had domestic-violence programs, nine offered programs for rape survivors, and nine provided programs for women's health education.

BOX **9.2**   **Platforms against Women's Discrimination**

Check these out. . . . (All can be found at the Web site for the
United Nations: www.un.org)

Beijing Declaration and Platform for Action

Convention against Torture and Other Cruel, Inhuman or Degrading Treatment
or Punishment

International Covenant on Civil and Political Rights (ICCPR)

International Convention on the Elimination of All Forms of Racial Discrimination (CERD)

Convention on the Elimination of All Forms of Discrimination Against Women (CEDAW)

Certainly physical-health care and perhaps mental-health care evoke the sameness/difference debate. Men do not need the same kinds of physical-health care that women need. Therefore, sameness/difference is not about receiving the same things; it is about receiving services based on the individual needs of the genders.

Violence Within the Institution

Women's prisons tend to witness much less violence than men's prisons do. Fights between inmates do break out, and other sorts of violent altercations occur. However, for the most part, hard-core violence in women's prisons does not take place between or among the prisoners. As Friedman (1995) writes,

> In 20 years, I've seen a dozen women who really scared me. . . . The rest may be frustrated as hell, and they may make a lot of noise, but they're not violent the way men are. . . . No serious student of crime or criminal justice has the slightest doubt that women, in general, just do not go in for serious crimes, especially crimes of bodily harm, of violence, of bloodshed (p. 234).

So where is the violence? Most often, it erupts between the prisoners and those who guard them. Men make up about 40 percent of the guards in women's prisons; until recently, other guards, administrators, and even some inmates have largely ignored their behavior. We assume that because these women are in prison, male guards have the right to search them, strip-search them, and monitor their every action. The problem is that some guards step over their boundaries.

Innumerable reports about male guards' abuse of women in prisons and jails have come to the public's attention recently. One of the most informative reports was published by Amnesty International (1999b). *Not Part of My Sentence: Violations of the Human Rights of Women in Custody* contains cases documenting male guards' sexual and physical abuse of incarcerated women. The stories are horrible, and some of them have resulted in lawsuits against specific guards, wardens, and departments of corrections. Sadly, some women inmates do not report such behavior for fear of retaliation; they are, after all, captives. What kinds of behavior are we talking about? Rape, gang rape, male prisoners playing guards to let them rape women prisoners (in the few co-ed prisons in the United States), stripping women nude and watching them in their cells, the conducting of endless "gynecological exams." The civilian world abhors such behavior but has ignored it in our prisons. Inefficient investigative and grievance procedures only make matters worse. Correctional employees rarely worry about losing their job or even being held accountable. Thus the behavior is largely invisible.

Emotionality

Another big difference between women's and men's institutions relates to emotions. Women tend to be more emotional than men in prison; they exhibit more mood swings, develop greater attachments to other inmates, put more effort into expressing their feelings. Research has found that many women inmates tend to internalize messages that devalue them. Hence they think of themselves as irrational, immoral, overly emotional, dependent, and submissive (Ogle, Katkin, & Bernard, 1995). Doubtless these thoughts influence their emotional state as well.

Education and Vocational Training

Though an inverse relationship exists between education received in prison and recidivism, women's prisons do not offer extensive educational experiences. Nearly all correctional institutions provide basic education courses, and over half offer some college courses (generally at the associate level, or A.A.). However, many inmates need to get their GED, or learn to read, before they can try their hand at the college-level classes.

In addition to inadequate education, most women's prisons provide only gender-specific vocational training. Women learn skills that place them in low-paying "women's work"—cosmetology, cooking, clerical jobs, and so forth. These programs are not meeting the socioeconomic needs of prisoners, and probably will not help them on the road to financial independence—a goal that becomes critical to them during incarceration. Institutions that have offered nontraditional programming—construction and electrical training, for example—find that female inmates do not prefer them. Interestingly, many women inmates possess traditional ideas about "femaleness"; such ideas do not support training in nontraditional fields such as construction or electrical work. To help these women, programs need to support them and their children once they leave prison. Feinman (1994) and others have pointed out that rehabilitation programs in women's institutions conform to white, middle-class cultural expectations. These programs' designers assume that women should learn how to become "good little wives and mothers"; a legacy of the "Lady Visitors," true womanhood, and assumptions about separate spheres. However, most of these women will never achieve this kind of middle-class life. Why? Because the reality of social class in the United States is that although many people are upwardly mobile, that mobility is minimal. The likelihood of poor women who are ex-convicts reaching middle-class status is quite slim. They may become working-class folks but that, too, is different from the middle class. It is a failure on the part of the correctional system, and the criminal-justice system in general, not to work toward programming that would benefit women prisoners in the long run. Often, policy makers justify inadequate programming for financial reasons; that is, it costs too much. But in reality, a little "front-end work" in the prisons would lower the rate of recidivism. Education and training save money in the long run.

Here's a final irony: Instead of putting money into educational and vocational training, prisons let women remain idle and grow bored. Because most prisons lack recreational facilities, they offer women board games and television instead. No matter how much you might like Monopoly, imagine playing it all day, every day—for years.

The Essence of the Chapter

The history of women's prisons and their inmates is one of neglect and invisibility. Whether we are discussing the development of the prison system and women's place in it, or the treatment of women prisoners yesterday and today, the criminal-justice system has struggled with issues of sameness and difference. Initially treating women the "same," the system lumped them togther with men and children. But once the idea of "difference" gained currency, no one followed it up with a clear discussion of women's unique needs when they are in prison. Except for the reformers—middle-class white women who felt they had it figured out—both prison administrators and policy makers have seen women as a negligible part of the system. In actuality, the system could learn something if it would only listen: Why do women constitute only 20 percent of those arrested and 6 percent of those incarcerated? Why do women engage in so much less criminality than men? I've raised these questions before, but they must be asked again over and over—until we identify some answers.

Quadraplexation offers a powerful analysis here. All four of its variables can help us understand something about women prisons and could help us structure a better prison system for them. *Production*—women's labor—often has direct links to why women end up in prison in the first place. Marginal jobs, often characterized as "women's work," do not support most women and their families. In prison, training women to master more productive, self-sufficient economic roles would better their and their families' position.

Reproduction is also a primary issue. Most women in prison are mothers, yet we punish them for having a hairbrush and do not let them see their children. We must formulate a better family policy, or what Dressel, Porterfield, and Barnhill (1998) call a "family-success paradigm."

Sexuality has defined women criminals from the beginning. Because society considers non-normative women of any kind "sluts" and "whores," *legally* non-normative women fall into the same boat. Furthermore, many theories about women's criminality centers on sexuality.

Finally, *socialization* as a quadraplexation variable tells us much about what incarcerated women desire—their families, traditional roles and jobs, a sense of femininity, and—something most of us want—self-respect.

10 Closing Remarks

Let's start this final chapter by revisiting our original question: What is justice? To answer this question, recall all the different definitions of justice that this book has touched on. What, if anything, do they have in common? What do they not have in common?

Miller (1976) believes that we can discuss the notion of justice only if three conditions are met. Outside of these conditions, something cannot be considered "just" or "unjust." The three conditions are:

1. There are at least two living, breathing people involved in a situation.
2. One person is carrying a burden, while the other is not.
3. That burden was created by human beings.

In other words, Miller sees justice as something within human control.

Rousseau (1990) conceives of two kinds of inequality, one that is "natural" or "physical," and one that is a "moral" or "political inequality." We can't do anything about the first one, because people are born with it; "the consent of men" authorizes the second one. This latter kind of inequality stems from "different privileges enjoyed by some at the expense if others." In other words, like Miller, Rousseau sees justice as something that human beings create and can control.

Mill (1990) suggests that it is "unjust to deprive anyone of [his] personal liberty, [his] property, or any other thing which belongs to [him] by law." And if the law does deprive one of such things, "the law . . . may be a bad law" (p. 195). And because human beings create laws, Mill also sees justice as something that lies within our control.

Sandel (1990) believes that "the principles of justice are the products of choice" (p. 138), and that such choices derive from the acceptance of moral principles. Because we humans identify moral principles and agree on them, Sandel, too, sees justice as coming under human control.

Hobbes (1990) discusses the difference between the justice of manners and the justice of actions. "The injustice of manners is the disposition or aptitude to do injury" (p. 90) and causes harm even before any physical injury results from it. Injust actions may be directed at a certain individual, but they often hurt others as well. Whether we are discussing injustice of manners or actions, humans engage in both, and both affect other humans. Therefore, Hobbes sees justice as something that humans create and can control.

Wolgast (1990) argues, "We imagine that justice is an ideal or standard from which injustice departs" (p. 348). She disagrees and instead urges us to consider "justice" in a broader context. She suggests "looking not at the concept by itself but more broadly at its grammar, at the ways and contexts in which justice is invoked" (p. 348). The ways justice is invoked . . . by humans.

Von Hayak (1990) asserts that "the initial chances of different individuals are often very different; they are affected by circumstances of their physical and social environment which are beyond their control but in many particular respects might be altered by some governmental action" (p. 219). Human creation and control, again.

Rawls (1990) purports, "Justice is to be understood in its customary sense as representing but one of the many virtues of social institutions" (p. 125), institutions created by humans for humans. "Justice is not to be confused with an all-inclusive vision of a good society; it is only one part of any such conception" (p. 125); society, after all, creates justice.

The commonality? It appears that humans may create justice or injustice. Thus, if we are talking about women and (in)justice, we are addressing something that humans have constructed together. It would stand to reason, then, that we could deconstruct it and put it back together in a different way. We've discussed many instances of injustice in this book; how might we remake it and thus transform it into justice?

This book has attempted to bring together the civil and criminal-justice issues that affect women's lives. I have woven the following ideas throughout:

1. Women's lives are powerfully affected by the social conditions, ideas, and people in place at any given time. Some eras are more or less conservative or liberal than other eras. Ideas and legal changes during such times reflect those qualities. Social change does not occur in a vacuum.

2. Women's lives are affected by the four quadraplexation variables of production, reproduction, sexuality, and socialization. This is true whether we are talking about paid labor or pornography, motherhood or sexual harassment.

3. All women, whether they like to believe it or not, are affected by the social and legal changes of the past *and* the practices of today. Individuals today may think that they haven't experienced discrimination, for example. But if their sisters have, then *all* women have been affected.

4. Women must keep trying to change the inequities and injustices which remain in society.

Let's revisit Otten's questions about the law (and justice) that we saw in Chapter 2:

1. Has U.S. law protected the interests of the powerful (men) from the powerless (women)?
2. The "primary thrust of our law is the promise to protect each person. . . ." Has U.S. law kept this promise to women?
3. How effective is the law as a tool of redress for women?

How would you answer these questions after reading this book? I would argue that although some loosening of the laws and case decisions regarding gender has occurred in the last several decades, much work remains. Witness the ongoing struggles that battered women and rape survivors face, the continuing episodes of sexual harassment, and poor women's struggle with rules concerning social welfare programs. All of these realities reveal a system that protects men's interests much more than women's. All of the quadraplexation variables are at work here. Men (the powerful) protect their interests over women (the powerless) by using sexuality as a weapon, by reinforcing patriarchal teachings about socialization, by enforcing notions regarding work (production) and reproduction so that they (men) may keep their privileged place(s) in society.

Thus on some levels the law has not kept its promise to protect people, especially women. Granted, some women benefit more from the law than other women do. However, both advantage and disadvantage have accumulated. All women are harmed by laws that fail to protect every woman. Of course, there is an interesting play on words here, because "protection" often translates into "restriction." In this paragraph, however, it represents a positive—watching out for women's interests and lives, and keeping them truly safe and well.

Finally, the law has a spotty record as a tool of redress. It took until *Reed v. Reed* (1971) before women could use an equal-protection argument to their benefit. Other case decisions and statutes have recognized that women's rights were violated. On the other hand, many rape survivors would say that their second raping by the justice system is hardly an adequate tool of redress. The law needs some work. We must keep trying.

I would suggest we can use quadraplexation to create new policies and laws. Whether we are examining women in prison, poor women, women on the job, or women in school, we must keep these variables in mind and *use them as a guideline*. For example, we know that women in prison face many inadequacies; if we compare them to men in prison, the inadequacies become even more apparent. How can we use quadraplexation to help women in prison? Well, we know that female inmates' educational and vocational training opportunities are poorer than men's. We also believe that women who hold well-paying jobs engage in crime less frequently. Providing better training for women behind bars would help society; better-trained individuals mean lower recidivist rates—we all win.

Women in prison need better parenting classes, more positive time with their children while they are in prison, more help in strengthening their relationships with their children. Controlling women in prison should not cost children—society, women, and kids all lose out in that situation. Women in prison must also be able to feel safe with their sexuality in prison. Prison rape and unwanted pregnancy should never occur. If it does, courts and administrators should hold perpetrators accountable (and should be held accountable themselves).

Family, friends, and the media have socialized many women in prison into traditional roles; education can help move them out of this mind set. We need to empower women to realize their own self-worth, and to know that their worth does not stem solely from physical attractiveness and sensuality but from who they are and what they do with their lives. If prisons can provide adequate educational and vocational training that helps women support themselves and their families, then socialization training may well change automatically. Though there is nothing wrong with choosing to value traditional images of womanhood, women in prison must also realize that they need to support themselves. Some gendered attitudes can make that difficult.

We can also use quadraplexation to construct new social and legal policy—if we choose. Again, because we ourselves create justice, we *can* choose the new path. We can engage in the same kind of analysis for all the different topics we've discussed in this book *and* deisgn policies to change current circumstances—if we choose.

A lovely book by Donna Jackson, *How to Make the World a Better Place for Women in Five Minutes a Day*, can assist in bringing quick justice to women's lives while we continue the work to change legal and social policies. Jackson offers quick suggestions we can actively engage in while we go about our daily lives. They include things like:

- Stick a "This Insults Women" sticker on sexist posters and ads.
- Start a phone tree for family (and women) friendly laws.
- Put up a poster on harassment.
- Don't ignore sexist slurs.
- Go to women headhunters who help break the glass ceiling.
- Make sure the local PTA owns the film *Shortchanging Girls, Shortchanging America*.

We can remake the social structures that harm women. Government policy, segregated labor markets, gendered family roles and lives, subtle and blatant discrimination—these are just a few examples of how we have socially created injustice. But we can make changes—and we must keep trying.

Peace.

BIBLIOGRAPHY

Adler, F. 1975. *Sisters in Crime*. New York: McGraw-Hill.

Agonito, R. 1988. *History of Ideas on Woman: A Sourcebook*. New York: Perigree Books/ G.P. Putnum's Sons.

Allen, D. W. 1992. Marriage and divorce: Comment. *American Economic Review*, 82(3), 679–686.

American Association of University Women. 1991. *Shortchanging Girls, Shortchanging America*. Washington, DC: AAUW.

American Association of University Women. 1998. *Gender Gaps: Where Schools Still Fail Our Children*. Washington, DC: AAUW.

American Bar Association. 2000. *A Snapshot of Women in the Law in the Year 2000*. abanet.org/women/snapshots.pdf.

American Bar Association: Committee on Women in the Profession. 2000. *Goal IX Update: An Annual Report on Women's Advancement into Leadership Positions in the ABA*. Washington, DC: ABA.

Amnesty International. 1999(a). *Interact: A Bulletin about Women's Human Rights*. Spring. New York: Amnesty International USA.

Amnesty International. 1999(b). *Not Part of My Sentence: Violations of the Human Rights of Women in Custody*. March. New York: Amnesty International.

Andersen, M. A. 2000. *Thinking About Women: Sociological Perspectives on Sex and Gender*, Fifth Edition. Boston: Allyn and Bacon.

Aries, P. 1962. *Centuries of Childhood*. New York: Vintage.

Baer, J. A. 1992. How Is Law Male: A Feminist Perspective on Constitutional Interpretation. In L. F. Goldstein, (Ed.), *Feminist Jurisprudence: The Difference Debate*. Lanham: Rowman & Littlefield. pp. 147–171.

Barash, D. 1982. *Sociobiology and Behavior*, Second Edition. London: Hodder and Stroughton.

Baron, A. 1987. Feminist Legal Strategies: The Powers of Difference. In B. B. Hess and M. M. Ferree (Eds.), *Analyzing Gender: A Handbook of Social Science Research*. Newbury Park: Sage. pp. 474–503.

Bartfield, J. 2000 (May). Child Support and the Postdivorce Economic Well-Being of Mothers, Fathers and Children. *Demography*, 37(2), 203

Beccaria, C. 1963. *Essays on Crimes and Punishments*. Translated, with an introduction by Henry Paolucci. Indianapolis: Duxbury Press.

Becker, H. S. 1963. *Outsiders: Studies in the Sociology of Deviance*. New York: Free Press.

Becker, M. 1992. Prince Charming: Abstract Equality. In L. F. Goldstein (Ed.), *Feminist Jurisprudence: The Difference Debate*. Lanham: Rowman & Littlefield. pp. 99–146.

Belknap, J. 1996. *The Invisible Woman: Gender, Crime and Justice*. Belmont: Wadsworth.

Beneke, T. 1982 . *Men on Rape*. New York: St. Martin's Press.

Benston, M. 1969. The Political Economy of Women's Liberation. *Monthly Review*, 21, 13–27.

Bentham, J. 1789. *An Introduction to the Principles of Morals and Legislation*. New York: Oxford University Press.

Blackstone, W. E. 1999 (1766). Of the Nature of Laws in General, Book I, Section II. In H. Broom and E. A. Hadley (Eds.), *Commentaries on the Laws of England*. Holmes Beah: Gaunt.

Cavan, R. S. and J. T. Cavan. 1968. *Delinquency and Crime: Cross-Cultural Perspectives*. Philadelphia: Lippincott.

Chambliss, W. J. 1973. The Saints and the Roughnecks. *Society*, 11, 24–31.

Church, G. J. 1990. The View from Behind Bars: The Number of Women Inmates Tripled in the Past Decade. *Time*, 136(19), 20–23.

Collins, S. D. 2000 (September). Washington's New Poor Law: Welfare "Reform's" Legacy and Real Welfare Reform. *Uncommon Sense*, 23.

Commission on Obscenity and Pornography. 1971. *Report of the Presidential Commission on Obscenity and Pornography*. Washington, DC: Government Printing Office.

Crittendon, A. 2001. *The Price of Motherhood: Why the Most Important Job in the World Is Still the Least Valued*. New York: Metropolitan Books.

Current Issues in the Operation of Women's Prisons. 1998. Boulder: National Institute of Corrections.

Dataline. 1991. *The Three Levels of the Glass Ceiling: Through the Looking Glass*. San Fransisco: Dataline. http://www.cyberwerks.com:70/0h/dataline.mapping/thethree.html.

Davis, A. 1983. *Women, Race and Class*. New York: Vintage Books.

Davis, A. 1989. *Women, Culture and Politics*. New York: Random House.

Davis, K. 1937. The Sociology of Prostitution. *American Sociological Review*, 2, 744–755.

DeKeseredy, W. S. 2000. *Women, Crime and the Canadian Criminal Justice System*. Cincinnati: Anderson Publishing Co.

Dressel, P., J. Porterfield, and S. K. Barnhill. 1998 (December). Mothers Behind Bars. *Corrections Today*, 60, 90–95.

Dusky, L. 1996. *Still Unequal: The Shameful Truth about Women and Justice in America*. New York: Crown Publishers.

Dworkin, R. 1998. Natural Law and Legal Reasoning. In S. Brewer (Ed.), *Moral Theory and Legal Reasoning*. New York: Garland Press. pp. 79–94.

Feinman, C. 1994. *Women in the Criminal Justice System*, Third Edition. Westport: Praeger.

Firestone, S. 1970. *The Dialectic of Sex*. New York: Morrow.

Flexner, A. 1969. *Prostitution in Europe*. Montclair: Patterson Smith.

Fox, G. L. 1977. Nice Girl: Social Control of Women through a Value Construct. *Signs*, 2(4), 805–817.

Friedman, L. 1995 (February 20). As quoted in T. Albor and B. Gage, The Women Get Chains . . . No Family Values Here. *The Nation*, 234–238.

Garrison, M. 1990. The Economics of Divorce: Changing Rules, Changing Results. In S. D. Sugarman and H. H. Kay (Eds.), *Divorce Reforms at the Crossroads*. New Haven: Yale University Press. pp. 30–43.

Gatland, L. 1997 (April). Putting the Blame on No-Fault. *ABA Journal*, 83, 50–54.

Giallombardo, R. 1966. *Society of Women: A Study of a Women's Prison*. New York: Wiley.

Glenn, N. 1999 (August). Further Discussion on the Effects of No-Fault Divorce on Divorce Rates. *Journal of Marriage and the Family* 61(3), 800–803.

Glueck, S. and E. Glueck. 1934. *Five Hundred Delinquent Women*. New York: A. A. Knopf.

Goffman, E. 1979. *Gender Advertisements*. New York: Harper and Row.

Goldstein, L. F. 1992. *Feminist Jurisprudence: The Difference Debate*. Lanham: Rowman & Littlefield.

Gordon, L. 1994. Heroes of Their Own Lives: The Politics and History of Family Violence: Boston 1880–1960. In A. Jones (Ed.), *Next Time She'll Be Dead: Battering and How to Stop It*. Boston: Beacon Press. pp. 96–97.

Graglia, C. 1995 (Spring). The Housewife as Pariah. *Harvard Journal of Law and Public Policy,* 18(2), 509–521.

Grall, T. 2000. *Child Support for Custodial Mothers and Fathers 1997.* Current Population Reports. Washington, DC: U.S. Census Bureau.

Grana, S. and J. Ollenburger. 1999. *The Social Context of Law*. Upper Saddle River: Prentice Hall.

Greenfield, L. A. and T. L. Snell. 1999. *Bureau of Justice Statistics Special Report: Women Offenders*. U.S. Department of Justice. Washington, DC: Bureau of Justice Statistics. NCJ 175688.

Greif, G. L. and M. S. Pabst. 1988. *Mothers Without Custody*. Lexington, MA: Lexington Books/D.C. Heath and Co.

Griffin, S. 1986. *Rape: The Politics of Consciousness*. San Francisco: Harper and Row.

Groth, N. 1990. *Men Who Rape: The Psychology of the Offender*. New York: Plenum Press.

Hamner, J. and M. Maynard. 1987. *Women, Violence and Social Control*. Atlantic Highlands: Humanities Press International.

Harris, J. 1991. *Marking Time: Letters from Jean Harris to Shana Alexander*. New York: Scribner's.

Hartmann, H. K. Allen and C. Owens. 1999. *Equal Pay for Working Families*. A joint research project of the AFL-CIO and the Women's Policy Research Institute. Washington, DC: IWPR.

Headlee, S. and M. Elfin. 1996. *The Cost of Being Female*. Westport: Praeger.

Herrerias, C. 1995 (Spring). Noncustodial Mothers Following Divorce. *Marriage & Family Review,* 20(1), 233–256.

Hobbes, T. 1990. The Leviathan. In R. C. Solomon and M. C. Murphy (Eds.), *What Is Justice? Classic and Contemporary Readings*. New York: Oxford University Press. pp. 80–92.

Hohengarten, W. M. 1994 (April). Same Sex Marriage and the Right of Privacy. *Yale Law Journal,* 103(6), 1495–1531.

Howard, J. 1957 (1777). *State of Prisons*. London: Dent and Sons.

Hungerford, G. P. 1996 (Summer–Fall). Caregivers of Children Whose Mothers Are Incarcerated: A Study of the Kinship Placement System. *Children Today*, 24(1), 23–28.

Hunter, N. 1983. Child Support and Policy: The Systematic Imposition of Costs on Women. *Harvard Women's Law Journal,* (1), 2–27.

Jackson, D. 1992. *How to Make the World a Better Place for Women in Five Minutes a Day*. New York: Hyperion.

Jacobson, J. L. 1992. Gender Bias: Roadblock to Sustainable Development. *World Watch Paper* No. 110, pp. 5–60. Washington, DC: World Watch Institute.

James, J. 1977. *The Politics of Prostitution: Resources for Legal Change.* Seattle: Social Research Associates.

Jones, A. 1994. *Next Time She'll be Dead: Battering and How to Stop It.* Boston: Beacon Press.

Kappeler, V. E ., M. Blumberg, and G. W. Potter. 1996. *The Mythology of Crime and Criminal Justice,* Second Edition. Prospect Heights: Waveland Press, Inc.

Karlsen, C. 1987. *The Devil in the Shape of a Woman: Witchcraft in Colonial New England.* New York: Norton.

Kellman, S. 1995. Child Custody and Support: Does the System Serve the Children's Best Interest? *CQ Researcher, 5*(2), 27–43.

Kennedy, F. 1972. *Pathology of Oppression.* Sound recording. University of Iowa Lecture Series.

Kerber, L. K. and J. S. DeHart. 2000. *Women's America: Refocusing the Past,* Fifth Edition. New York: Oxford University Press.

Lemert, E. M. 1951. *Social Pathology.* New York: McGraw-Hill.

Leonard, E. 1995. Theoretical Criminology and Gender. In B. R. Price and N. J. Sokoloff (Eds.), *The Criminal Justice System and Women: Offenders, Victims and Workers.* New York: McGraw-Hill. pp. 54–70.

Lindgren, R. and N. Taub. 1993. *The Law of Sex Discrimination,* Second Edition. Minneapolis: West Publishing.

Littleton, C. 1987. Rethinking or Reconstructing Sexual Equality. *California Law Review,* 75, 201.

Littleton, C. 1993. Reconstructing Sexual Equality. In P. Smith (Ed.), *Feminist Jurisprudence.* New York: Oxford University Press. pp. 110–135.

Lombroso, C. 1920 (1895). *The Female Offender.* New York: Appleton.

Luchetti, C. and C. Olwell. 1982. *Women of the West.* New York: Orion.

Lyons, N. 1993. Women's Education. In R. Lindgren and N. Taub (Eds.) *The Law of Sex Discrimination,* Second Edition. Minneapolis: West Publishing. pp. 264–267.

MacKinnon, C. 1979. *Sexual Harassment of Working Women.* Cambridge: Harvard University Press.

MacKinnon, C. 1983. Feminism, Marxism, Method and the State: Toward Feminist Jurisprudence. *Signs,* 8(2), 644.

MacKinnon, C. 1993. Sexual Harassment: Its First Decade in Court. In P. Smith (Ed.), *Feminist Jurisprudence.* New York: Oxford University Press. pp.145–157.

Malamuth, N. M. and E. I. Donnerstein. 1984. *Pornography and Sexual Aggression.* Orlando: Academic Press.

Margolis, M. L. 2000. *True to Her Nature: Changing Advice to American Women.* Prospect Heights: Waveland.

Martin, S. 1989. *Women on the Move? The Status of Women in Policing.* Washington, DC: Police Foundation.

McBride, A. 1973. *The Growth and Development of Mothers.* New York: Harper and Row.

McCaughey, M. *Rape Culture.* Via private email correspondence. Spring, 1998.

McClellan, D. 1994. Disparity in the Discipline of Male and Female Inmates in Texas Prisons. *Women and Criminal Justice,* 5, 71–97.

Merlo, A. V. and J. M. Pollack. 1995. *Women, Law and Social Control.* Boston: Allyn and Bacon.

Merton, R. K. 1938. Social Structure and Anomie. *American Sociological Review,* 3, 672–682.

Mill, J. S. 1990. Utilitarianism. In R. C. Solomon and M. C. Murphy (Eds.), *What Is Justice? Classic and Contemporary Readings.* New York: Oxford University Press. pp. 258–260.

Miller, D. 1976. *Social Justice.* Oxford: Oxford University Press.

Miller, J. B. 1982 (April). Psychological Recovery in Low Income Single Parents. *American Journal of Orthopsychiatry,* 52, 346–352.

Minow, M. 1993. Justice Engendered. In P. Smith (Ed.), *Feminist Jurisprudence.* New York: Oxford University Press. pp. 217–243.

Mitchell, J. 1966 (November/December). Women: The Longest Revolution. *New Left Review,* 40, 11–37.

Mitchell, J. 1971. *Woman's Estate.* New York: Pantheon.

Ogle, R. S., D. M. Katkin, and T. J. Bernard. 1995. A Theory of Homicidal Behavior among Women. *Criminology,* 33, 173–187.

Otten, L. A. 1993. *Women's Rights and the Law.* Westport: Praeger.

Owen, B. and B. Bloom. 1995 (June). Profiling Women Prisoners: Findings from National Surveys and a California Sample. *The Prison Journal,* 75, 165–177.

Pagelow, M. D. 1984. *Family Violence.* New York: Praeger.

Parkman, A. M. 1992. *No-Fault Divorce: What Went Wrong?* Boulder: Westview Press.

Pence, E. 1994. As cited in A. Jones, *Next Time She'll Be Dead: Battering and How to Stop It.* Boston: Beacon Press. pp. 99–100.

Pertman, A. 1994 (February 13). Justice Has Different Definitions: Men, Women Often View Facts of Legal Cases Differently. *Duluth News Tribune,* 9A.

Peters, H. E. 1986. Marriage and Divorce: Informational; Constraints and Private Contracts. *American Economic Review,* 76, 437–545.

Pleck, E. 1994. Cited in A. Jones, *Next Time She'll Be Dead: Battering and How to Stop It.* Boston: Beacon Press. pp. 164.

Pollak, O. 1950. *The Criminality of Women.* Philadelphia: University of Pennsylvania Press.

Pollock-Byrne, J. M. 1990. *Women, Prison and Crime.* Belmont: Wadsworth.

Rape Statistics. 1992. National Center for Victims of Crime. Arlington, VA.

Rawls, J. 1990. A Theory of Justice. In R. C. Solomon and M. C. Murphy (Eds.), *What Is Justice? Classic and Contemporary Readings.* New York: Oxford University Press. pp. 305–312.

Reiman, J. 1998. *The Rich Get Richer and the Poor Get Prison: Ideology, Class and Criminal Justice.* Boston: Allyn and Bacon.

Rich, A. 1976. *Of Woman Born.* New York: Norton.

Richardson, L. 1988. *The Dynamics of Sex and Gender: A Sociological Perspective,* Third Edition. New York: Harper and Row.

Rodgers, J. L., P. A. Nakonezny, and R. D. Shull. 1999 (August). Does No-Fault Legislation Matter? Definitely Yes and No. *Journal of Marriage and the Family,* 61(3), 803–811.

Rotherberg, P. (Ed.). 1995. *Race, Class and Gender in the United States: An Integrated Study,* Third Edition. New York: St. Martin's Press.

Rousseau, J. J. 1990. The Discourse on the Origin of Inequality. In R. C. Solomon and M. C. Murphy (Eds.), *What Is Justice? Classic and Contemporary Readings.* New York: Oxford University Press. pp. 101–116.

Rush, G. E. 2000. *The Dictionary of Criminal Justice*, Fifth Edition. Guilford, CT: Dushkin/McGraw-Hill.

Russell, D. E. H. 1990. *Rape in Marriage*. Bloomington: Indiana University Press.

Sadker, M. and D. M. Sadker. 1980. *Between Teacher and Student: Overcoming Sex Bias in Classroom Interaction*. Washington, DC: U.S. Department of Education.

Sandel, M. 1990. Liberalism and the Limits of Justice. In R. C. Solomon and M. C. Murphy (Eds.), *What Is Justice? Classic and Contemporary Readings*. New York: Oxford University Press. pp. 138–146.

Scales, A. C. 1993. The Emergence of Feminist Jurisprudence: An Essay. In P. Smith (Ed.), *Feminist Jurisprudence*. New York: Oxford University Press.

Scott, H. 1985. *Working Your Way to the Bottom: The Feminization of Poverty*. London: Pandora Press.

Shanley, M. L. and R. Battistoni. 1992. Afterword: Sexual Difference and Equality. In L. F. Goldstein (Ed.), *Feminist Jurisprudence: The Difference Debate*. Lanham: Rowman & Littlefield. pp. 263–273.

Sheffield, C. J. 1987. Sexual Terrorism: The Social Control of Women. In B. B. Hess and M. M. Ferree (Eds.), *Analyzing Gender: A Handbook of Social Science Research*. Newbury Park: Sage. pp. 171–189.

Simon, R. J. 1977. *Women and Crime*. Lexington: Lexington Books.

Smart, C. 1976. *Women, Crime and Criminology: A Feminist Critique*. Boston: Routledge and Kegan Paul.

Smith, P. 1993. *Feminist Jurisprudence*. New York: Oxford University Press.

Solomon, R. C. 1990. Justice and the Passion for Revenge. In R. C. Solomon and M. C. Murphy (Eds.), *What Is Justice? Classic and Contemporary Readings*. New York: Oxford University Press. pp. 292–304.

Sourcebook of Criminal Justice Statistics Online. Arrest Statistics, 1999. Originally Table 4.8. http://www.albany.edu/sourcebook/1995/pdf/t48.pdf.

Steffensmeier, D. 1995. Trends in Female Crime: It's Still a Man's World. In B. R. Price and N. J. Sokoloff (Eds.), *The Criminal Justice System and Women: Offenders, Victims and Workers*. New York: McGraw-Hill.

Stetson, D. M. 1997. *Women's Rights in the USA: Policy Debates and Gender Roles*, Second Edition. New York: Garland.

Stevens, D. J. 1998. Incarcerated Women, Crime and Drug Addition. *Criminologist*, 22(1), 3–20.

Stohr, M. K., G. L. Mays, N. P. Lovrich, and A. M. Gallegos. 1996. *Parallel Perceptions: Gender, Job Enrichment and Job Satisfaction Among Correctional Officers in Women's Jails*. Paper presented at the Academy of Criminal Justice Sciences.

Stout, K. 1991 (Fall). A Continuum of Male Controls and Violence against Women: A Teaching Model. *Journal of Social Work Education*, 27(3), 305–319.

Sutherland, E. H. 1947. *Principles of Criminology*, Fourth Edition. Philadelphia: Lippincott.

Swerdlow, A. R., R. Bridenthal, J. Kelly, and P. Vine. 1980. *Household and Kin*. Old Westbury, New York: Feminist Press.

Thomas, W. I. 1907. *Sex and Society*. Boston: Little, Brown.

Thomas, W. I. 1923. *The Unadjusted Girl*. New York: Harper.

Tilley, L. A. and J. W. Scott. 2000. Cited in M. A. Andersen, *Thinking about Women: Sociological Perspectives on Sex and Gender*, Fifth Edition. Boston: Allyn and Bacon. 100.

Title IX: 25 Years of Progress. 1997. Washington, DC: U.S. Department of Education.

U.S. Census Bureau. Current Population Reports—1999. Washington, DC.

U.S. Commission on Civil Rights. 1995. The Problem: Discrimination. In P. Rothenberg (Ed.), *Race, Class and Gender in the United States: An Integrated Study,* Third Edition. New York: St. Martin's Press. pp. 70–80.

U.S. Department of Education. 2001. Table 248—Earned Degrees Conferred by Degree Granting Institutions, by Level of Degree and Sex of Student, 1869–2010. *Digest of Education Statistics, 2000.* Washington, DC.

U.S. Department of Education. 1997. *Title IX: 25 Years of Progress.* Washington, DC.

U.S. Department of Justice. 1986. *Attorney General's Commission on Pornography Final Report.* Washington, DC: Government Printing Office.

U.S. Department of Justice. 1991. *Women as Correctional Officers in Men's Maximum Security Facilities: A Survey of the Fifty States.* Washington, DC: Government Printing Office.

Valian, V. 1998. *Why So Slow? The Advancement of Women.* Cambridge: MIT Press.

von Berckefeldt, K. 2000. The Vandy Girl. *Vanderbilt University Commodore 2000.* Dallas: Taylor Publishing.

von Hayek, F. 1990. The Mirage of Social Justice. In R. C. Solomon and M. C. Murphy (Eds.), *What Is Justice? Classic and Contemporary Readings.* New York: Oxford University Press. pp. 212–220.

Walby, S. 1990. *Theorizing Patriarchy.* Cambridge: Blackwell.

Walker, L. E. 1980. *The Battered Woman.* New York: HarperPerennial.

Watterson, K. 1996. *Women in Prison: Inside the Concrete Womb.* Boston: Northeastern University Press.

Weitzman, L. 1985. *The Divorce Revolution.* New York: The Free Press.

Welter, B. 1966. The Cult of True Womanhood. *American Quarterly,* 18, 151–174.

West, R. 1993. Jurisprudence and Gender. In P. Smith (Ed.), *Feminist Jurisprudence.* New York: Oxford University Press.

Wilson, E. O. 1975. *Sociobiology: The New Synthesis.* Cambridge: Harvard University Press.

Wolgast, E. 1990. The Grammar of Justice. In R. C. Solomon and M. C. Murphy (Eds.), *What Is Justice? Classic and Contemporary Readings.* New York: Oxford University Press. pp. 348–350.

Wright, K. N. and W. G. Saylor. 1991 (Spring). Male and Female Perceptions of Prison Work: Is There a Difference? *Justice Quarterly,* 4, 505–524.

Zimmer, L. E. 1986. *Women Guarding Men.* Chicago: University of Chicago Press.

INDEX

Abortion
    and Constitution Equality Amendment, 57
    ongoing debate about, 132–133
Acceptance approach, 48
Acceptance standard, 57
Accommodation approach, 48
Actus reus, 20
Adams, Abigail, 24, 41
Adams, John Quincy, 24, 41
Adaptation in society, 35–36
Advertising
    genderisms in, 150–151
    and pornography, 153–154
    and sexuality, 148
Affirmative action, 102–104
Aid to Families with Dependent
    Children (AFDC), 27, 124
Alice in Wonderland, 97
Alimony, 68–69
    case citations, 65
Andersen, Margaret, 2
Androgyny model of sameness, 47
Appearance
    atavistic characteristics of women
        criminals, 31
    and gender schemas, 10
    and rape, 145
Apprenticeship, 96
Arrest statistics, 28–29
Assimilation model of sameness, 47
Asymmetrical approach to equality, 48
Athletics, and Title IX, 86–88

Barash, David, 8
Baron, Ava, 40
Battered women. *See* Violence against
    women
Beccaria, Ceasare, 34
Bentham, Jeremy, 34
Biblical image of women, 11
Bill of Rights, 41, 45
Biological determinism, 8–9
Biology
    and accommodation approach, 48

and deviant behavior, 31
Blackstone, Sir William, 18
Bona fide occupational qualification
    (BFOQ), 100
Brown v. Topeka Board of Education,
    52, 82

Capitalism
    and women and poverty, 122
    and women as criminals, 34
Career. *See* Work
Case citations
    contraception, 132
    employee discrimination, 115
    Equal Protection Clause, 54
    family, 67
    Muller v. State of Oregon, 92
    Reed v. Reed (equal protection), 176
    Roe v. Wade, 133
    same-sex marriage, 70
    Title IX, 86, 101
    Title VII, 101
    welfare, 124
    women admittance to the bar, 112
Catch-22. *See* Walking the line
Child support, 76–78
    case citations, 65
Childcare
    nursing and women, 12
    and quadraplexation, 73–74
    and women criminals, 78–79, 168
Chivalry hypothesis, 32
Civil law, 20–21
Civil rights
    Brown v. Topeka Board of Education,
        52, 82
    Title VII, 98–101
Civil War Amendments, 24, 45
    equal protection clause, 51–55
College
    compliance with Title IX, 88
    first to admit women, 81
Common law
    challenges to system, 23–24
    and civil and criminal law, 20–21

187